POSTER ART

ROCKPORT
PUBLISHERS

ROCKPORT PUBLISHERS, INC.
ROCKPORT, MASSACHUSETTS

FIRST PUBLISHED AND DISTRIBUTED IN THE UNITED STATES OF AMERICA BY:
ROCKPORT PUBLISHERS, INC.
146 GRANITE STREET
ROCKPORT, MASSACHUSETTS 01966-1299
TELEPHONE: (508) 546-9590
FAX: (508) 546-7141

ISBN 1-56496-290-3

10 9 8 7 6 5 4 3 2 1

ART DIRECTOR LYNNE HAVIGHURST
DESIGNER SARA DAY GRAPHIC DESIGN
COVER CONTRIBUTORS TOP ROW, IMAGES; CENTER ROW, KAN TAI-KEUNG DESIGN AND ASSOCIATES LTD.; BOTTOM LEFT, SIBLEY/PETEET DESIGN; BOTTOM RIGHT, SUBURBIA STUDIOS

Manufactured in Singapore by Welpac

Introduction

Posters—they're big. Not only does their size afford the designer the latitude to convey his message, but they're big in another sense—they're popular. Posters publicize local happenings; they make political statements; they promote educational programs; they give directions with loud, arresting visuals. And, when a designer has done his job well, they become collector's items.

Whether a poster promotes a multi-million-dollar film or just a meat sale at the corner market, the design can be great. The graphics must overpower; the text, in the split-second that it holds the reader's attention, must embed its message into his memory.

This volume celebrates the best posters Rockport has seen in recent years. Designers of international renown are featured, and though many of the events have come and gone, the posters' relevance remains: with effective graphics that get their message across, they will serve as an example and an inspiration to those conceiving their own poster designs.

Save me, please. I'm here.

Save me, please. I'm here.

Design Firm Nippon Design Center, Inc.
Art Director Kazumasa NAGAI
Designer Kazumasa NAGAI
Client Japan Graphic Designers Association
Purpose Exhibition promotion
Size 40.5" x 28.5" (103cm x 72.8cm)

Save me, please. I'm here.

May 1 2 3 4 5 6 7 8 9 10 11 12 13 14 15 16 17 18 19 20 21 22 23 24 25 26 27 28 29 30 31

QUEEN CITY PRINTERS

Design Firm Kaiserdicken
Art Director Craig Dicken
Designer Debra Kaiser
Illustrator Tolya Kats
Client Queen City Printers
Purpose Promotional calendar
Size 25.75" x 20.75" (65.4cm x 52.7cm)

This brilliant painting was done by a
6-year-old from Russia, made available through
the Children's Art Exchange—a non-profit
organization which "helps children create,
strengthen and celebrate global connections
through the universal language of art."

5

THE GOOD SON

MOVIE COMPANY
Twentieth Century Fox
(International)
DISTRIBUTOR OF FILM
Twentieth Century Fox
(International)
DESIGN FIRM/AGENCY
Frankfurt Balkind Partners
ART DIRECTOR
Rima Sinno
DESIGNERS
Rima Sinno, Robert Rainey
CREATIVE DIRECTOR
Peter Bemis

Image was converted to
a blue duotone, using a
gaussin blur on the whole
face except for the eye,
which allowed the
eye to stand out.

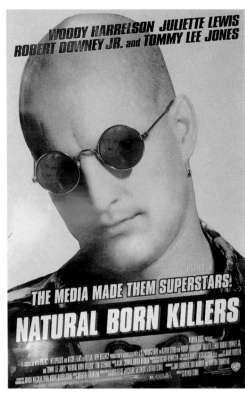

NATURAL BORN KILLERS

MOVIE COMPANY
Regency Enterprises
DISTRIBUTOR OF FILM
Warner Bros.
DESIGN FIRM
BLT & Associates Inc.
ART DIRECTOR
BLT & Associates Inc.
DESIGNER
BLT & Associates Inc.
PHOTOGRAPHER
Sidney Baldwin
DIGITAL IMAGING
BLT & Associates Inc.

The designers used red
and yellow accents on
this six-color design.

SLEEPING WITH THE ENEMY

MOVIE COMPANY
Twentieth Century Fox
DISTRIBUTOR OF FILM
Twentieth Century Fox
DESIGN FIRM
Mike Salisbury
Communications Inc.
ART DIRECTOR
Chris Pula
DESIGNER
Mike Salisbury

This concept was executed in
print from a television trailer.

6

DESIGN FIRM TOM FOWLER, INC.
ART DIRECTOR THOMAS G. FOWLER
DESIGNER THOMAS G. FOWLER
ILLUSTRATORS SAMUEL TOH,
   THOMAS G. FOWLER
CLIENT CONNECTICUT GRAND OPERA
   & ORCHESTRA
PURPOSE OPERA PERFORMANCE PROMOTION
SIZE 16" x 28" (40.6CM x 71.1CM)

ADOBE ILLUSTRATOR WAS USED FOR
THIS DESIGN. THE COLOR PALETTE WAS
INFLUENCED BY TRADITIONAL JAPANESE
WOOD BLOCK PRINTS.

CONNECTICUT GRAND OPERA & ORCHESTRA

P R E S E N T S

MADAMA ✹ BUTTERFLY

BY GIACOMO PUCCINI

SATURDAY, SEPTEMBER 24, 1994, 8PM ■ KLEIN MEMORIAL AUDITORIUM, BRIDGEPORT
SATURDAY, OCTOBER 1, 1994, 8PM ■ THE PALACE THEATRE, STAMFORD
CALL 203.359.0009 FOR TICKETS

DESIGN FIRM RICHARDS & SWENSEN, INC.
ART DIRECTOR MICHAEL RICHARDS
DESIGNERS MICHAEL RICHARDS, CONNIE CHRISTENSEN
ILLUSTRATOR CONNIE CHRISTENSEN
CLIENT NOVELL, INC.
PURPOSE "BICYCLE TO WORK DAY" PROMOTION
SIZE 14" x 22" (35.6cm x 55.9cm)

A ROUGH DRAWING WAS SCANNED AND RECREATED IN ADOBE ILLUSTRATOR 5.5 THEN RASTERIZED INTO ADOBE PHOTOSHOP 3.0 WHERE THE BASIC COLORS WERE APPLIED. THROUGH ADOBE PHOTOSHOP'S LAYERS AND CHANNELS THE DESIGNER APPLIED SHADOWS AND LIGHT EFFECTS TO MAKE THE COLORS PLAY OFF EACH OTHER. LASTLY, THE TYPE WAS MERGED WITH THE IMAGE AGAIN IN ADOBE ILLUSTRATOR AT A ONE-TO-ONE RATIO. THEN THE FILE WAS RUN OUT TO FILM FOR OFFSET PRINTING THROUGH ADOBE SEPARATOR.

DESIGN FIRM SEGURA
ART DIRECTOR CARLOS SEGURA
DESIGNER CARLOS SEGURA
ILLUSTRATOR TONY KLASSEN
CLIENT [T-26] DIGITAL TYPE FOUNDRY
PURPOSE PROMOTION
SIZE 24" x 36" (60.9cm x 91.4cm)

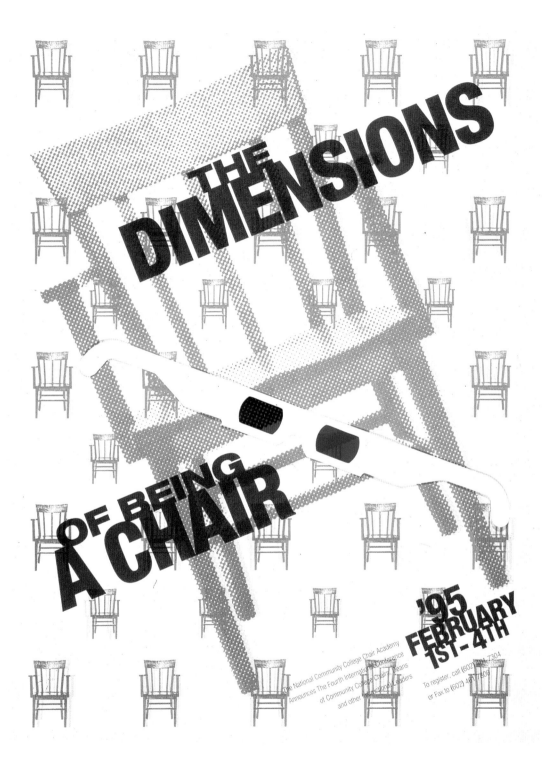

THE DIMENSIONS OF BEING A CHAIR

'95 FEBRUARY 1ST–4TH

The National Community College Chair Academy
Announces The Fourth International Conference
of Community College Chair, Deans
and other Instructional Leaders

To register, call (602) 461-7304
or Fax to (602) 461-7804

DESIGN FIRM AFTER HOURS CREATIVE
ART DIRECTOR RUSS HAAN
DESIGNER TODD FEDELL
CLIENT NATIONAL COMMUNITY COLLEGE CHAIR ACADEMY
OBJECTIVE TO ATTRACT ATTENDEES TO THE FOURTH NATIONAL
COMMUNITY COLLEGE CHAIR ACADEMY CONFERENCE

TO BREAK THROUGH THE CLUTTER OF MAIL AND
ACADEMIC BUREAUCRACY, A LIGHT-HEARTED, INTERACTIVE
APPROACH IS ADOPTED. THE POSTER, WHEN VIEWED THROUGH
ITS ATTACHED THREE-DIMENSIONAL GLASSES, BRINGS THE
CONFERENCE THEME TO LIFE AND DEMONSTRATES THE HOST'S
COMMITMENT TO FRESH, PARTICIPATORY THINKING.

Design Firm Sibley/Peteet Design
Art Director Derek Welch
Designers Derek Welch, John Evans
Illustrator Derek Welch
Client Texas Special Olympics
Purpose Summer games promotion
Size 24" x 25" (61cm x 63.5cm)

APRIL 1995

DESIGN FIRM SIBLEY/PETEET DESIGN
ART DIRECTOR REX PETEET
DESIGNERS DEREK WELCH, REX PETEET, TOM HOUGH
ILLUSTRATORS DEREK WELCH, REX PETEET, TOM HOUGH
CLIENT TEXAS STATE PRESERVATION BOARD
PURPOSE OPENING CELEBRATION OF RENOVATED CAPITOL
SIZE 24" X 37" (61CM X 94CM)

[LEFT AND FACING PAGE]

DESIGN FIRM SULLIVANPERKINS
ART DIRECTOR ART GARCIA
DESIGNER ART GARCIA
PHOTOGRAPHER ROBB DEBENPORT
COPYWRITERS MARK PERKINS, DAVY WOODRUFF
CLIENT DAKA (VAN SAXON & ASSOCIATES)
PURPOSE PROMOTION
SIZE 23" X 23.25" (58.4CM X 59.1CM)

ALL TYPOGRAPHY WAS SHOT AS PART OF THE
PHOTOGRAPH TO GIVE A DIMENSION THAT COULD
NOT BE ACHIEVED MECHANICALLY.

JOHNNY HANDSOME

MOVIE COMPANY MGM
DISTRIBUTOR OF FILM MGM
DESIGN FIRM MIKE SALISBURY
COMMUNICATIONS INC.
ART DIRECTOR MIKE SALISBURY
DESIGNER TERRY LAMB
ILLUSTRATOR/ARTIST ROD DYER

THE DESIGN WAS ILLUSTRATED BY
HAND FROM PHOTOGRAPHS.

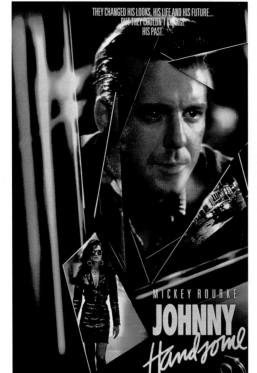

SPELL BINDER

MOVIE COMPANY MGM
DISTRIBUTOR OF FILM
MGM
DESIGN FIRM
MIKE SALISBURY
COMMUNICATIONS INC.
ART DIRECTORS
RICK LOPER, MIKE SALISBURY
DESIGNER
MIKE SALISBURY
ILLUSTRATOR/ARTIST
JEFF WACK

THIS GRAPHIC WAS CREATED
USING AIRBRUSH OVER
PHOTOGRAPHY.

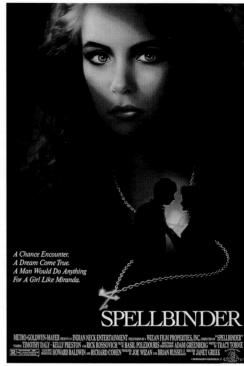

DOLORES CLAIBORNE

MOVIE COMPANY
CASTLE ROCK ENTERTAINMENT
DISTRIBUTOR OF FILM
COLUMBIA PICTURES
DESIGN FIRM
FRANKFURT BALKIND PARTNERS
CREATIVE DIRECTOR
PETER BEMIS
DESIGNERS
BRETT WICKENS, KIM WEXMAN
ILLUSTRATOR/ARTIST
EMERALD CITY

PHOTOGRAPHIC ELEMENTS WERE
SCANNED AND INPUT IN TO A
SILICON GRAPHICS
WORKSTATION, COMPOSED,
COLOR-MANIPULATED, AND
GRAINED FOR EFFECT.

SLIVER

MOVIE COMPANY
PARAMOUNT PICTURES
DESIGN FIRM
FRANKFURT BALKIND PARTNERS
ART DIRECTOR
KIM WEXMAN
DESIGNER
KIM WEXMAN
CREATIVE DIRECTOR
PETER BEMIS
COPYWRITER
KIM WEXMAN

THREE DIFFERENT SCENES WERE
MERGED TOGETHER AND
CROPPED IN THE SHAPE OF A
"SLIVER." KIM TRIED TO KEEP
THE TYPE MINIMAL SO AS NOT
TO INTERFERE WITH THE
CONCEPT OF THE SLIVER SHAPE
IN THE CENTER.

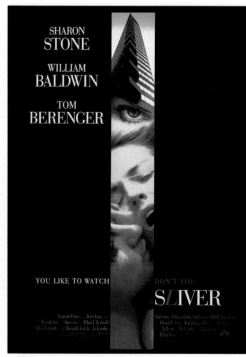

DESIGN FIRM FRANK HEYMANN
ALL DESIGN FRANK HEYMANN
CLIENT NEVES ENSEMBLE
(CHAMBER MUSIC)
PURPOSE PROMOTION

DESIGN FIRM FRANK HEYMANN
ILLUSTRATORS HYLNUR HALLSON,
FRANK HEYMANN
CLIENT IH HANNOVER
IB KUNST & DESIGN
PURPOSE END OF WORLD
WAR II COMMEMORATION

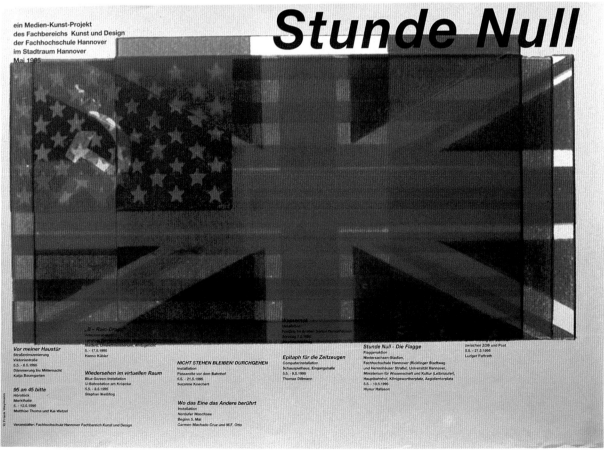

DESIGN FIRM KAN TAI-KEUNG DESIGN & ASSOCIATES LTD.
ART DIRECTOR KAN TAI-KEUNG DESIGN & ASSOCIATES LTD.
DESIGNER KAN TAI-KEUNG DESIGN & ASSOCIATES LTD.
PURPOSE SELF-PROMOTION

THE INK STONE AND THE PALE YELLOW PAPER REPRESENT TAIWAN
AND MAINLAND CHINA, RESPECTIVELY. THE BRUSH STROKES
RESEMBLE THE LETTER "T" AND THE FIRST CHARACTER
OF A TAIWAN CHINESE NAME. THE STONE ALSO SUGGESTS THE
MEANING OF EDUCATIONAL EXCHANGE, FOR THERE IS A CHINESE
SAYING, "EVEN THE STONE OF ANOTHER MOUNTAIN HAS
SOMETHING FOR YOU TO LEARN."

DESIGN FIRM KAN TAI-KEUNG DESIGN & ASSOCIATES LTD.
ART DIRECTOR FREEMAN LAU SIU HONG
DESIGNERS FREEMAN LAU SIU HONG,
VERONICA CHEUNG LAI SHEUNG
CLIENT KAN TAI-KEUNG DESIGN & ASSOCIATES LTD.
PURPOSE SELF-PROMOTION

THESE POSTERS WERE DESIGNED FOR AN INVITATIONAL SHOW IN
TAIWAN. EVERY CHINESE CHARACTER HAS ITS OWN MEANING. THE
DESIGNER BREAKS DOWN SEVERAL CHARACTERS AND REORGANIZES
THEM TO MAKE A NEW CHARACTER WITH A NEW MEANING.

DUTCH GRAPHIC DESIGN POSTER

DESIGN FIRM STOLTZE DESIGN
ALL DESIGN CLIFFORD STOLTZE

THIS IS A TWO-COLOR POSTER, BUT THE
FLUORESCENT CHANGES FROM ONE SIDE
TO THE OTHER TO GIVE IT MORE IMPACT.
THE PRINTING WAS DONATED.

Design Firm Greteman Group
Art Director Sonia Greteman
Designer Sonia Greteman
Illustrator Sonia Greteman
Client John Coultis
Purpose Christmas promotion
Size 12" x 20" (30.5 cm x 50.8 cm)

DESIGN FIRM SACKETT DESIGN ASSOCIATES
ART DIRECTOR MARK SACKETT
DESIGNERS MARK SACKETT, WAYNE SAKAMOTO,
JAMES SAKAMOTO, MIRJAM PATSCHEIDER,
TAMAR KONDY, CHANDRA CRISSMAN
CLIENT BRAINFOOD CREATIVE PROGRAMS
PURPOSE PROMOTION
SIZE 5" x 30" (12.7CM x 76.2CM)

FOUND IMAGES OF ANTIQUE DOLLS
AND LABELS WERE SCANNED IN AND ARRANGED
INTO A BACKGROUND COLLAGE. THE POSTER
DEMONSTRATES HOW DIVERSE ONE'S RESEARCH
CAN BE WHEN LOOKING
FOR CREATIVE INSPIRATION.

DESIGN FIRM MARLA MURPHY/LA
DESIGNER MARLA MURPHY
ILLUSTRATOR MARLA MURPHY
CLIENT ESU REPTILE, ENERGY SAVERS
UNLIMITED, INC.
PURPOSE INTRODUCE REPTILE LINE
TO PET INDUSTRY
SIZE 22.875" x 29.125" (58.1CM x 74CM)

ILLUSTRATION IS A SOFT PASTEL
DRAWING. FIRST IN A SERIES
FOR THE CLIENT, TWO MORE POSTERS
ARE PLANNED FOR NEW PRODUCTS.

Event Annual Charity Polo Event
Design Firm Boelts Bros. Design Inc.
Art Director Jackson Boelts, Eric Boelts
Designer Jackson Boelts, Eric Boelts
Illustrator Eric Boelts

Event Annual Charity Polo Event
Design Firm Boelts Bros Design Inc.
Art Director Jackson Boelts, Eric Boelts
Designer Jackson Boelts, Eric Boelts
Illustrator Jackson Boelts

POLO

EVENT ANNUAL CHARITY POLO EVENT
DESIGN FIRM BOELTS BROS. DESIGN INC.
ART DIRECTOR JACKSON BOELTS, ERIC BOELTS
DESIGNER JACKSON BOELTS, ERIC BOELTS
ILLUSTRATOR JACKSON BOELTS

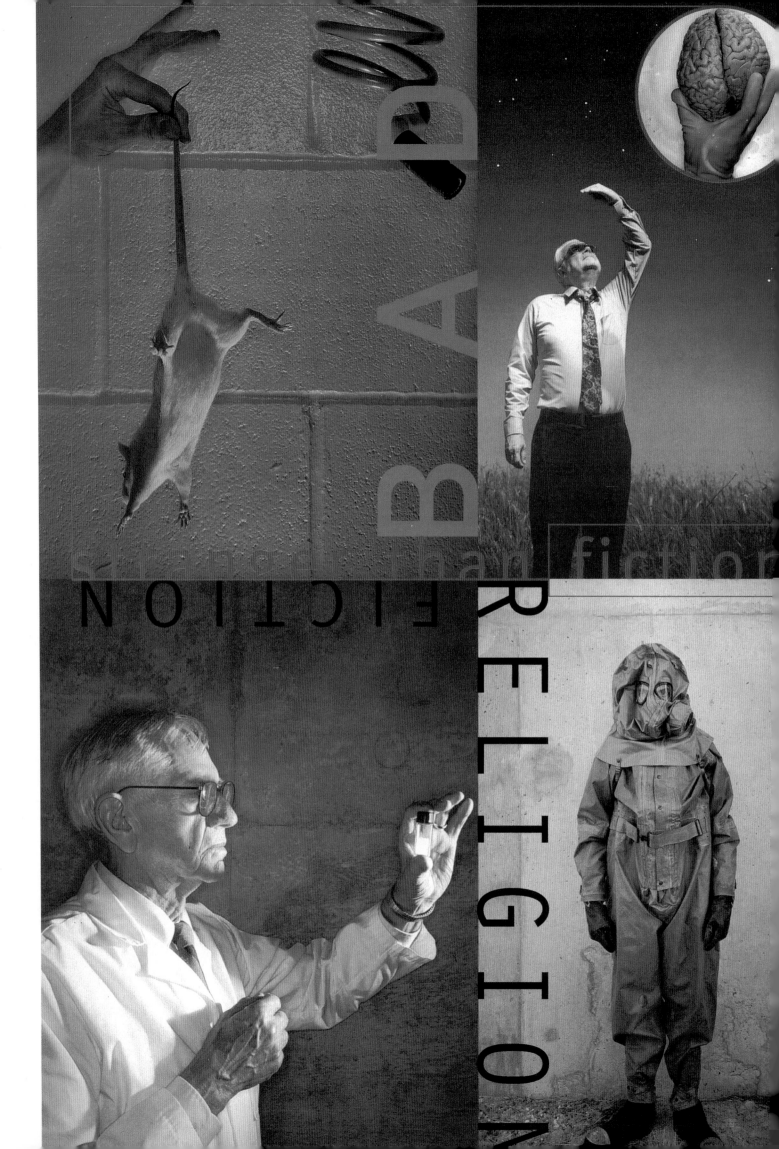

BAD RELIGION

FICTION

RELIGION

strange than fiction

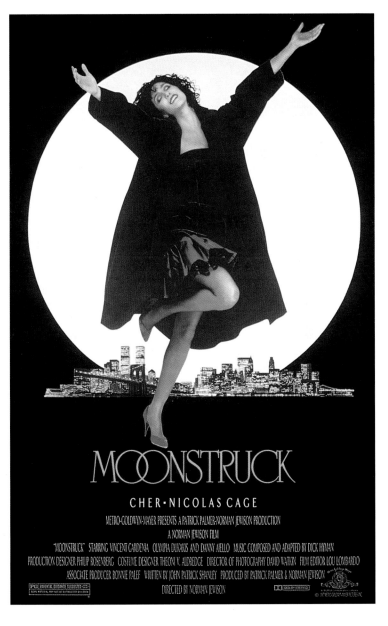

MOONSTRUCK

MOVIE COMPANY MGM
DISTRIBUTOR OF FILM MGM
DESIGN FIRM MIKE SALISBURY
    COMMUNICATIONS INC.
ART DIRECTOR MIKE SALISBURY
DESIGNER TONY SEINIGER
PHOTOGRAPHER HERB RITTS

PHOTOGRAPHY WAS BASED ON
ORIGINAL SKETCH DRAWINGS.

FOUR WEDDINGS AND A FUNERAL

MOVIE COMPANY POLYGRAM
FILMED ENTERTAINMENT
DISTRIBUTOR OF FILM
GRAMERCY PICTURES
DESIGN FIRM BRD DESIGN
ART DIRECTOR SAMANTHA HART
DESIGNERS NEVILLE BURTIS,
PETER KING ROBBINS

THIS FOUR-COLOR DESIGN INCLUDES
MULTIPLE PHOTOGRAPHS THAT WERE
COMPOSITED ON QUANTEL PAINTBOX®.

DESIGN FIRM DESIGN/ART INC.
ALL DESIGN NORMAN MOORE
PHOTOGRAPHER DAN WINTERS
CLIENT ATLANTIC RECORDS
PURPOSE RECORD PROMOTION
SIZE 24" X 36" (61CM X 91.4CM)

[FACING PAGE]
HIGH-RESOLUTION SCANS WERE SET UP
ALONG WITH AND TYPE IN QUARKXPRESS.

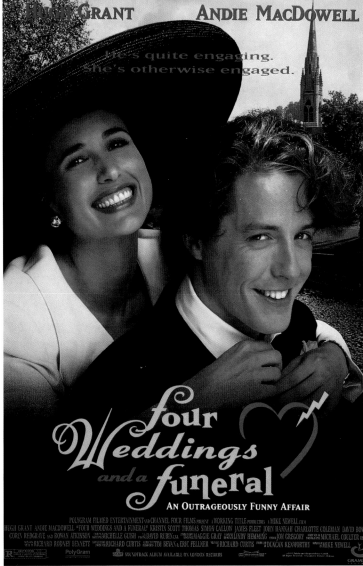

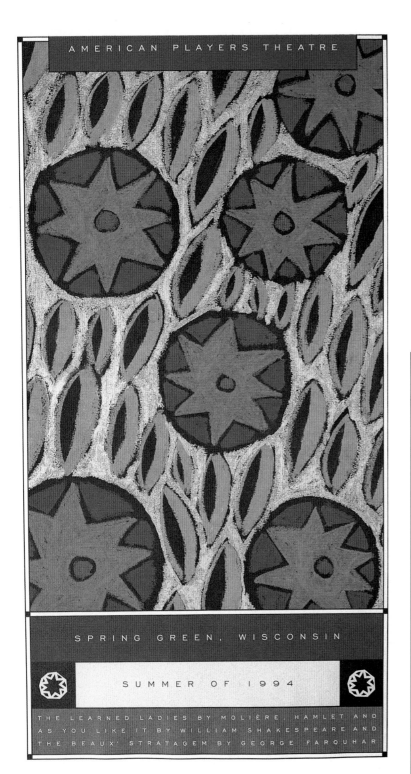

AMERICAN PLAYERS THEATRE

SPRING GREEN, WISCONSIN

SUMMER OF 1994

THE LEARNED LADIES BY MOLIÉRE, HAMLET AND
AS YOU LIKE IT BY WILLIAM SHAKESPEARE AND
THE BEAUX' STRATAGEM BY GEORGE FARQUHAR

AMERICAN PLAYERS THEATRE

SUMMER OF 1993

MOLIÉRE'S THE SCHOOL FOR WIVES, SHAKESPEARE'S THE MERCHANT
OF VENICE, THE TAMING OF THE SHREW AND KING HENRY IV, PART I

DESIGN FIRM PLANET DESIGN CO.
ART DIRECTORS DANA LYTLE, KEVIN WADE
DESIGNERS [THIS PAGE] DANA LYTLE, RAELENE MERCER
[FACING PAGE] DANA LYTLE, MARTHA GHRAETTINGER
ILLUSTRATOR DANA LYTLE
CLIENT AMERICAN PLAYERS THEATRE
PURPOSE THEATRE SEASON PROMOTION
SIZE [THIS PAGE] 26" X 24"
[FACING PAGE] 19" X 35.5"

THE ILLUSTRATION WAS DONE USING CATTLE MARKERS, OIL
PASTELS, AND CHARCOAL. THE DESIGNER ALSO USED
QUARKXPRESS ON A MACINTOSH QUADRA 700 FOR THE
DESIGN OF THIS SERIES OF THREE POSTERS.

MICHAEL KEATON

BATMAN
RETURNS

JUNE 19

24

BATMAN RETURNS

MOVIE COMPANY WARNER BROS.
DISTRIBUTOR OF FILM WARNER BROS.
DESIGN FIRM/AGENCY THE IDEA PLACE
ART DIRECTOR MASEEH RAFANI
DESIGNERS JIMMY WACHTEL,
VICTOR MARTIN
PHOTOGRAPHER JACK PEDOTA
ILLUSTRATORS/ARTISTS
MYRA WOOD, PAGE WOOD

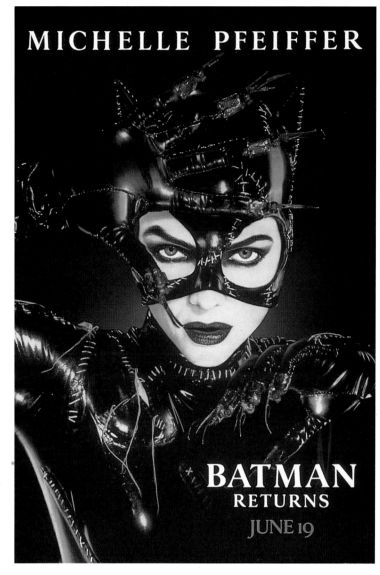

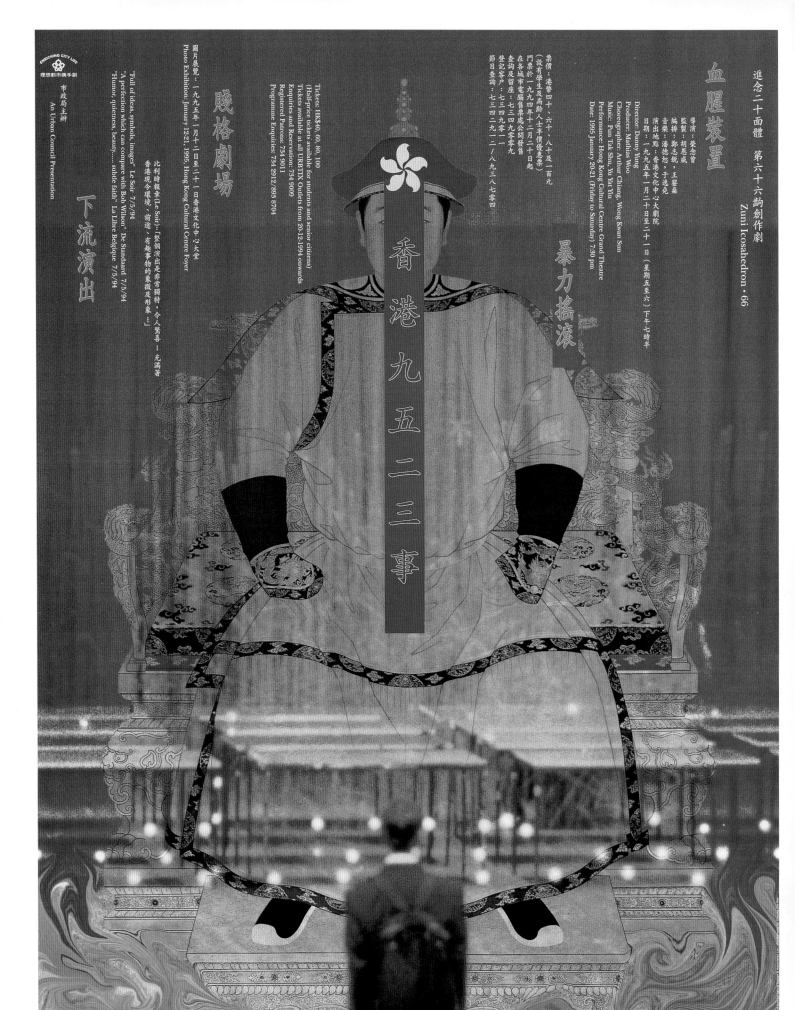

Two or Three Events .... of No Significance, Hong Kong 1995

DESIGN FIRM KAN TAI-KEUNG DESIGN & ASSOCIATES LTD.
ART DIRECTOR FREEMAN LAU SIU HONG
DESIGNERS FREEMAN LAU SIU HONG, VERONICA CHEUNG LAI SHEUNG
PHOTOGRAPHER CHEUNG CHI WAI
CLIENT ZUNI ICOSAHEDRON
PURPOSE DRAMA PROMOTION

[FACING PAGE]
THIS POSTER PROMOTES A DRAMA ABOUT THE POLITICAL
CRISIS THAT THE HONG KONG WILL FACE IN 1997. THE PERSON
STANDING IN FRONT REPRESENTS A HONG KONG CITIZEN. HE FEARFULLY
AND HELPLESSLY FACES THE GHOST, VISUALIZED AS AN ANCIENT CHINESE
EMPEROR, WHICH SYMBOLIZES THE TOTALITARIANISM.

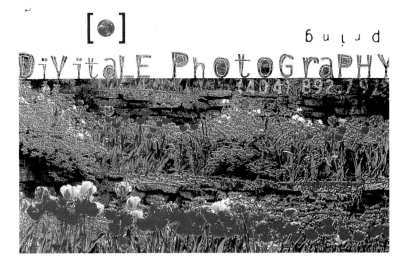

DESIGN FIRM FUSE
ART DIRECTOR RICH GODFREY
DESIGNER RICH GODREY
ILLUSTRATOR JIM DIVITALE
PHOTOGRAPHER DIVITALE PHOTOGRAPHY
DIGITAL MANIPULATOR JIM DIVITALE
CLIENT DIVITALE PHOTOGRAPHY
PURPOSE SELF-PROMOTION
SIZE [LEFT] 10" X 14" (25.4CM X 35.6CM)
[ABOVE] 16" X 20" (40.64CM X 50.8CM)

[ABOVE] DESIGNERS CONSTRUCTED AN INTERESTING
LAYOUT WITH TYPE AROUND AN EXCITING PHOTOGRAPH.
ORIGINAL TYPOGRAPHY FONTS CREATED IN ALTSYS
FONTOGRAPHER AND ADOBE ILLUSTRATOR WERE OUTPUT
TO LINO. THE SPECIAL EFFECTS SHOWN IN THE IMAGE
WERE ACHIEVED BY THE PHOTOGRAPHER, USING
TRADITIONAL DARKROOM TECHNIQUES.

[LEFT] THE DESIGNER USED ALTSYS FONTOGRAPHER TO
CREATE ORIGINAL TYPE WHICH HAD TO WORK THROUGH
A REPETITIVE MOTIF AND MULTIPLE COLORS WITHOUT
OVERSHADOWING THE IMAGE. THE ADVERTISING
MESSAGE WAS DELIVERED THROUGH THE TYPE AND
LAYOUT WITHOUT TAKING AWAY FROM THE VISUAL
IMPACT OF THE IMAGE. THE IMAGE ITSELF WAS
CREATED ON THE COMPUTER WITH ADOBE
PHOTOSHOP, ALDUS GALLERY EFFECTS, KAI'S
POWER TOOLS, AND FRACTAL DESIGN PAINTER.

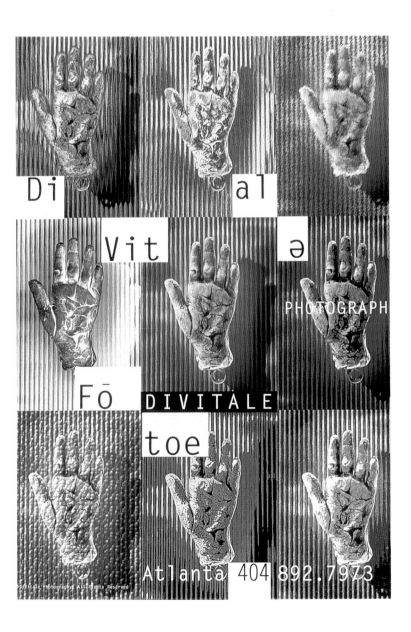

Event Annual Halloween Party
Design Firm Boelts Bros. Design Inc.
Art Director Jackson Boelts, Eric Boelts
Designer Jackson Boelts, Eric Boelts,
   Kerry Stratford
Illustrator Eric Boelts

Posters are silkscreened.

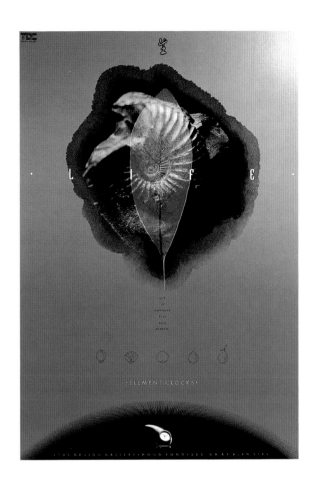

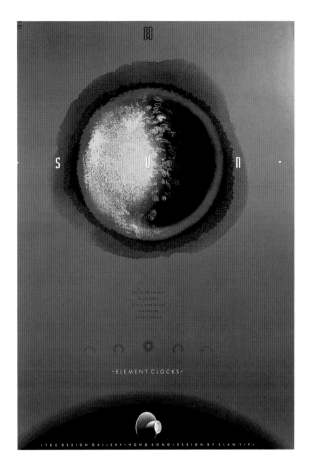

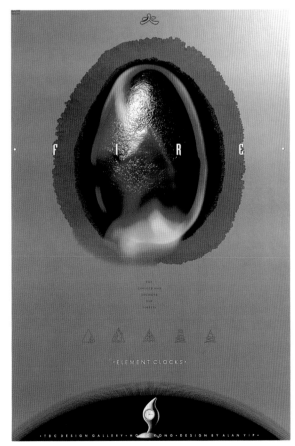

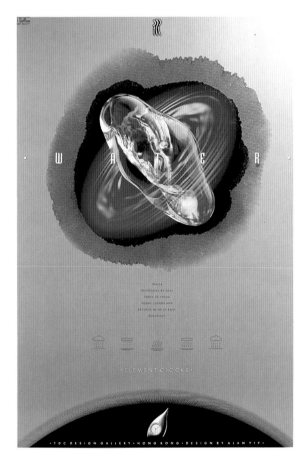

DESIGN FIRM KAN TAI-KEUNG DESIGN & ASSOCIATES LTD.
ART DIRECTORS KAN TAI-KEUNG, EDDY YU CHI KONG
DESIGNERS KAN TAI-KEUNG, EDDY YU CHI KONG
COMPUTER ILLUSTRATOR BENSON KWUN TIN-YAU
PHOTOGRAPHER C K WONG

CLIENT HONG KONG TRADE DEVELOPMENT COUNCIL
PURPOSE CLOCK PROMOTION

THE DESIGN OF THE POSTERS IS BASED ON THE
IDEA OF ORIENTAL PHILOSOPHICAL THINKING TO
PROMOTE AN UTTERLY MODERN PRODUCT.

DESIGN FIRM YELLOW M
ART DIRECTORS CRAIG FALCONER, LEE MANSON
DESIGNERS CRAIG FALCONER, LEE MANSON
COPYWRITER DAWN COULTER
PHOTOGRAPHER MOY WILLIAMS
CLIENT NORTH TYNESIDE & TYNEMOUTH COLLEGE
PURPOSE College recruitment
SIZE 60" x 40" (152.4CM x 101.6CM)

THE FISH AND FROG WERE MODELLED IN RESIN AND HAND-PAINTED. THE BANANA WAS HAND-MODELLED AND -PAINTED USING AN ACTUAL BANANA.

GO YOUR OWN WAY

AT NORTH TYNESIDE COLLEGE AND TYNEMOUTH

COLLEGE YOU CAN CHOOSE FROM OVER 600 COURSES.

SO IF YOU WANT THE **FREEDOM** TO USE YOUR OWN MIND,

GO YOUR OWN WAY.

GO TO COLLEGE

FOR MORE INFORMATION ABOUT GOING TO COLLEGE CONTACT
TYNEMOUTH COLLEGE: 257 8414 OR NORTH TYNESIDE COLLEGE: 262 5000

TYNEMOUTH
COLLEGE

NORTH
TYNESIDE
COLLEGE

SAN FRANCISCO INTERNATIONAL FILM FESTIVAL

MOVIE COMPANY
SAN FRANCISCO FILM SOCIETY
DESIGN FIRM
PRIMO ANGELI INC.
ART DIRECTORS
CARLO PAGODA,
PRIMO ANGELI
DESIGNER
PRIMO ANGELI
ILLUSTRATORS/ARTISTS
PAUL TERRILL,
MARCELO DE FREITAS

THE POSTER WAS CREATED USING ADOBE ILLUSTRATOR. THE TEXTURED LOOK IN THE COLLAGE BACKGROUND WAS ACHIEVED THROUGH A UNIQUE APPLICATION OF WD-40 DIRECTLY TO THE CAL-COMP PRINT-OUT. THE COLLAGE WAS THEN PHOTOGRAPHED AND RESCANNED INTO THE LAYOUT AND THE SAN FRANCISCO FILM SOCIETY TRADEMARK WAS SUPERIMPOSED AT A DIAGONAL.

DESIGN FIRM
KAN TAI-KEUNG DESIGN
& ASSOCIATES LTD.
ART DIRECTOR
FREEMAN LAU SI
DESIGNERS
FREEMAN LAU SIU HONG,
VERONICA CHEUNG
LAI SHEUNG
PHOTOGRAPHER
C K WONG
CLIENT
ZUNI ICOSAHEDRON
PURPOSE
DRAMA PROMOTION

[FACING PAGE]
THIS POSTER WAS CREATED
FOR AN AVANT-GARDE DRAMA.

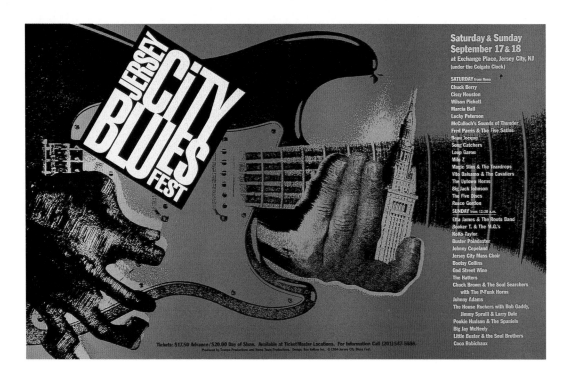

Design Firm Ron Kellum, Inc.
All Design Ron Kellum
Client Tramps Production
Purpose Music festival promotion
Size 33" x 21" (83.8cm x 53.3cm)

Poster was created with the use of Xerox collage with stencils and spray paint.

Design Firm Emerson,
Wajdowicz Studios, Inc.
Art Director Jurek Wajdowicz
Designer Lisa LaRochelle,
Jurek Wajdowicz
Illustrator Jacqui Morgan
Client UNIFEM
Purpose Conference
Size 19" x 28" (48.3cm x 71.1cm)

Design Firm Images
Art Director Walter McCord,
Julius Friedman
Designer Walter McCord,
Julius Friedman
Photographer Craig Guyon
Client Images
Purpose Self-promotion
Size 20" x 30" (50.8cm x 76.2cm)

Design Firm Images
Art Director Walter McCord,
Julius Friedman
Designer Walter McCord,
Julius Friedman
Photographer Joe Boone
Client Randolph Caldecott Medal
Purpose Children's
literature promotion
Size 19.5" x 27" (49.5cm x 68.6cm)

The Randolph Caldecott Medal Honoring Excellence in Illustration for Children

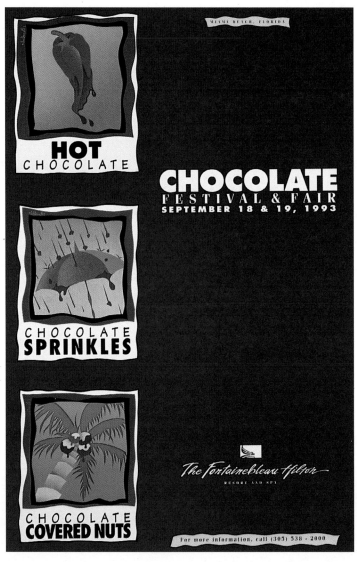

[CLOCKWISE FROM TOP LEFT]

EVENT CITY FAIR OPENING
DESCRIPTION CAMPAIGN MATERIALS
DESIGN FIRM SULLIVANPERKINS
ART DIRECTOR RON SULLIVAN
DESIGNER LINDA HELTON
ILLUSTRATOR LINDA HELTON

EVENT CHOCOLATE FESTIVAL AND FAIR
DESIGN FIRM SCHWARTZ AND KAPLAN ADVERTSING
ART DIRECTOR RENEE KUCI
DESIGNER RENEE KUCI
ILLUSTRATOR SID DANIELS

THIS EVENT WAS HELD AT THE FONTAINEBLEAU HILTON RESORT
AND SPA IN MIAMI BEACH, FLORIDA.

EVENT 1994 TEJANO CONJUNTO FESTIVAL
DESCRIPTION AIRBRUSH GOAUCHE
COMPUTER SOFTWARE CORELDRAW **4**
DESIGNER RICHARD O. MENCHACA
ILLUSTRATOR RICHARD O. MENCHACA
PHOTOGRAPHER ANSEN SEALE

THIS POSTER WAS ENTERED IN THE 13TH ANNUAL STATEWIDE
TEJANO CONJUNTO FESTIVAL CONTEST.

Event 30th Leonard J. Waxdock Bird Calling Contest
Design Firm Bartels & Company Inc.
Art Director David Bartels
Designer Brian Barclay
Illustrator James Marsh

DESIGN FIRM HEINS CREATIVE, INC.
ART DIRECTORS JOE HEINS, JIM HEINS
DESIGNER JOE HEINS
ILLUSTRATOR JOE HEINS
CLIENT PRESTONWOOD TOWN CENTER
PURPOSE HOLIDAY MALL PROMOTION
SIZE 12" x 24" (30.5CM x 61CM)

DESIGNERS USED TRADITIONAL TECHNIQUES, INCLUDING HAND-ILLUSTRATION WITH CHALK PASTELS, FOR THIS POSTER DESIGN. THREE OF THE NINE COLORS WERE USED IN A SPLIT-FOUNTAIN BLEND CREATED ON PRESS.

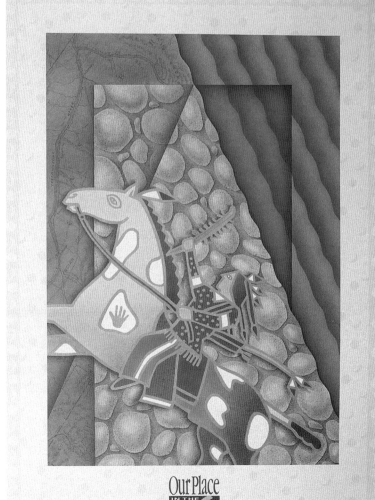

DESIGN FIRM HEINS CREATIVE, INC.
ART DIRECTORS JIM HEINS, JOE HEINS
DESIGNER JIM HEINS
ILLUSTRATOR JIM HEINS
CLIENT WESTERN HERITAGE CENTER
PURPOSE EXHIBIT PROMOTION
SIZE 17" x 25.5" (43.2CM x 64.8CM)

FOR THIS PROMOTION, TRADITIONAL TECHNIQUES WERE USED, INCLUDING HAND-ILLUSTRATION WITH AN AIRBRUSH AND COLORED PENCILS.

Places, Pasts & Images of the Yellowstone Valley, 1880–1940   Western Heritage Center, Billings, Montana
Funding from the National Endowment for the Humanities

Design Firm Tracy Sabin Graphic Design
Art Director Jim Gordon
Designer Tracy Sabin
Illustrator Tracy Sabin
Client Gordon Screen Printing
Purpose Self-promotion calendar
Size 19" x 34" (48.3cm x 86.4cm)

Design Firm Yamamoto Moss
Art Director Gregory Pickman
Designer Gregory Pickman
Illustrator Mercedes McDonald
Client Twin Cities Marathon
Purpose Race announcement
    and commemoration
Size 22" x 32" (55.9cm x 81.2cm)

The illustrator used vibrant chalk pastel colors for this race poster.

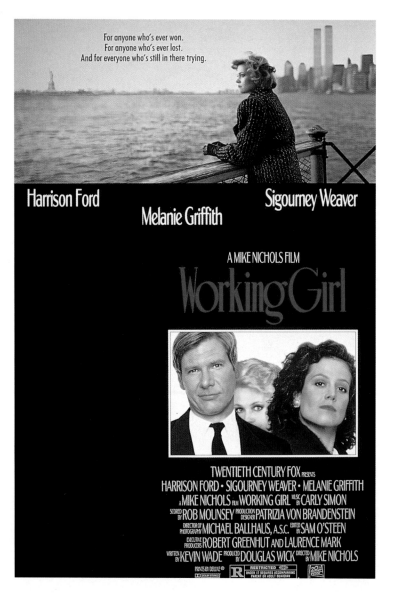

WORKING GIRL

MOVIE COMPANY TWENTIETH CENTURY FOX
DISTRIBUTOR OF FILM TWENTIETH CENTURY FOX
DESIGN FIRM MIKE SALISBURY COMMUNICATIONS INC.
ART DIRECTOR CHRIS PULA
DESIGNERS MIKE SALISBURY, MIKE NICHOLS,
   TERRY LAMB, BRIAN FOX

DESIGNERS WIDENED THE PHOTOGRAPH OF MELANIE GRIFFITH AND ADDED THE IMAGE OF THE STATUE OF LIBERTY AND THE BOAT RAILING IN THE COMPUTER.

BURY ME HIGH

MOVIE COMPANY GOLDEN HARVEST
DISTRIBUTOR OF FILM GOLDEN HARVEST
DESIGN FIRM PPA DESIGN LIMITED
ART DIRECTOR BYRON JACOBS
DESIGNER NICK RHODES

THE TYPOGRAPHY AND ARTWORK WAS CREATED IN ALDUS FREEHAND THEN SCANNED IN AND ILLUSTRATED ON QUANTEL PAINTBOX®. ALL MATERIALS WERE PRINTED OFFSET, AND THE TITLE ART WAS APPLIED TO LOBBY CARDS AND POSTERS.

Design Firm Pentagram Design
All Design Woody Pirtle
Client Art Directors Club, NYC
Purpose Call for entries
Size 20" x 36" (50.8cm x 91.4cm)

WINNING

It's not the will to win that matters - everyone has that - it's the will to prepare to win that matters.

PAUL "BEAR" BRYANT

CHANGE

We have always held to the hope, the belief, the conviction that there is a better life, a better world, beyond the horizon

FRANKLIN D. ROOSEVELT

LEARNING

The real voyage of discovery consists not in seeking new lands but in seeing with new eyes.

PROUST

SUCCESS

Coming together is a beginning. Keeping together is progress. Working together is success.

HENRY FORD

DESIGN FIRM SUBURBIA STUDIOS
ALL DESIGN RUSS WILLMS
CLIENT PRIORITY MANAGEMENT
PURPOSE RETAIL
SIZE 18" x 24" (45.7CM x 61CM)

DESIGN FIRM KEILER DESIGN GROUP
ART DIRECTOR CHRISTOPHER PASSEHL
DESIGNER CHRISTOPHER PASSEHL
PHOTOGRAPHER WOODRUFF/BROWN
CLIENT HARTFORD STAGE
PURPOSE PLAY ANNOUNCEMENT
SIZE 20.5" x 34" (52.1CM x 86.4CM)

INSIGHT, *the* COMBINATION *of*
REAL WORLD KNOWLEDGE
and AN INSTINCT *for* TOMORROW'S
BUSINESS PROBLEMS.

ORACLE

DESIGN FIRM FRAZIER DESIGN
ALL DESIGN CRAIG FRAZIER
CLIENT ORACLE CORPORATION
PURPOSE PROMOTION
SIZE 24" x 32" (61CM x 81.3CM)

DESIGN FIRM FRAZIER DESIGN
ALL DESIGN CRAIG FRAZIER
CLIENT ORACLE CORPORATION
PURPOSE PROMOTION
SIZE 24" x 32" (61CM x 81.3CM)

LISTENING,
the KEY *to*
SUCCESSFULLY ROUTING *a* PROBLEM
TOWARD *its*
RIGHTFUL SOLUTION.

ORACLE

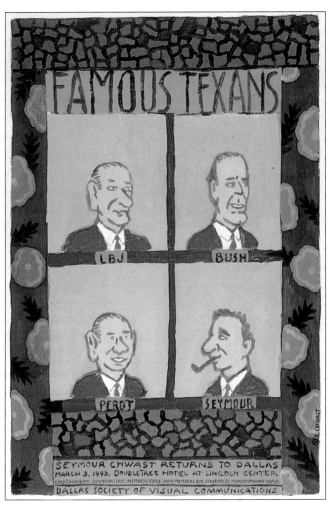

EVENT EARTH DAY NYC
DESIGN FIRM THE PUSHPIN GROUP, INC.
ART DIRECTOR SEYMOUR CHWAST
DESIGNER SEYMOUR CHWAST
ILLUSTRATOR SEYMOUR CHWAST

THIS DESIGN FOR EARTH DAY 1991 WAS
PRINTED ON THE BACK OF REMAINING
EARTH DAY 1990 POSTERS.

EVENT "FAMOUS TEXANS"/SPEAKING ENGAGEMENT,
    DALLAS SCHOOL OF VISUAL COMMUNICATION
DESIGN FIRM THE PUSHPIN GROUP
ART DIRECTOR SEYMOUR CHWAST
DESIGNER SEYMOUR CHWAST
ILLUSTRATOR SEYMOUR CHWAST

JANIS, POSTER

MOVIE COMPANY
UNIVERSAL PICTURES
DISTRIBUTOR OF FILM
UNIVERSAL PICTURES
PHOTOGRAPHER
JIM MARSHALL
ILLUSTRATOR/ARTIST
CHARLIE WILD

TO GIVE THIS DOCUMENTARY
FILM A FEATURE FEELING, THE
DESIGNERS USED INNOVATIVE
TYPE AND A CLEAN
BACKGROUND.

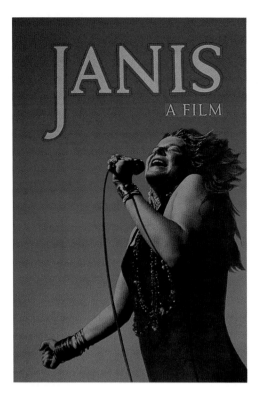

ACTRESS

MOVIE COMPANY
GOLDEN HARVEST
DISTRIBUTOR OF FILM
GOLDEN HARVEST
DESIGN FIRM
PPA DESIGN LIMITED
ART DIRECTOR
BYRON JACOBS
DESIGNER
BYRON JACOBS

THE PHOTOGRAPHIC IMAGES AND
MECHANICAL ARTWORK,
INCLUDING TYPE PREPARED WITH
ALDUS FREEHAND, WERE COLOR-
SEPARATED AND OFFSET PRINTED.

RACHEL-RACHEL

MOVIE COMPANY
WARNER BROS.
DISTRIBUTOR OF FILM
WARNER BROS.
DESIGN FIRM
MIKE SALISBURY
COMMUNICATIONS INC.
ART DIRECTOR
MIKE SALISBURY
DESIGNER
DWIGHT SMITH
ILLUSTRATOR/ARTIST
JEFF WACK

THIS RE-RELEASE POSTER WAS
DEVELOPED WITH AIRBRUSH
OVER PHOTOGRAPHY.

BARCELONA

MOVIE COMPANY
CASTLE ROCK ENTERTAINMENT
DISTRIBUTOR OF FILM
FINE LINE FEATURES
DESIGN FIRM
BLT & ASSOCIATES INC.
ART DIRECTOR
BLT & ASSOCIATES INC.
DESIGNER
BLT & ASSOCIATES INC.
PHOTOGRAPHERS
BOB MARSHAK, ERIC ROBERT
DIGITAL IMAGING
IMAGIC

THE DESIGNERS USED A CUSTOM
METALLIC YELLOW ACCENT AND
A MOTHER-OF-PEARL TITLE
TREATMENT ON THIS SIX-
COLOR DESIGN.

BASIC INSTINCT

MOVIE COMPANY
TRISTAR PICTURES

DISTRIBUTOR OF FILM
TRISTAR PICTURES

DESIGN FIRM
MIKE SALISBURY
COMMUNICATIONS INC.

ART DIRECTORS
BILL LOPEZ, MIKE SALISBURY

DESIGNER
MIKE SALISBURY

ILLUSTRATOR/ARTIST
JACK UPSOM

IMAGES OF THE ACTORS'
HEADS WERE COMBINED BY
COMPUTER WITH BODY-
DOUBLE IMAGES
FOR THIS GRAPHIC.

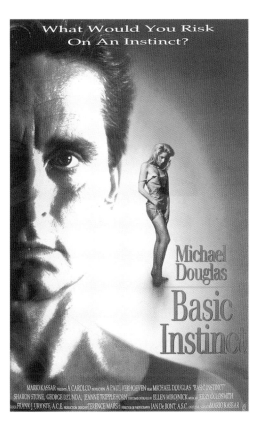

THE RIVER RAT

MOVIE COMPANY
PARAMOUNT PICTURES

DISTRIBUTOR OF FILM
PARAMOUNT PICTURES

DESIGN FIRM
MIKE SALISBURY
COMMUNICATIONS INC.

ART DIRECTOR
MIKE SALISBURY

DESIGNER
TERRY LAMB

ILLUSTRATOR/ARTIST
JEFF WACK

THE IMAGES WERE DEVELOPED
WITH THE USE OF PAINT OVER
PHOTOGRAPHS.

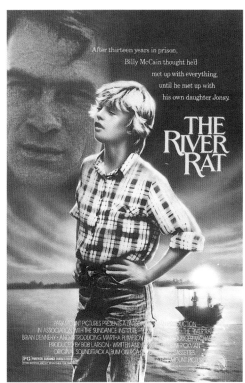

THE CUTTING EDGE

MOVIE COMPANY
MGM

DISTRIBUTOR OF FILM
MGM

DESIGN FIRM
MIKE SALISBURY
COMMUNICATIONS INC.

ART DIRECTOR
BILL COPER

DESIGNER
MIKE SALISBURY

DESIGNERS COMBINED IMAGES
OF THE ACTORS' HEADS,
OLYMPIC RINGS, AND UNIT
STILLS, ALONG WITH AIRBRUSH,
TO DEVELOP THIS DESIGN.

THE UNDERNEATH

MOVIE COMPANY
GRAMERCY PICTURES

DISTRIBUTOR OF FILM
GRAMERCY PICTURES

DESIGN FIRM
MIKE SALISBURY
COMMUNICATIONS INC.

ART DIRECTOR
MIKE SALISBURY

DESIGNERS
RON BROWN, MIKE SALISBURY

ILLUSTRATOR/ARTIST
RON BROWN

ALL GRAPHICS WERE CREATED IN
QUARKXPRESS FROM VARIOUS
STILL PHOTOGRAPHS.

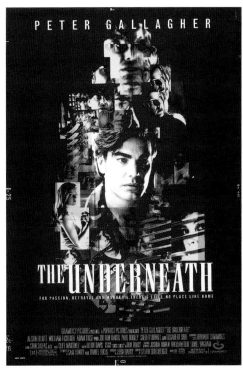

SPORTS EVENT

DESIGN FIRM MULLER + COMPANY
DESIGNE DAVID SHULT
ART DIRECTO DAVID SHULTZ
PHOTOGRAPHER STEVE CURTIS

FIVE DIFFERENT COMPANIES, INCLUDING THE DESIGNER,
PHOTOGRAPHER, COMPUTER RETOUCHER, FILM HOUSE,
AND PRINTER, DONATED THEIR SERVICES FOR THIS PIECE.

THE BUCK BUCHANAN SPORTS FESTIVAL

SATURDAY, FEBRUARY 11, 1995, 1-5 P.M. AT THE KANSAS CITY MERCHANDISE MART, 115TH & METCALF

KC BLUES & JAZZ FESTIVAL JUL. 29.30.31

PENN VALLEY PARK SPONSORED BY PEPSI

BLUES & JAZZ POSTER

DESIGN FIRM MULLER + COMPANY
ALL DESIGN JOHN MULLER

THIS ILLUSTRATION WAS CREATED SIMPLY WITH OPAQUE MARKERS
AT A SMALL SCALE, THEN ENLARGED AT THE SEPARATOR.
TYPOGRAPHY WAS INCORPORATED INTO THE ART, AND OTHER
TYPESETTING WAS KEPT TO A MINIMUM. THE PAPER WAS DONATED.

ILLUSTRATION ACADEMY

DESIGN FIRM MULLER + COMPANY
DESIGNER JON SIMONSEN
ART DIRECTORS JOHN MULLER, JON SIMONSEN
PHOTOGRAPHER MIKE REGNIER

SINCE THIS DESIGN WAS CREATED FOR AN
ILLUSTRATION SCHOOL, THE DESIGN FIRM WAS ABLE
TO ACQUIRE ALL DESIGN WORK AT NO FEE.

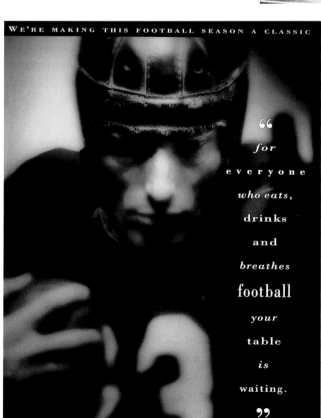

WE'RE MAKING THIS FOOTBALL SEASON A CLASSIC

"

for

everyone

who eats,

drinks

and

breathes

football

your

table

is

waiting.

"

HOULIHAN'S FOOTBALL POSTER

DESIGN FIRM MULLER + COMPANY
DESIGNE CHARLES HOFFMAN
ART DIRECTO CHARLES HOFFMAN
PHOTOGRAPHER WILLIAM HAWKES

A CMYK READING WAS TAKEN AT TWO POINTS IN THE
SINGLE TRANSPARENT IMAGE. THE TWO COLORS CHOSEN
BECAME THE TRAP COLORS IN THE TYPE, THUS LIMITING
ADDITIONAL PRINTING COSTS.

Design Firm Antero Ferreira Design
Art Director Antero Ferreira
Designers Antero Ferreira,
Eduardo Sotto Mayor
Illustrator Eduardo Sotto Mayor
Purpose Clothing promotion
Size 26.8" x 18.9" (68cm x 48cm)

Design was completed on an Apple Macintosh with Aldus FreeHand and Adobe Photoshop software.

Design Firm Antero Ferreira Design
Art Director Antero Ferreira
Designer Antero Ferreira
Illustrators Sofia Assalino, Joana Alves
Photographer Oscar De Almeida
Client A.C. Pimenta
Purpose Pimentinha Winter
Collection promotion
Size 18" x 9" (46cm x 22cm)

Design was completed using 3-D illustration, photographs, and Aldus FreeHand and Adobe Photoshop software.

Event "JOHN SAYLES POSTER SERIES"
Design Firm SAYLES GRAPHIC DESIGN
Art Director JOHN SAYLES
Designer JOHN SAYLES

THIS SERIES OF POSTERS PROMOTES TALKS
BY GRAPHIC DESIGNER JOHN SAYLES.

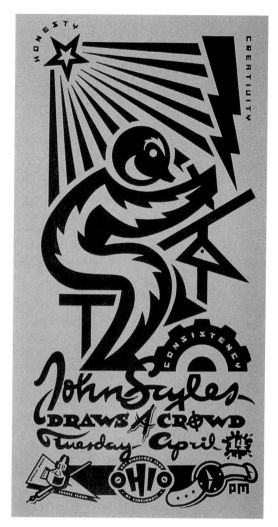

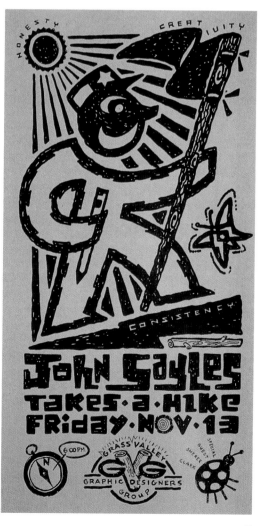

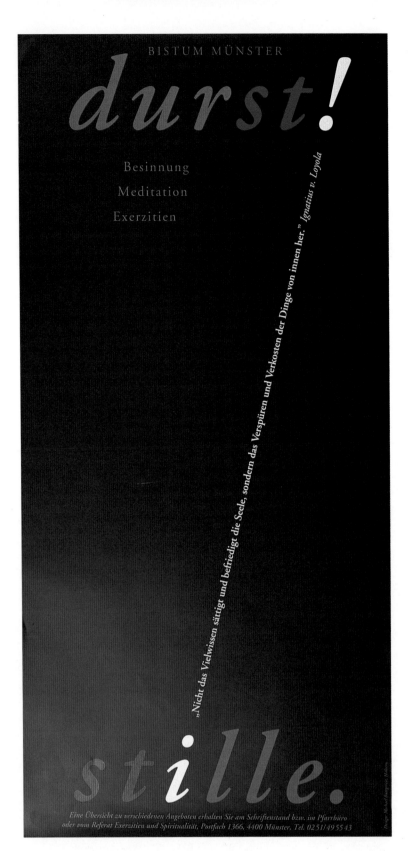

DESIGN FIRM BUTTGEREIT & HEINDENREICH
ART DIRECTOR MICHAEL BUTTGEREIT
DESIGNER MICHAEL BUTTGEREIT
CLIENT BISTUM MÜNSTER
PURPOSE INVITATION TO SPIRITUAL EXERCISES
SIZE 33" X 15.75" (84CM X 40CM)

DESIGNERS USED ALDUS FREEHAND 3.11
TO COMPLETE THIS POSTER.

DESIGN FIRM BUTTGEREIT & HEINDENREICH
ART DIRECTOR MICHAEL BUTTGEREIT
& WOLFRAM HEIDENREICH
DESIGNER MICHAEL BUTTGEREIT
& WOLFRAM HEIDENREICH
CLIENT BUTTGEREIT & HEIDENREICH,
KOMMUNIKATIONS-DESIGN
PURPOSE ANTI-VIOLENCE AND
ANTI-RACISM POSTER

DESIGN CREATED WITH THE USE
OF ALDUS FREEHAND 3.11.

How Strong Is Your Portfolio?

Design Firm Paper Shrine
All Design Paul Dean

The budget for this flyer was essentially non-existent. Copyright-free illustrations from a rescue book were used. Once designed, the piece was photocopied, in black, onto 8.5- by 14-inch pieces of manilla cardstock cut from some discarded folders.

Attention Aspiring Graphic Designers

Design Firm Paper Shrine
All Design Paul Dean

This piece was designed with copyright-free illustrations and was photocopied in colors, red and black, onto recycled paper trimmed from another, larger job.

How STRONG is your portfolio?

Pump it up for PORTFOLIO REVIEW! All junior and senior graphic design majors must submit a portfolio to room 118 of the Art Building by 5P.M., Thursday, December 1st!

Juniors must submit 8 to 10 pieces and a resumé is optional!
Seniors must submit 10 to 12 pieces and a resumé is required!
Contact your graphic design professor for more information!

Design Firm Vaughn Wedeen Creative Inc.
Art Director Steve Wedeen
Designers Steve Wedeen,
Lucy Hitchcock, Dan Flynn
Illustrator Vivian Harder
Client US West Foundation
Purpose Internal sales promotion
Size 24" x 36" (61cm x 91.4cm)

Design Firm Vaughn Wedeen Creative Inc.
Art Directors Rick Vaughn, Steve Wedeen
Designer Rick Vaughn
Illustrator Rick Vaughn
Client Vaughn Wedeen Creative Inc.
Purpose Self-promotion
Size 19.5" x 35.5" (49.5cm x 90.2cm)

GLENN CLOSE   CHRISTOPHER WALKEN

Sarah
PLAIN AND TALL

GLENN CLOSE AND CHRISTOPHER WALKEN IN "SARAH, PLAIN AND TALL"

THE 175TH PRESENTATION OF THE HALLMARK HALL OF FAME

SATURDAY, DECEMBER 19, 1992 ON CBS TELEVISION

CLOSED CAPTIONED FOR THE HEARING IMPAIRED

Hallmark Hall of Fame

SARAH PLAIN AND TALL
DISTRIBUTOR OF FILM
A SELF PRODUCTIONS, INC.
& TRILLIUM PRODUCTIONS, INC.
PRODUCTION
DESIGN FIRM
MULLER + COMPANY
ART DIRECTOR
JOHN MULLER
ILLUSTRATOR/ARTIST
MARK ENGLISH

FOUR SEPARATE PHOTOS WERE
ASSEMBLED AND OUTPUT AS A
16- BY 20-INCH PRINT. THE
ASSEMBLED PRINT WAS THEN
DRAWN UPON AND SCANNED
CONVENTIONALLY.

OUT OF TOWN
LARRY GROSSMAN

Design Firm Larry Grossman
All Design Larry Grossman
Client Posner Fine Arts
Purpose Gallery retail

Poster created on a 7100 Power Macintosh
with Adobe Photoshop software.

ON THE TOWN
LARRY GROSSMAN

Design Firm Primo Angeli Inc.
Art Directors Primo Angeli, Carlo Pagoda
Designer Primo Angeli
Computer Illustrators Marcelo De Freitas, Paul Terrill
Client San Francisco Film Society
Purpose San Francisco International Film Festival
Size 34" x 23" (86.4cm x 58.4cm)

The poster was created using Adobe Illustrator. The textured look in the collage background was achieved through a unique application of WD-40 directly to the Cal-Comp print-out. The collage was then photographed and re-scanned into the layout and the San Francisco Film Society trademark was superimposed at a diagonal.

Design Firm Primo Angeli Inc.
Art Director Primo Angeli
Designer Primo Angeli
Computer Illustrator Marcelo De Freitas
Photographer June Fouche
Client Pendleton (San Francisco)
Purpose Pendleton Mission
Dolores Blanket
Size 42" x 17.25" (106.7cm x 43.8cm)

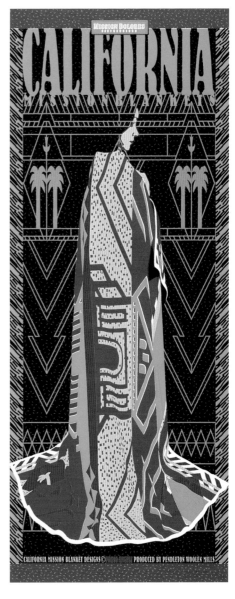

BECKY SHARP

DESIGN FIRM GLUEBOY INTERNATIONAL
DESIGNER TAL LEMING
ILLUSTRATOR DAVID HOTSTREAM

THE DESIGN WAS DONE IN EXCHANGE FOR FREE
ADMISSION TO THE SHOW. THE POSTER WAS GIVEN A
"DIRTY" LETTERPRESS LOOK SINCE IT HAD TO BE
PHOTOCOPIED. THE ORANGE CHARACTERS WERE
SPRAY-PAINTED USING A STENCIL. THE TOP AND
BOTTOM WERE THEN TRIMMED TO GIVE THE
POSTERS A "PRINT-SHOP TRASH" LOOK.

BECKY SHARP

DESIGN FIRM GLUEBOY INTERNATIONAL
DESIGNER TAL LEMING
PHOTOGRAPHER U.S. ARMY

DESIGN FOR THIS BAND PROMOTION WAS
DONATED IN EXCHANGE FOR FREE ADMISSION
TO SHOWS AND AN OCCASIONAL GUITAR SOLO
ON THE LAST SONG AT SOME SHOWS. THE
POSTERS WERE DESIGNED TO BE REPRODUCED ON
A PHOTOCOPIER USING BLACK, BLUE, AND RED
TONER ON A VARIETY OF COLORED PAPERS.

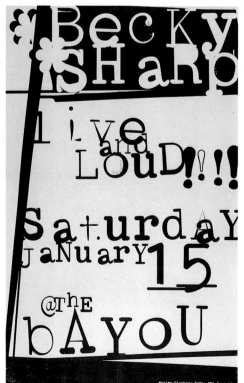

THEATER SCHMEATER

DESIGN FIRM STUDIO M D
DESIGNER RANDY LIM
ART DIRECTORS RANDY LIM, JESSE DOQUILO, GLENN MITSUI
ILLUSTRATOR RANDY LIM

WITH THE BUDGET CONSTRAINTS OF A SMALL LOCAL THEATER, THE BLACKLINE DIAZO PROCESS WAS CHOSEN TO PRODUCE ECONOMICAL LARGE-FORMAT POSTERS. BLACK IS VERY BOLD AND CAN EASILY BE SEEN FROM A DISTANCE.

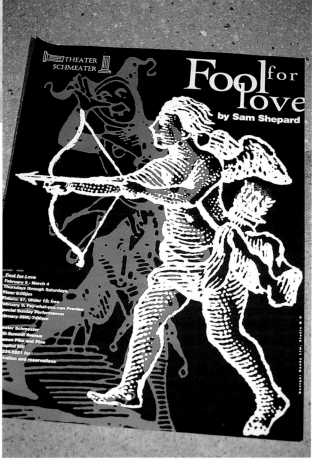

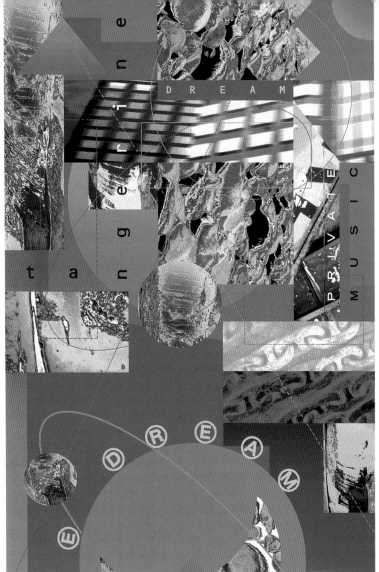

Design Firm Design/Art Inc.
All Design Norman Moore
Client Laura Tamburino/
III Sound & Stage
Purpose Art show announcement
Size 24" x 36" (61cm x 91.4cm)

[FACING PAGE]
A photo of industrial pipes was scanned
to a Photo CD and reversed to a negative
and greyscale. The windows were added in
Adobe Photoshop, while the type and
layout were finished in QuarkXPress.

Design Firm Design/Art Inc.
All Design Norman Moore
Client Private Music
Purpose Record promotion
Size 24" x 36" (61cm x 91.4cm)

Desktop scans of photos were
manipulated in Adobe Photoshop.

Design Firm Design/Art Inc.
All Design Norman Moore
Client Design/Art Inc.
Purpose Self promotion
Size 24" x 36" (61cm x 91.4cm)

Desktop scans of photographs were
manipulated in Adobe Photoshop,
while the layout and type were
created in QuarkXPress.

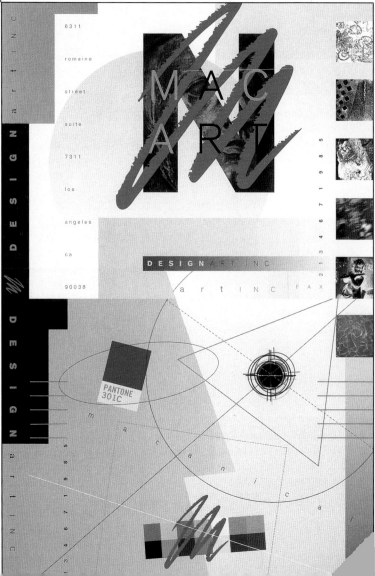

111 SOUND & STAGE
and LAKELORD PRODUCTIONS

presents

DECEMBER 1993-FEBRUARY 1994

XX XART

111 gallery, 111 leroy street, NY

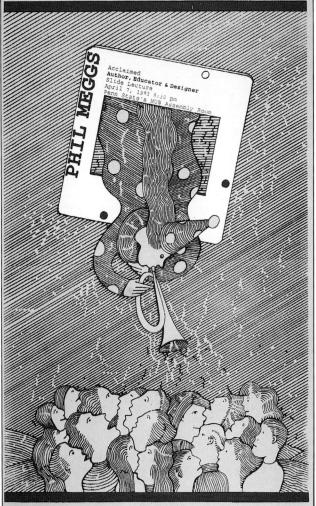

EVENT LECTURE SERIES
DESIGN FIRM SOMMESE DESIGN
ART DIRECTOR LANNY SOMMESE
DESIGNER LANNY SOMMESE

LECTURE SERIES WAS MADE UP OF WRITERS
FROM EASTERN EUROPE.

EVENT COSTUME BALL FOR ARCHITECTURE STUDENTS
DESIGN FIRM SOMMESE DESIGN
ART DIRECTOR LANNY SOMMESE
DESIGNER LANNY SOMMESE
ILLUSTRATOR LANNY SOMMESE

EVENT PHIL MEGGS LECTURE
DESIGN FIRM SOMMESE DESIGN
ART DIRECTOR LANNY SOMMESE
DESIGNER LANNY SOMMESE
ILLUSTRATOR LANNY SOMMESE

LECTURER IS AN EXPERT ON GRAPHIC DESIGN HISTORY.

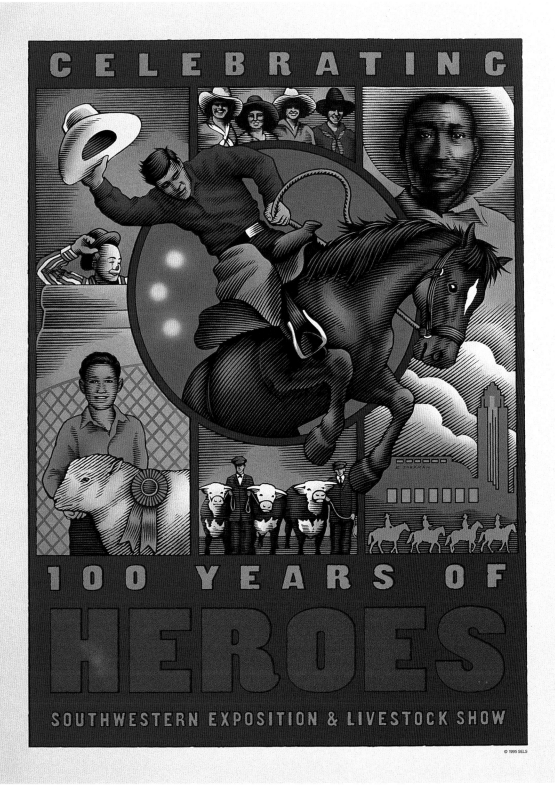

DESIGN FIRM WITHERSPOON ADVERTISING
ART DIRECTOR KYLE MIZE
DESIGNER KYLE MIZE
ILLUSTRATOR ERWIN SHERMAN
CLIENT SOUTHWESTERN EXPOSITION &
    LIVESTOCK SHOW
PURPOSE 100 YEARS OF HEROES
SIZE 16" X 21.5" (40.7CM X 54.2CM)

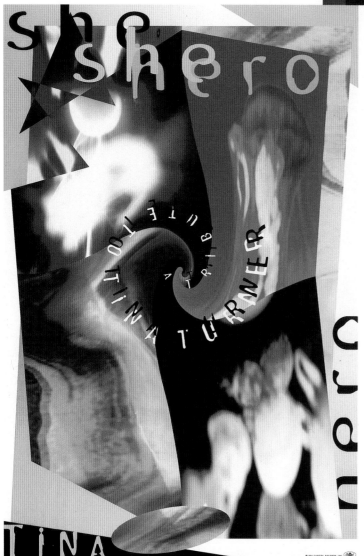

DESIGN FIRM DESIGN/ART, INC.
ALL DESIGN NORMAN MOORE
CLIENT CAPITOL RECORDS
PURPOSE RECORD PROMOTION
SIZE 24" x 36" (61CM x 91.4CM)

DESKTOP SCANS OF PHOTOS WERE
MANIPULATED IN ADOBE PHOTOSHOP.
TYPE AND LAYOUT WERE COMPLETED IN
QUARKXPRESS USING SKETCHPAD EXTENSION.

DESIGN FIRM DESIGN/ART, INC.
ALL DESIGN NORMAN MOORE
PHOTOGRAPHER DOUGLAS BROTHERS
CLIENT EPITAPH RECORDS
PURPOSE RECORD PROMOTION
SIZE 24" x 36" (61CM x 91.4CM)

HIGH-RESOLUTION SEPIA-TONED PHOTO
LETTERING WAS DONE IN ALDUS FREEHAND 4.0.
LAYOUT WAS COMPLETED IN QUARKXPRESS.

Design Firm Planet Design Co.
Art Directors Dana Lytle, Kevin Wade
Designers Dana Lytle, Martha Graettinger
Client Milwaukee Ballet
Purpose Season announcement
Size 14" x 24" (35.6cm x 70cm)

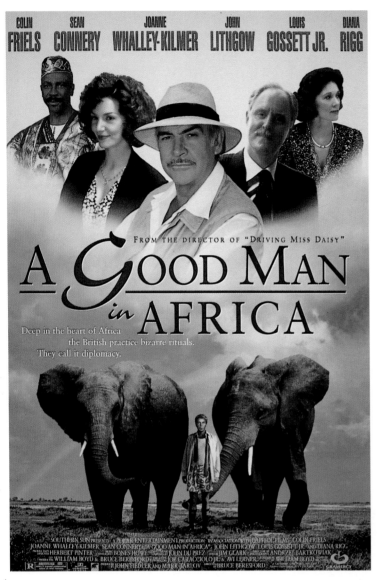

A GOOD MAN IN AFRICA

MOVIE COMPANY UNIVERSAL PICTURES
DISTRIBUTOR OF FILM GRAMERCY PICTURES
DESIGN FIRM BRD DESIGN
ART DIRECTOR NEVILLE BURTIS
DESIGNER NEVILLE BURTIS

DESIGNERS COMPOSITED THE MAJORITY OF IMAGERY
FROM THE UNIT IN QUANTEL PAINTBOX®.

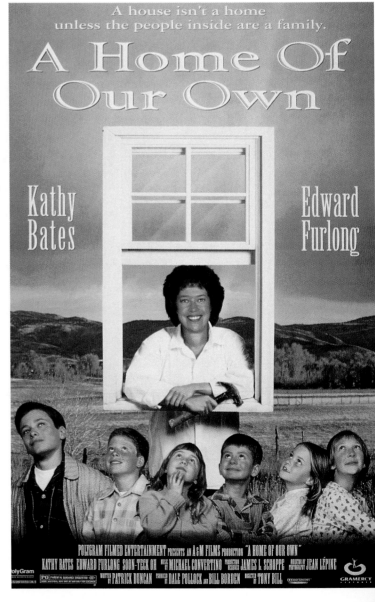

A HOME OF OUR OWN

MOVIE COMPANY
POLYGRAM FILMED ENTERTAINMENT
DISTRIBUTOR OF FILM GRAMERCY PICTURES
DESIGN FIRM BRD DESIGN
ART DIRECTORS TABITHA DELATORRE,
PETER KING ROBBINS
DESIGNER PETER KING ROBBINS

PHOTOGRAPHERS USED A BODY DOUBLE FOR
ACTRESS KATHY BATES AND STRIPPED THE IMAGE
OF THE MODEL'S HEAD IN QUANTEL PAINTBOX®.
THE WINDOW WAS PART OF THE BODY-DOUBLE
SHOOT AND THE IMAGES OF CHILDREN WERE
COMPOSITED IN QUANTEL PAINTBOX®.

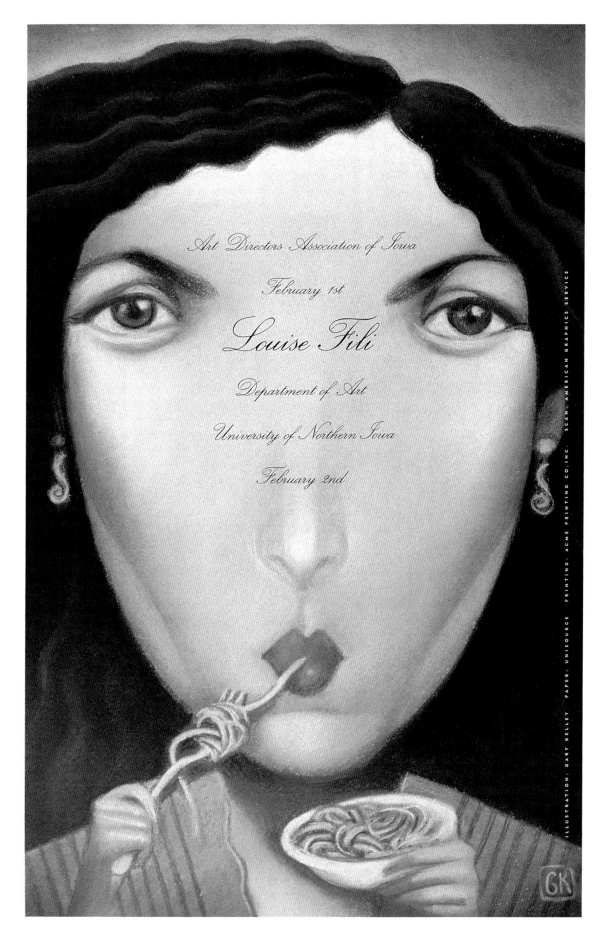

Art Directors Association of Iowa

February 1st

Louise Fili

Department of Art

University of Northern Iowa

February 2nd

Design Firm Louise Fili Ltd.
Art Director Louise Fili
Designer Louise Fili
Illustrator Gary Kelley
Client University of
    Northern Iowa
Purpose Lecture announcement
Size 11" x 17" (27.9cm x 43.2cm)

A pastel illustration was used for this piece along with computer-generated type.

ILLUSTRATION: GARY KELLEY ~ PAPER: UNISOURCE ~ PRINTING: ACME PRINTING CO. INC. ~ SCAN: AMERICAN GRAPHICS SERVICE

Come to the Q101 party, and you could end up in Barcelona...

Counting Crows

uno dos tres quatro

The countdown to our
annual party is underway.

Join us on Tuesday, September 20th,
1994, from 5:30 pm until 9:00 pm at
Lucky's, 213 West Institute Place, for
fun food and music. You might win a
six-night, seven-day trip to Barcelona,
Spain to catch the Counting Crows. It
all includes airfare, hotel and tickets
to the show.

Please R.S.V.P. soon to Diana Cazares
at 312. 245. 1254.

From your friends at Chicago's New Rock Alternative

UNO DOS TRES QUATRO

DESIGN FIRM SEGURA, INC.
DESIGNER CARLOS SEGURA
ART DIRECTOR CARLOS SEGURA

THIS PROMOTIONAL CONCERT POSTER WAS PRINTED IN
TWO COLORS, YELLOW AND BLACK. SCANNED IMAGES
WERE DISTORTED IN ADOBE PHOTOSHOP, THEN THE
VISUAL WAS USED IN LAYERS AND PRINTED 2-COLOR.

Design Firm Masterline Communications, Ltd.
Art Directors Grand So, Kwong Chi Man
Designer Kwong Chi Man
Illustrator James Fong
Photographer K.K. Wong
Client Wah Shing Sports Trading Co., Ltd.
Purpose Advertisement
Size 20" x 28" (50.8cm x 71.2cm)

Designers used computer retouching to mix and match several photos and illustrations together.

Design Firm Grand Design Co.
Art Directors Grand So, Kwong Chi Man
Designers Grand So, Raymond Au, Terry Lam, Kwong Chi Man
Client Superbowl - The Art of Eating Congee
Purpose Advertisement
Size 15" x 21" (37.7cm x 53.3cm)

This is the first high-class congee shop in Hong Kong. The concept comes from 1950s Hong Kong. It aims to educate Hong Kong people to appreciate congee.

Here kitty kitty...

YOU CAN TRY IT...BUT WE WOULDN'T

RECOMMEND IT. YOU CAN TRY DESIGNING

AND PRODUCING YOUR OWN BROCHURE

TOO...BUT WE DON'T RECOMMEND THAT

EITHER. AT DCE DESIGN WE HAVE AWARD-

WINNING DESIGNERS AND ILLUSTRATORS

THAT CAN HELP TELL YOUR STORY IN A WAY

YOU'LL BE PLEASED TO SHOW ANYONE.

SO BEFORE YOU GRAB A YOU-KNOW-WHAT

BY THE TAIL, CALL US. IT DOESN'T

HAVE TO BE A JUNGLE OUT THERE.

DCE GRAPHICS • 581-6114

Sit...stay...rollover...nice poochy!

SOMETIMES YOU KNOW EXACTLY WHAT

YOU WANT TO SAY, BUT THE MESSAGE

DOESN'T GET THROUGH. WE CAN HELP.

AT DCE GRAPHICS, OUR AWARD-WINNING

DESIGNERS AND ILLUSTRATORS

WORK CLOSELY WITH YOU TO CREATE

BROCHURES AND PROMOTIONAL PIECES

THAT TELL YOUR STORY AND LOOK

GREAT TOO. BEFORE YOU GET BITTEN

BY THE UNKNOWN, CALL US. WE JUST

MAY GIVE YOU A NEW LEASH ON LIFE.

DCE GRAPHICS • 581-6114

DESIGN FIRM DCE DESIGN
ART DIRECTOR SCOTT GREER
DESIGNER DAVID MEIKLE
ILLUSTRATOR DAVID MEIKLE
CLIENT DCE MARKETING/DESIGN
PURPOSE SELF PROMOTION
SIZE 9" X 16.5" (22.86 CM X 42 CM)

THE ILLUSTRATION FOR THIS POSTER WAS CREATED BY
HAND, USING ACRYLIC ON GESSOED ETCHING PAPER.

You wanted warm and fuzzy...

WHAT YOU GOT WAS WARM AND FUZZY

WITH TEETH, CLAWS AND AN ATTITUDE.

IF YOU ARE CONSIDERING A NEW BROCHURE

OR PROMOTIONAL PIECE WE CAN HELP.

AT DCE DESIGN OUR AWARD-WINNING

DESIGNERS AND ILLUSTRATORS

WORK CLOSELY WITH YOU TO ENSURE YOU

GET EXACTLY WHAT YOU WANT. A NEW

BROCHURE DOESN'T HAVE TO BE A

GRISLY EXPERIENCE. CALL US.

WE'LL MAKE IT BEARABLE.

DCE GRAPHICS • 581-6114

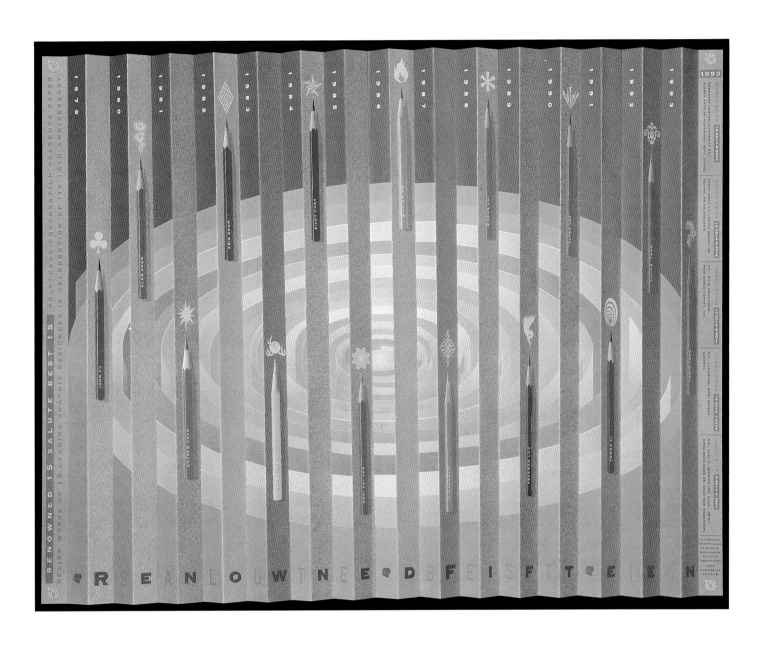

Design Firm Kan Tai-keung Design & Associates Ltd.
Art Director Freeman Lau Siu Hong
Designers Freeman Lau Siu Hong,
Veronica Cheung Lai Sheung
Computer Illustrator Benson Kwun Tin Yau
Client Polytrade Corporation
Objective To produce a poster announcing
the 15th anniversary of a paper company

Innovation A single poster displays three different
perspectives. In the right view, 15 pencils represent
the 15 designers and their celebratory icons. In the
left view, 15 sheets of paper form an unending
spiral, representing the client's concept of
synergy. From the front, pencils and spiral join
to form a 15th-birthday cake for the client.

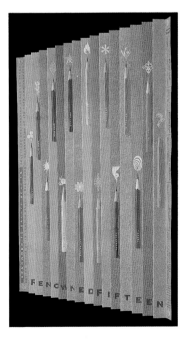

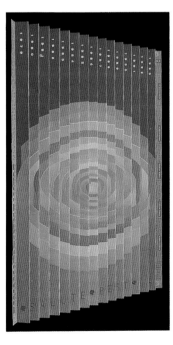

Design Firm Vaughn Wedeen Creative, Inc.
Art Director Rick Vaughn
Designer Rick Vaughn
Illustrator Rich Vaughn
Photographer Valerie Satagto
Client US West Foundation
Purpose Internal sales promotion
Size 24" x 36" (61cm x 91.4cm)

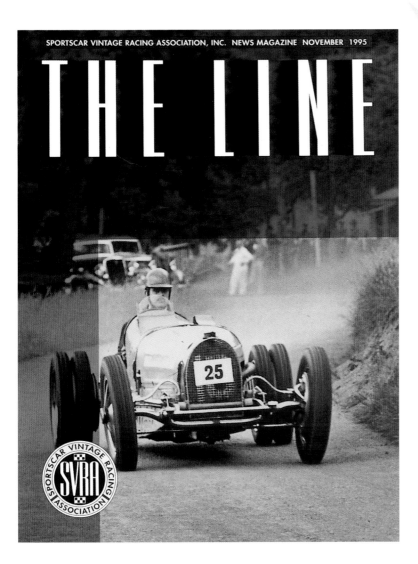

SPORTSCAR VINTAGE RACING ASSOCIATION, INC. NEWS MAGAZINE NOVEMBER 1995

THE LINE

SPORTSCAR VINTAGE RACING ASSOC.

DESIGN FIRM MULLER + COMPANY
DESIGNERS JOHN MULLER, JENNIFER BROSNAHAN
PHOTOGRAPHER KLEMANTASKI

THESE COVERS WERE GANGED TOGETHER ON ONE PRESS FORM AND USED COMMON COLORS. THE PHOTOGRAPHS WERE DONATED FROM A VINTAGE COLLECTION TO SAVE USAGE FEES, AND THE DESIGN FORMAT WAS KEPT CONSISTENT, DECREASING DESIGN TIME AND SIMPLIFYING PRODUCTION TECHNIQUES.

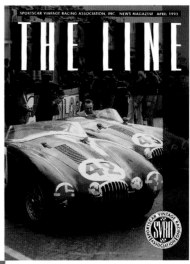

SPORTSCAR VINTAGE RACING ASSOCIATION, INC. NEWS MAGAZINE APRIL 1995

THE LINE

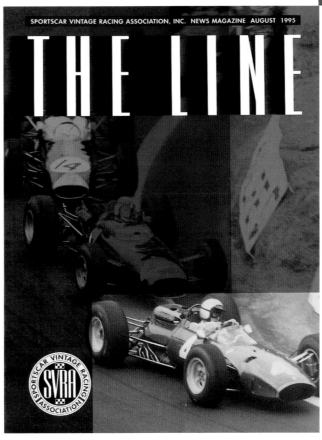

SPORTSCAR VINTAGE RACING ASSOCIATION, INC. NEWS MAGAZINE AUGUST 1995

THE LINE

DESIGN FIRM TREND DESIGN LTD.
ART DIRECTOR FRANKIE CHEUNG
DESIGNER FRANKIE CHEUNG
PHOTOGRAPHER KENNETH YEUNG
CLIENT URBAN COUNCIL, HONG KONG
PURPOSE 1950S DRAMATIC FILM PROMOTION
SIZE 28" X 18" (71 CM X 46 CM)

A TRADITIONAL LADIES' HANDKERCHIEF COMMONLY CARRIED BY LADIES OF THE PERIOD WAS USED AS THE MAIN VISUAL, ECHOING THE THEME "TIME FOR TEARS" — A PARADE OF FAMOUS SAD MOVIES BY THREE FAMOUS DIRECTORS.

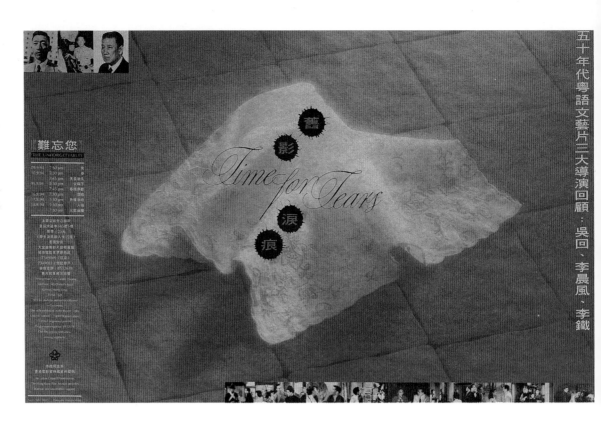

DESIGN FIRM TREND DESIGN LTD.
ART DIRECTOR FRANKIE CHEUNG
DESIGNER FRANKIE CHEUNG
PHOTOGRAPHER KENNETH YEUNG
CLIENT URBAN COUNCIL, HONG KONG
PURPOSE 1950S DRAMATIC FILM PROMOTION
SIZE 20" X 30" (50.8CM X 76.2CM)

IMAGES WERE RETRIEVED FROM ORIGINAL BLACK AND WHITE FILMS AND REPRODUCED INTO BLACK AND WHITE PRINTS WITH THE 1950S BORDER. PROPS WERE USED, INCLUDING COINS OF THE SAME PERIOD, TO DELIVER THE 1950S MOOD.

SLEEPLESS IN SEATTLE

MOVIE COMPANY TriStar Pictures
DISTRIBUTOR OF FILM TriStar Pictures
DESIGN FIRM BLT & Associates Inc.
ART DIRECTOR BLT & Associates Inc.
DESIGNER BLT & Associates Inc.
PHOTOGRAPHER Timothy White
DIGITAL IMAGING Imagic

DESIGNERS USED A 6-COLOR PROCESS
FOR THIS IMAGE.

SHADOWLANDS

MOVIE COMPANY
SAVOY PICTURES ENTERTAINMENT
DISTRIBUTOR OF FILM
SAVOY PICTURES ENTERTAINMENT
AGENCY B.D. FOX &
FRIENDS, INC. ADVERTISING
ART DIRECTORS CINDY LUCK,
GARRETT BURKE, BRIAN D. FOX
DESIGNER GARRETT BURKE
PHOTOGRAPHER KEITH HAMSHERE
ILLUSTRATOR METAFOR
COPYWRITER KATE COX

Design Firm NBA Properties, Inc.
Art Director Tom O'Grady
Designer Suzanne Gulbin
Illustrator Diane Borowski
Client NBA Properties, Inc
Purpose NBA All-Star Weekend promotion
Size 18" x 36" (45.7cm x 91.4cm)

Design Firm TBC Design
Art Director Lenny Rosenthal
Illustrator Gary Yealdhall
Client Babe Ruth Museum
Purpose Babe Ruth Museum
     opening promotion
size 16" x 30" (40.6cm x 76.2cm)

DESIGN FIRM SULLIVANPERKINS
ART DIRECTOR RON SULLIVERN, LORRAINE CHARMAN
DESIGNER LORRAINE CHARMAN
PHOTOGRAPHER ROBB DEBENPORT
COPYWRITER CHRISTINE LOWRANCE
CLIENT MARCH OF DIMES NORTH TEXAS CHAPTER
PURPOSE WALKAMERICA POSTER
SIZE 19" X 19" (48.3CM X 48.3CM)

THE POSTER COMBINES PHOTOGRAPHY WITH TYPESETTING
AND DESIGN CREATED IN ADOBE ILLUSTRATOR 5.0.

DESIGN FIRM SULLIVANPERKINS
ART DIRECTOR ART GARCIA
ILLUSTRATOR ART GARCIA
COPYWRITER MARK PERKINS
CLIENT DSVC
PURPOSE PROMOTION
SIZE 23.5" X 25.5" (59.7CM X 59.7CM)

ALL ART WAS PICKED UP FROM ORIGINAL ART
FROM ART CHANTRY AND COMPOSED AS A
PORTRAIT. BASE ART WAS PRINTED BLACK
WITH PMS COLORS AS BACKGROUND SOLIDS.

Blast Off To The 21st Century

Design Firm Kiku Obata & Company
Designer Kiku Obata & Company
Art Director Rich Nelson
Illustrator Rich Nelson
Photographer Rich Nelson

The retro-style illustration of this invitation utilizes flat colors to keep film trapping to a minimum. The savings on film allowed for five colors instead of two or three. The invitation, program cover, and RSVP card were designed for the same five colors so that printing could be done in a single press run. Stock was bought at a discount in exchange for the paper merchant's printed credit on all materials.

Design Firm Keiler Design Group
Art Director Mike Scricco
Designer Jeff Lin
Photographer Frank Marchese
Client Connecticut Public Television
Purpose Wine auction promotion
Size 34" x 24" (86.4cm x 61.0cm)

Design Firm Clifford Selbert
Design Collaborative
Art Director Melanie Lowe
Designer Melanie Lowe
Illustrator Marco Ventura
Client Massachusetts
Horticultural Society
Purpose Flower show promotion
Size 23" x 16" (58.4cm x 40.6cm)

123rd New England
Presented by THE MASSACHUSETTS
HORTICULTURAL SOCIETY SPRING
FLOWER SHOW

MARCH 5-13, BAYSIDE EXPO
A World of Color
SPONSORED BY
The Boston Globe

TO CHARGE TICKETS CALL 1 800 442 1854 · ALSO AVAILABLE AT STOP & SHOP STORES

ADDITIONAL SPONSORSHIP BY BELMONT SPRINGS WATER CO. · FOR INFORMATION CALL 617 536-9280

Pat Duimst

"That's why they call it a DINING ROOM!"

*A less stress, more love
approach to family meal times*

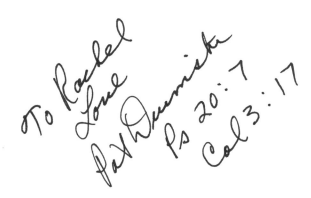

ISBN No. 09774324-3-2
Copyright 2010 by Golden Apple Greetings

Interior photos by Leslie Mulder, Cathy Runyon, Chris Selley
Cover photos by Jeffrey Cunningham

GOLDEN APPLE GREETINGS
5066 Lake Michigan Drive, Allendale, Michigan 49401
www.goldenapplegreetings.com

Dedication ♥ ♥ ♥

This book is dedicated to all homemakers

who really do believe in the concept

that caring for a family's needs is a privilege

and an honorable profession

rather than a chore and a second-class career.

God has placed them in families to use the gifts He gave them,

just as He places others in different ministries.

In serving others, we serve Him.

CONTENTS

Butterscotch Pie ❤ ❤ ❤

I had never heard those two words used together before, but as I took my first bite of that creamy, delicious pie*, I saw the sparkle in Pat's eye.

As a chef, I know that sparkle. It is the look that good cooks get when they see someone enjoy their creations, fueling the passion to get out the pots and pans and do it all over again.

After tasting many of Pat's dishes over the years, I wasn't too surprised to hear she was writing a cookbook. But I must say, after looking at the recipes and seeing the work and detail involved, I was very impressed and inspired. I know this book will inspire you to get in the kitchen and try these recipes out, just as it has me.

This book shows the vast experience Pat has with food and the satisfaction she feels by making people happy through their stomachs. It's easy to follow and will give you many new fun and tasty ideas to try out.

And who knows.

Maybe you will get that sparkle, too.

　Cheers,
　"Chef Jeff"
　Jeffrey Brandon

Recipe for Grandma's Easy Butterscotch Pie, p. 161

Jeffrey Brandon was executive chef for the Frederick Meijer Gardens for 5 years and is currently a corporate chef for Superior Foods in Grand Rapids, MI. He and his wife, Amy, have three boys to cook for. Visit his Web site, www.fixingyourmeals.com.

Photo by Ryan Start of RMS Photography. Used by permission.

It's about the love ♥ ♥ ♥

One day my husband and I visited my daughter and had the privilege of being served a delicious dinner. It was evident she had given much thought and time to prepare and serve it just right.

Part way through the meal, the youngest child asked to be excused since he had eaten all he planned to eat and wanted to go and play. His father told him he needed to wait until we were finished and he complied without complaining.

As he sat politely waiting for us to finish, I mentioned to him how fortunate he was to have a mom who cared enough to fix him a delicious meal. Then I asked him, "How many of your friends eat their meals all together as a family?"

He thought a minute and said "None."

How sad! Cooking, for me, has always been my artistic outlet and gives me much satisfaction. I enjoy nothing more than putting together a mouthwatering meal and presenting it in style to my family and friends. The joy of taking a batch of oatmeal raisin cookies to my pastor or making a pot of soup for a neighbor gives me much pleasure indeed. Through the years, I have spent as much time as possible mentoring my own children in the art of cooking because I wanted them to enjoy it as much as I did.

With that in mind, you can imagine my surprise when another daughter called me one day and tearfully confessed she was exhausted with trying to think up something to serve, tired of cooking and couldn't imagine doing this the rest of her life. At the same time, she wanted to make sure her family was taken care of. She felt guilty because she didn't cook from "scratch" and just didn't seem to know how to make meals come out right and on time.

As we talked, I came to realize my enjoyment in cooking wasn't only about the food; it was about the joy of serving those I loved. It never mattered to my family if I made them a bowl of chili or a complicated meal with all the trimmings; their reaction was the same. We enjoyed eating together, the kids often helped cook, and we had a good time in the kitchen. Many of our best memories are of making cookies on snow days when schools were closed, cooking for holidays, or making a meal for a sick friend, but the food was never the topic of conversation. It was always the activity surrounding the food that we remembered.

Over the next few months I spent some time helping Janet simplify her cooking duties and showed her how to use some convenience products and offered some other tips for making it easier to fix meals for her family. The time I spent with Janet, and realizing that many young women shared her frustration, became the inspiration for this book.

We are living in a society that is burdened with appointments, extra-curricular activities and stress. One of the things that has been affected is family meal times, evidenced by my grandson's remark. Moms are over-booked with running children to activities and often, working outside the home. Dads find themselves, of necessity, preparing food for young children. Parents have little time to think about menus. They may have to prepare meals that can be eaten in shifts. This book is meant to help you successfully prepare meals that are delicious and appealing to your family and to encourage you to come together at some point in the day just to be together. Mealtime is a good time, since everyone has to eat sometime.

The act of preparing a meal is not necessarily about the food; it's about meeting the needs of your family without begrudging the service. Most any parent would tell you that is very important to them.

This book also in intended to be a teaching tool for beginning cooks, most often young women, to help them successfully prepare meals for their families with confidence. The meals are not necessarily balanced by most standards but instead are meals that families will enjoy and will eat. The food need not be gourmet fare and doesn't need to be made from "scratch." Many recipes use ready-to serve products from the grocery store. What is essential is preparation by someone who is interested in demonstrating through an act of caring how important fellowship among family members is.

My desire also is that young women will once again believe that the role of being a homemaker is an honorable profession blessed by God, and that they are equipped by their Creator to fill this role.

I am hoping this book will help young cooks understand that caring for a family and mentoring children is an honorable and enjoyable profession that God instituted and that He has given them special gifts to accomplish that purpose. You don't need to be a gourmet cook or make dishes with a long list of ingredients. The main ingredient is the time spent with those you love. When time is in short supply, these recipes will help you make the most of that most precious gift.

I've put some menus together in this book to help you get ideas as well as some other recipes. Most recipes are very easy and some are a little more challenging for when you feel like spending some time experimenting.

The most important thing to remember is that it isn't about the food,
 it's about the love.

Love,

Grandma Pat

Some Instructions for Using This Book

1. Along with the menu section you will find a <u>grocery list</u> for each menu. (I haven't included <u>salt and pepper</u> in any of the grocery lists since I believe they are a given and you need to always have them on hand.)Take the time to make sure you have all the ingredients for each meal you are going to fix. Nothing is more frustrating than to get halfway through fixing cranberry chicken and find out you don't have any cranberry sauce.

2. I haven't always given instructions to <u>grease or spray any pans</u> or dishes. It is assumed for any dish you prepare. I prefer to use food release spray, but you may use whatever you choose to lubricate your pans and dishes to make cleanup easier.

3. <u>Recipes are only an idea to start with</u>. You may read a recipe and think to yourself that it would taste better if you added a different spice, meat or other ingredient. By all means, experiment and make it your own.

4. The recipes found in this book are <u>basic, simple food recipes</u>. They are mostly quick to prepare or make use of a slow cooker. There are a few more complicated recipes for you to try when you are feeling more creative, but for the most part, they are for you to use for your family when you have ball games, church meetings, or other obligations that require a quick meal with little fuss.

5. The menus in this book are not necessarily "balanced meals" since most families simply don't eat that way due to time, budget or food preferences. <u>The most well-balanced meal in the world is useless if your family doesn't like it</u>.

6. There is nothing that says you need to prepare everything yourself or that you need to cook everything from "scratch." <u>Take advantage of the great prepared mixes, frozen items and other convenience products</u> that are available to help you fix a great meal and save you time. There is nothing virtuous about slaving over a hot stove all day unless it is something you particularly enjoy. You can still prepare a great meal for your family using all the shortcuts available.

7. I haven't put <u>serving sizes</u> on most of the recipes since what I may view as eight servings may only be four servings to your family.

8. Container or can sizes may vary slightly with brands, but should not affect recipe quality.

Have a great time with this book and enjoy mealtimes with your family!

MENUS
for the
FAMILY TABLE

GRILLED REUBEN SANDWICH MEAL

MENU

- ♥ *Grilled Reuben Sandwiches*
- ♥ *Green Salad*
- ♥ *Sherri's Brownies*

GRILLED REUBEN SANDWICH MEAL
grocery list
- ☐ Dark rye bread
- ☐ Swiss cheese
- ☐ Corned beef
- ☐ Thousand Island dressing
- ☐ Dressing for salad
- ☐ Sauerkraut
- ☐ Butter
- ☐ Greens, tomatoes, cucumber, onion
- ☐ Sugar
- ☐ Flour
- ☐ Cocoa
- ☐ Eggs
- ☐ Powdered sugar
- ☐ Vanilla
- ☐ Nuts (Optional)

GRILLED REUBENS

(If you have a Foreman grill, plug it in to heat.)

For each sandwich:
2 slices dark rye bread
2 slices corned beef from the deli
1 slice Swiss cheese
1/4 cup sauerkraut, rinsed and drained
Thousand Island dressing

Butter each slice of bread on one side. On the unbuttered side of one slice, layer the ingredients as given. Top with the other slice of bread, buttered side out. Grill in a Foreman grill, nonstick pan or on a griddle until toasted and hot through.

GREEN SALAD

Chopped lettuce (Two or three kinds of lettuce and greens mixed together make a nice salad.)
Cherry tomatoes
1 cucumber, sliced
1/4 medium red onion, sliced

Assemble ingredients and serve with dressing of your choice.

(recipes continued on next page)

SHERRI'S BROWNIES

When my daughter Sherri was in the 4th grade she came home from school one day and said she had decided to make brownies. This is the recipe she made and we have used it ever since!

Oven temperature: 325 degrees

2 cups sugar
1/3 cup unsweetened cocoa powder
1 ½ cups flour
2 sticks butter or margarine, melted
4 eggs, slightly beaten
1 teaspoon vanilla
1/2 teaspoon salt

Mix dry ingredients. Add remaining ingredients and stir just until mixed. Pour into a 9"x13" baking pan. Bake at 325 degrees approximately 25 minutes. Brownies should be soft in the middle. When cool, frost with butter cream frosting.

BUTTER CREAM FROSTING

4 cups powdered sugar
1 stick (8 tablespoons) soft butter or margarine
1/8 teaspoon salt
1/2 cup unsweetened cocoa powder
Approximately 5 to 6 tablespoons evaporated or chocolate milk

Mix all ingredients together and frost cooled brownies. Top with chopped nuts, if desired.

COMPANY PORK LOIN DINNER

MENU

- ♥ *Butterflied Pork Loin*
- ♥ *Peas and Rice*
- ♥ *Applesauce*
- ♥ *Baked Dessert*

COMPANY PORK LOIN DINNER
grocery list
- ☐ Pork loin
- ☐ Fresh basil leaves
- ☐ Roasted red peppers
- ☐ Sun dried tomatoes
- ☐ Herbed goat cheese
- ☐ Chive cream cheese
- ☐ Rice
- ☐ Onion
- ☐ Garlic or garlic powder
- ☐ Chicken broth
- ☐ Italian seasoning
- ☐ Dried basil leaves
- ☐ Frozen baby peas
- ☐ Grated Parmesan cheese
- ☐ Applesauce

COMPANY PORK LOIN

Oven temperature: 425 degrees

You will need approximately 4 to 6 ounces of meat for each person you are going to serve. This recipe is for a roast weighing approximately three pounds.

Prepare pork loin the night or day before you are going to serve it.
Cut the pork loin almost in half, but not all the way through. Lay it out flat.
Pat dry with paper towels. Spread the following ingredients in thin, even layers on the pork:

1 jar, about 10 ounces, roasted red peppers (located in the section with pizza ingredients or by the spaghetti sauces)
Six to eight sun dried tomatoes, cut up with scissors
1 4-ounce tube herbed goat cheese (found in the deli gourmet cheese case)
8 ounces cream cheese with chives (found in round tubs with other cream cheese)
10 large basil leaves, briefly dipped into boiling water

Roll the loin halves back together. Using butcher string or kite string, tie the roast in several places. Roll in plastic wrap and put into the refrigerator overnight.

When ready to roast the pork, drizzle a little olive oil over the surface and rub it in. Sprinkle with a little salt and pepper. Roast in a shallow pan about 45 minutes depending on the size. A meat thermometer inserted into the middle of the roast should read 150 degrees. Take out and cover with foil and let rest for approximately fifteen minutes, then slice.

(recipes continued on next page)

PEAS and RICE

1½ cups long grain white rice
3/4 cup chopped onion
2 garlic cloves, minced
2 (14½-ounce) cans chicken broth
1/3 cup water
3/4 teaspoon Italian seasoning
1/2 teaspoon dried basil
1/2 cup frozen baby peas, thawed (put in a
    strainer and run hot water over them)
1/4 cup grated Parmesan cheese

Combine rice, onion and garlic in slow cooker.

In saucepan, mix chicken broth and water. Bring to a boil. Add the Italian seasoning and basil. Stir into rice mixture in slow cooker. Cover and cook on low two to three hours until liquid is absorbed. Stir in peas. Cover and cook a little longer until hot through. Add cheese and stir well.

APPLESAUCE

Use a good brand of commercial applesauce from the store. To get a "homemade" taste, add one or more of the following ingredients: cinnamon, sugar, nutmeg, cloves, orange zest, lemon zest, orange juice, lemon juice or melted butter. Experiment!

BAKED DESSERT

Purchase a good quality yellow, white or angel food cake from the bakery, and frozen strawberries. Serve slices of cake with strawberries and whipped topping.

FOUR BEAN & SAUSAGE MEAL

MENU

- ♥ *Four Bean & Sausage Casserole*
- ♥ *Biscuits*
- ♥ *Cream Cheese Bars*

FOUR BEAN & SAUSAGE CASSEROLE

15-ounce can great northern beans, drained
15½-ounce can black beans, rinsed and drained
16-ounce can red kidney beans, drained
15-ounce can butter beans, drained
1½ cups ketchup
1/2 cup chopped onion
1 green pepper, chopped (if you like)
1 pound smoked sausage, Polish sausage, smoky links or ham
1/4 cup brown sugar
1 teaspoon garlic powder
1 teaspoon Worcestershire sauce
1/2 teaspoon dry mustard or 1 teaspoon regular mustard
Dash of Tabasco sauce (if you like)

Combine all ingredients in a slow cooker and cook on medium for approximately 7 hours, depending on your slow cooker.

BISCUITS

Follow the directions for biscuits on the Bisquick or store brand baking mix box.

CREAM CHEESE BARS

Yellow cake mix
1 stick butter or margarine, melted
1 egg

8-ounce package cream cheese, softened
1 pound (3 to 4 cups) powdered sugar
3 eggs

Mix together cake mix, butter and egg. Spread on greased and floured 9"x13" baking pan. Mix together the remaining ingredients and pour on top of the cake batter. Bake 350 degrees for 40 minutes.

KENTUCKY HOT BROWN MEAL

MENU

- ♥ *Kentucky Hot Brown*
- ♥ *Fresh Green Beans*
- ♥ *Malt Shoppe Pie*

KENTUCKY HOT BROWN

Oven temperature: 350 degrees

1/4 cup butter or margarine
4 tablespoons flour
2 cups whole or 2% milk
1 cup shredded Cheddar cheese
1/4 teaspoon salt
1/2 teaspoon Worcestershire sauce
1 pound thin-sliced turkey
6 slices toasted bread
3 tomatoes, sliced
10 strips of thick bacon, cooked but not crisp

In a saucepan over low heat, melt the butter and stir in the flour. Whisk in the milk and stir until mixture thickens. Add the cheese, salt and Worcestershire sauce. Stir till heated through and smooth.

Arrange the toast in the bottom of a 9"x13" baking dish. Top the toast with the sliced turkey, cheese sauce, tomatoes and bacon. Bake at 425 degrees for approximately 20 minutes or until bubbly and hot through.

SOUTHERN GREEN BEANS

10-ounce bag of frozen green beans
1/2 of a peeled onion, cut into pieces
1 teaspoon salt

1 teaspoon liquid smoke flavoring
2 slices bacon cut into pieces

Put the green beans into a saucepan and cover with water. Add the salt, onion, smoke flavoring and raw bacon. Bring to a boil and cook for approximately 15 minutes or until beans are tender. Drain and discard the cooked bacon. Serve with a pat of butter on top.

(menus continued on next page)

MALT SHOPPE PIE

1 graham cracker pie crust
1 pint vanilla ice cream, softened
8 ounces whipped topping, thawed

8 ounces Whoppers malted milk balls candy
Topping for garnish

Crush all but 8 Whoppers. Soften the ice cream and mix with the whipped topping and the crushed Whoppers. Turn mixture into the pie crust. Top pie with the reserved Whoppers and freeze for about 4 hours. Serve with more whipped topping.Best if made the day before or night before it is served.

CREAMY CHICKEN SLOW COOKER MEAL

MENU

♥ *Creamy Slow Cooker Chicken over Rice or Noodles*

♥ *Corn*

♥ *Red Gelatin Dessert with Bananas*

CREAMY SLOW COOKER CHICKEN

1 envelope dried onion soup mix
2 cups sour cream
1 can cream of mushroom soup
6 skinless boneless chicken breast halves

Mix soup mix, sour cream and cream of mushroom soup together and put into a slow cooker. Add chicken breast halves, pushing down to make sure all are covered by the sauce. Cover and cook for 6 to 8 hours on low.

Cook rice or noodles according to package directions. (Instant or fresh mashed potatoes also may be used.) Spoon sauce and chicken over rice, noodles or potatoes on serving plates.

CORN

Purchase a package of frozen corn and cook according to package directions.

RED GELATIN DESSERT with BANANAS

Make a 6-ounce package of red gelatin dessert according to package directions. Put in the refrigerator to cool. When cooled but not firmly set, slice two bananas into the gelatin. Cover with plastic wrap and return to refrigerator. When set, cover with whipped topping and serve.

CRANBERRY CHICKEN SLOW COOKER MEAL

MENU

- ♥ *Cranberry Chicken*
- ♥ *Orange Salad*
- ♥ *Ice Cream Sundaes*

CRANBERRY CHICKEN MEAL

grocery list

- ☐ Chicken pieces
- ☐ Celery
- ☐ Onion or dry minced onion
- ☐ Whole berry cranberry sauce
- ☐ BBQ sauce
- ☐ Mixed green or baby spinach
- ☐ Mandarin oranges
- ☐ Red onion
- ☐ Salted pecans or walnuts
- ☐ Olive oil
- ☐ Honey
- ☐ Good vinegar
- ☐ Ice cream
- ☐ Ice cream toppings

CRANBERRY CHICKEN

About 3 pounds chicken pieces
1/2 teaspoon salt
1/4 teaspoon pepper
1/2 cup celery
1/2 cup diced onion or 1 tablespoon dry minced onion
16-ounce can whole berry cranberry sauce
1 cup barbecue sauce

Mix all ingredients together and put into slow cooker. Cook on low approximately 7 hours.

ORANGE SPINACH SALAD

8 cups, loosely packed, mixed greens or baby spinach
10-ounce can Mandarin orange segments, drained
1 cup salted pecans or walnuts
1/2 of a red onion, sliced

DRESSING:

1/2 cup olive oil
2 tablespoons honey
Pinch of salt
1 or 2 teaspoons red wine vinegar or apple cider vinegar

Whisk or shake well until combined.

ICE CREAM SUNDAES

Purchase your favorite ice cream and toppings and let everyone make their own sundaes.

SWEET AROMATIC CHICKEN SLOW COOKER MEAL

MENU

- ♥ *Sweet Aromatic Chicken*
- ♥ *Roasted Sweet Potatoes*
- ♥ *Pineapple Spears*

SWEET AROMATIC CHICKEN

1/2 cup coconut milk (found in the ethnic food section at your grocery store)
1/2 cup water
8 chicken thighs with skin
1/2 cup brown sugar
2 tablespoons soy sauce
1/8 teaspoon ground cloves
2 mashed garlic cloves or 1 teaspoon garlic powder

Combine the coconut milk and water in a slow cooker. Add the remaining ingredients in the order listed. Cook on low approximately 7 hours.

What to do with leftover coconut milk? Make ice cream sundaes with a couple of spoons full of coconut milk over ice cream and a maraschino cherry. Make non-alcoholic piña coladas by placing coconut milk in a pitcher and adding pineapple juice to taste, along with some ice cubes.

ROASTED SWEET POTATOES

Oven temperature: 400 degrees

Peel three medium sweet potatoes and cut into large cubes and place them in a bowl. Drizzle the sweet potato cubes with olive oil and sprinkle with salt and pepper. Mix well to make sure olive oil is on all the cubes. Pour out onto a baking sheet lined with tin foil and roast for approximately 45 minutes, stirring several times.

PINEAPPLE SPEARS

Purchase a fresh pineapple and cut away the outside rind. Cut the pineapple in half, then into fourths. Take out the core. Cut each piece into spears and place on a serving plate with several lettuce leaves to garnish. Cover with plastic wrap and leave at room temperature for several hours for best taste.

COWBOY MEAL

MENU

- ♥ *Cowboy Food*
- ♥ *Cornbread with Jalapenos*
- ♥ *Graham Cracker Cookies*

COWBOY MEAL
grocery list
- ☐ Ground chuck
- ☐ Onion
- ☐ Garlic powder
- ☐ Spanish rice
- ☐ Chili beans
- ☐ Cheddar cheese
- ☐ Cornbread mix
- ☐ Pickled jalapeno peppers
- ☐ Cake frosting
- ☐ Graham crackers

COWBOY FOOD

1 pound ground chuck
1/2 medium onion chopped
1/2 teaspoon salt
1/4 teaspoon pepper
1/2 teaspoon garlic powder
1 can Spanish rice
1 can chili beans
1½ cup shredded Cheddar cheese

Brown the ground beef with the seasonings in a large skillet and drain. Add Spanish rice and beans and return to heat until bubbly. Stir in cheese and melt.

CORNBREAD with JALAPENOS

1 box Jiffy cornbread mix
1/2 cup chopped pickled
    jalapeno peppers

Make mix according to directions and add the drained jalapenos. Bake according to directions.

GRAHAM CRACKER COOKIES

1 can cake frosting of your choice
Graham crackers

Spread the frosting between two graham crackers and serve. (I like chocolate graham crackers and chocolate frosting, but use what you like.)

GERMAN PORK MEAL

MENU

♥ *Pork Roast with Sauerkraut*

♥ *Apple Crisp*

I put this recipe together especially for my son-in-law, Tom Lesher, who is of German descent. He loves good food and I love to cook for him!

GERMAN PORK MEAL
grocery list
- ☐ Pork roast
- ☐ Sauerkraut
- ☐ Brown sugar
- ☐ Granny Smith or canned apples
- ☐ Potatoes
- ☐ Flour
- ☐ Sugar
- ☐ Butter
- ☐ Cinnamon

PORK ROAST with SAUERKRAUT

Oven temperature: 350 degrees

Butt pork roast – about 3 pounds
1 teaspoon sage
1 teaspoon salt
1/2 teaspoon pepper
2 tablespoons olive oil
2 (15-ounce) cans sauerkraut,
rinsed and drained

1/2 cup brown sugar
2 tart apples, such as Granny Smith, peeled,
  cored and sliced
8 red or white potatoes quartered; OR 8 white
  potatoes, peeled and quartered

Season pork roast with sage, salt and pepper. Heat oil in Dutch oven and brown the meat in the oil. Add the remaining ingredients and bake at 350 degrees at least 3½ hours or until meat begins to fall apart.

APPLE CRISP

Oven temperature: 375 degrees

Slice about six or eight good-sized apples in a 9"x13" baking pan. (You can peel or not peel the apples depending on your taste.)You may also substitute two 1-pound cans of sliced apples if you choose.

Mix together:
2 teaspoons cinnamon
1/2 teaspoon salt
1½ cups sugar

Stir into the apples then prepare the topping.

TOPPING:
2 cups flour
1 cup sugar
1 cup butter (two sticks)

Combine ingredients and mix with your hands or with a fork until topping is crumbly and will almost stick together when you squeeze it in your hands. Bake for approximately 1 hour.

ORIENTAL PEPPER STEAK SLOW COOKER MEAL

MENU

- ♥ *Pepper Steak with Rice*
- ♥ *Mud Pie*

ORIENTAL PEPPER STEAK

1 pound sirloin steak, sliced into thin strips
3 tablespoons soy sauce
1/2 teaspoon ground ginger
1 garlic clove, minced, or 1 teaspoon garlic powder
1 green pepper, sliced into strips
1 (4-ounce) can of mushrooms, drained, or 1 cup fresh mushroom slices
1 onion, thinly sliced
1/2 teaspoon crushed red pepper or a pinch of cayenne pepper or a few dashes Tabasco sauce

Combine all ingredients in slow cooker. Cover and cook on low 6 to 8 hours. Serve over cooked rice. Leftovers can be served on sub buns with Provolone cheese.

MUD PIE

1 prepared chocolate crumb pie crust
1 pint coffee flavored ice cream
1 jar prepared fudge topping
8 ounces whipped topping
Pecans

Spread the softened ice cream in the chocolate pie crust. Top with the fudge topping and whipped topping. Sprinkle with pecans.

BEEF STEW
SLOW COOKER MEAL

MENU

- ♥ *Beef Stew with Vegetables*
- ♥ *French Bread*
- ♥ *Cake*

BEEF STEW

3 pounds stew beef, or buy any inexpensive cut of beef
   (round steak or roast) cut into cubes
1 cup water or beef broth
1 cup red wine
1/4 cup flour
2-ounce envelope beef mushroom soup mix
   (in section with dry onion soup mix)
2 cups diced potatoes
1 cup thinly sliced carrots
10-ounce package frozen peas and onions (or use frozen peas and add fresh chopped onion.)

Layer all ingredients in the slow cooker. Cover and cook on low for at least 8 hours. You may put in any other vegetables you like or more of what is called for. If you want the stew thicker, turn cooker on high until it boils and thicken it with a little cornstarch mixed with water, as you would thicken gravy before serving.

FRENCH BREAD

Buy a loaf of French bread. Cut the bread into slices and butter it. Put it under the broiler or on high in the oven for about 2 or 3 minutes. Watch it all the time. Also good with some Mozzarella or Swiss cheese melted on it.

CAKE

Purchase a cake mix of your choice and a can of frosting. Bake according to directions and frost when cool.

HUNGARIAN GOULASH SLOW COOKER MEAL

MENU

- ♥ *Hungarian Goulash with Buttered Noodles*
- ♥ *Green Peas*
- ♥ *Easy Decadent Chocolate Pudding*

HUNGARIAN GOULASH MEAL
grocery list
- ☐ Round steak
- ☐ Onion powder
- ☐ Garlic powder
- ☐ Flour
- ☐ Paprika
- ☐ Tomato soup
- ☐ Sour cream
- ☐ Vegetable of your choice
- ☐ Half and half
- ☐ German chocolate
- ☐ Sugar
- ☐ Eggs
- ☐ Vanilla
- ☐ Whipped topping or whipping cream

HUNGARIAN GOULASH

2 pounds round steak, cut into cubes
1/2 teaspoon onion powder
1/2 teaspoon garlic powder
2 tablespoons flour
1/2 teaspoon salt
1/4 teaspoon pepper
1½ teaspoons paprika
1 can condensed tomato soup
1/2 soup can of water
1 cup sour cream
Cooked egg noodles

Mix meat, onion powder, garlic powder and flour together in slow cooker until meat is well coated. Add remaining ingredients **EXCEPT FOR SOUR CREAM.** Cover and cook on low for approximately 6 hours. Add sour cream about a half-hour before serving.

Cook egg noodles according to the package directions and serve with the goulash.

GREEN PEAS

Purchase a package of frozen green peas. Cook according to directions and serve.

EASY DECADENT CHOCOLATE PUDDING

1 cup half and half
4-ounce package German sweet chocolate, chopped in pieces
Optional whipped cream for topping
1 tablespoon sugar
3 beaten egg yolks
1 teaspoon vanilla

Separate eggs and throw away the whites. Put the yolks in a small bowl and beat up with a whisk. In a heavy small saucepan, combine light cream, chopped chocolate, sugar and salt. Cook and stir over medium low heat until smooth and just beginning to thicken. Gradually stir about half of the hot mixture into the beaten egg yolks, then put the egg yolk mixture into the pan with the rest of the chocolate mixture and return to the heat. Cook and stir over medium low heat 2 or 3 minutes more. Remove from heat, stir in vanilla. Pour into 4 small dishes. Cover and chill several hours or overnight. This dessert is unbelievably rich and creamy. Top with whipped cream if you like.

CORNED BEEF & CABBAGE MEAL

MENU
- ♥ *Corned Beef and Cabbage*
- ♥ *Pudding Cream Pie*

CORNED BEEF & CABBAGE MEAL
grocery list
- ☐ Corned beef brisket
- ☐ Onions
- ☐ Apple juice
- ☐ Brown sugar
- ☐ Orange (optional)
- ☐ Whole cloves
- ☐ Mustard
- ☐ Cabbage
- ☐ Potatoes
- ☐ Carrots
- ☐ Pie crust
- ☐ Pudding mix (and optional add-ins)
- ☐ Half and half
- ☐ Whipped topping

CORNED BEEF & CABBAGE

2 onions, sliced
3-pound corned beef brisket
1 cup apple juice
1/4 cup brown sugar
2 teaspoons orange peel (optional)
6 whole cloves
2 teaspoons prepared mustard
6 cabbage wedges
4 potatoes cut into chunks
3 sliced carrots

Layer all ingredients except cabbage in a slow cooker. Cover and cook on low four hours.

Add cabbage wedges to liquid, pushing down to moisten. Turn to high and cook an additional two to four hours.

PUDDING CREAM PIE

1 prepared pie crust (a graham cracker crust or a frozen pastry
   crust that has been baked and cooled.
6-ounce package instant pudding of your choice (coconut cream is delicious if you like coconut)
2 cups half and half
Half of an 8-ounce tub of whipped topping

Make the pudding using the half and half and fold the whipped topping into it. Put into the pie crust. Top with additional whipped topping.
*If you're using coconut pudding, add coconut to the mixture.
*If you're using chocolate pudding, you can add miniature marshmallows
*If you're using vanilla pudding, you can add chopped walnuts

POLISH KIELBASA & SAUERKRAUT MEAL

MENU

- ♥ *Polish Kielbasa and Sauerkraut*
- ♥ *Chocolate Upside-Down Cake*

POLISH KIELBASA & SAUERKRAUT MEAL
grocery list
- ☐ Green pepper
- ☐ Onion
- ☐ Brown sugar
- ☐ Stewed tomatoes
- ☐ Polish kielbasa
- ☐ Caraway seeds
- ☐ Sauerkraut
- ☐ Chocolate cake mix
- ☐ Butter
- ☐ Chocolate chips
- ☐ Miniature marshmallows

POLISH KIELBASA & SAUERKRAUT

Oven temperature: 350 degrees

1 green pepper, chopped
2 medium onions, chopped
3 tablespoons brown sugar
2 small cans stewed tomatoes
1 large ring (approximately 1 pound) Polish kielbasa, sliced
1/2 teaspoon caraway seeds
28-ounce jar sauerkraut, rinsed and drained

Sauté the green pepper and onions. Place in a large baking dish. Add the remaining ingredients and pour tomatoes over top. Bake at 350 degrees for about 1½ hours.

CHOCOLATE UPSIDE-DOWN CAKE

1 chocolate cake mix
1 tablespoon butter
2 cups chocolate chips
1 cup brown sugar
2 cups miniature marshmallows

Melt the butter in a 9"x13" baking pan. Add brown sugar, chocolate chips and marshmallows. Mix the cake mix according to the directions on the package and pour the batter over the mixture in the baking pan. Bake as directed on the cake mix package.

When done, take out to cool for approximately 10 minutes, then turn upside down onto a baking sheet covered with foil or other serving plate. (You can also just leave the cake in the pan if you like and cut it into squares.)

BEER BRISKET MEAL

MENU

- ♥ *Beer Baked Brisket*
- ♥ *Baked Beans*
- ♥ *Maple Blondies*

BEER BRISKET MEAL
grocery list
- ☐ Beef brisket or chuck roast
- ☐ Beer
- ☐ Onion
- ☐ Chili sauce
- ☐ Brown sugar
- ☐ Garlic cloves
- ☐ Bush's baked beans
- ☐ Ketchup
- ☐ Mustard
- ☐ Worcestershire sauce
- ☐ Bacon (optional)
- ☐ Eggs
- ☐ Butter
- ☐ White sugar
- ☐ Vanilla
- ☐ Flour
- ☐ Baking soda
- ☐ Baking powder
- ☐ Milk
- ☐ White chocolate
- ☐ Powdered sugar
- ☐ Cream cheese
- ☐ Real maple syrup
- ☐ Nuts
- ☐ Vanilla ice cream (optional)

BEER BAKED BRISKET

Oven temperature: 350 degrees

3- or 4-pound beef brisket (If you can't get a
    brisket, use a chuck roast.)
1 teaspoon salt
1/4 teaspoon pepper
1 large onion, sliced
1/2 cup chili sauce
2 tablespoons brown sugar
2 cloves garlic, crushed
12 ounces beer

Place the brisket in a Dutch oven. Season with salt and pepper and top with onion slices. Combine the rest of the ingredients and pour over the meat. Cover with a tight-fitting lid and bake for four hours.

BAKED BEANS

Oven temperature: 325 degrees

4 cans (15 ounces each) Bush's baked beans or
    two big cans (28 ounces)
1/2 cup ketchup or barbecue sauce
1 tablespoon mustard

1/4 cup brown sugar
1 tablespoon Worcestershire sauce
1 onion, chopped
4 slices bacon

Fry the bacon until it's approximately half-cooked. Take it out of the pan and fry the onions in the bacon grease. Remove the onions from the pan and mix with the bacon and all other ingredients. Pour into a large casserole dish and cover and bake approximately one hour. Remove the cover and bake until beans begin to thicken, approximately 1 more hour.

(menus continued on next page)

MAPLE BLONDIES

Oven temperature: 325 degrees

MAPLE BLONDIES:

4 egg whites	1 teaspoon baking soda
1/2 cup butter, softened (1 stick)	1/2 teaspoon baking powder
1/2 cup brown sugar	1/4 teaspoon salt
1/4 cup white sugar	1/2 cup milk
1 teaspoon vanilla	8 ounces white chocolate cut into chunks
2¼ cups flour	1/2 cup walnuts, chopped

To make the Blondies, whip the egg whites until they are stiff and form peaks. Set aside.

In another bowl, mix the softened butter, brown sugar, white sugar and vanilla with an electric mixer until smooth.

In a separate bowl sift together flour, baking soda, baking powder, and salt. Add the dry ingredients to the butter-sugar mixture ingredients and mix well until smooth. Mix in milk, white chocolate chunks and nuts. Gently fold in the egg whites and pour into a 9"x13" baking pan. Bake 40 to 45 minutes.

SAUCE:
1/2 cup softened butter (don't use margarine)
1/2 cup powdered sugar
1/2 cup cream cheese, softened
2 tablespoons real maple syrup
1/4 teaspoon salt

ORANGE CHICKEN SLOW COOKER MEAL

(reduced calorie)

MENU

- ♥ *Orange Chicken*
- ♥ *Rice*
- ♥ *Chocolate Cola Cake*

ORANGE CHICKEN

4 skinless boneless chicken breasts
4 tablespoons flour
1 jar low-sugar orange marmalade
3/4 cup barbecue sauce
1 tablespoon soy sauce
1 tablespoon grated ginger root (buy grated ginger root in a jar or grate fresh.)

Toss chicken with the flour and put into a slow cooker. Stir in all remaining ingredients. Cover and cook on low six to eight hours.

RICE

Prepare rice according to package directions. (Instant rice is very easy but regular rice is cheaper.)

CHOCOLATE COLA CAKE

1 chocolate cake mix
12 ounces diet cola

Mix together and put into a greased 9"x13" baking pan. Bake approximately 30 minutes. To serve, cut into squares and top with fat-free whipped topping

HAWAIIAN CHICKEN MEAL
(reduced calorie)

HAWAIIAN CHICKEN
grocery list
- ☐ Chicken
- ☐ Honey
- ☐ Canned sliced pineapple
- ☐ Heinz steak sauce
- ☐ Asparagus
- ☐ Olive oil
- ☐ Sugar-free pudding
- ☐ Sugar-free whipped topping

MENU
- ♥ *Hawaiian Chicken*
- ♥ *Roasted Asparagus*
- ♥ *Sugar Free Pudding*

HAWAIIAN CHICKEN

Oven temperature: 350 degrees

2 pounds chicken pieces
1 teaspoon salt
1/4 teaspoon pepper
1 tablespoon honey
8 ounce can sliced pineapple
2 tablespoons pineapple juice
1 tablespoon Heinz A1 steak sauce

Place chicken in foil lined baking pan. Season with the salt and pepper and bake 10 minutes.

Drain the pineapple and save the juice. Mix the juice, honey and the steak sauce in a bowl. Pour over the chicken and bake another 35 to 45 minutes. Arrange the pineapple slices over the chicken and baste with the sauce and continue to bake until the chicken pieces are done.

ROASTED ASPARAGUS

Oven temperature: 425 degrees

1 bundle of asparagus
Extra virgin olive oil
Kosher salt
Black pepper

Lay the asparagus on a baking sheet and drizzle with the olive oil. Sprinkle kosher salt and black pepper over all and mix until all spears are coated with the mixture. Roast in a 425 degree oven approximately 30 minutes or until fork tender. (You can prepare this in the oven while the Hawaiian chicken is cooking. Plan on at least 45 minutes.)

SUGAR-FREE PUDDING

Purchase your favorite flavor of sugar-free instant pudding and prepare according to package directions. Serve with fat-free whipped topping.

"WHOLE MEAL" CHICKEN MEAL

MENU

- ♥ *"Whole Meal" Chicken Casserole*
- ♥ *Mandarin Cake*

"WHOLE MEAL" CHICKEN CASSEROLE

Oven temperature :350 degrees

2 whole boneless skinless chicken breasts, approximately
   8 ounces each; or 4 smaller halves
4 boneless, skinless chicken thighs,
   approximately 4 ounces each
8 small red potatoes scrubbed and quartered
8 ounces fresh mushrooms quartered
1 large onion, thinly sliced
4 cloves garlic thinly sliced OR
1 tablespoon garlic powder
1/2 teaspoon crushed dried thyme
1/2 teaspoon dried rosemary
1/4 teaspoon pepper
1 tablespoon olive oil
1 small navel orange
1 large lemon

Wash orange and lemon. Do not peel. Slice thinly and remove seeds.

Rinse chicken pieces: remove and discard any visible fat. Pat the chicken pieces dry with paper towels. Arrange chicken in a baking pan and surround with potatoes and mushrooms. Scatter onion and garlic over the chicken and vegetables. Sprinkle with thyme, rosemary and pepper. Drizzle the olive oil over all. Arrange orange and lemon slices on top. Cover the pan tightly with a lid or foil and bake 45 minutes. Uncover the pan and continue to bake until browned.

MANDARIN CAKE

1 yellow cake mix
1 egg

1 small can mandarin oranges with juice
15-ounce can crushed pineapple drained

Mix the cake mix with the egg and oranges with the juice. Bake in a 9"x13" baking pan for approximately 30 minutes. Cool and cover with the crushed pineapple. Serve with fat-free whipped topping.

CHICKEN TORTELLINI MEAL

MENU

- ♥ *Chicken Tortellini Casserole*
- ♥ *Cashew Nut Salad*
- ♥ *Parfaits*

**CHICKEN TORTELLINI MEAL
grocery list**

- ☐ Tortellini
- ☐ Monterey jack cheese
- ☐ Boneless, skinless chicken breasts
- ☐ Flour
- ☐ Butter
- ☐ Olive oil
- ☐ Dried onion
- ☐ Chicken bouillon cubes
- ☐ Chicken broth
- ☐ Granulated sugar
- ☐ Cream of mushroom or cream of chicken soup
- ☐ Sour cream
- ☐ Lettuce
- ☐ Swiss cheese
- ☐ Cashews
- ☐ Vegetable oil
- ☐ Vinegar
- ☐ Mustard
- ☐ Poppy seeds
- ☐ Gelatin dessert mix
- ☐ Vanilla pudding
- ☐ Whipped topping

CHICKEN TORTELLINI CASSEROLE

Oven temperature: 350 degrees

8 ounces tortellini, chicken or cheese filled
1 pound Monterey jack cheese, shredded
4 boneless, skinless chicken breast halves
3 tablespoons flour
1/4 cup butter or margarine
3 tablespoons olive oil
2 teaspoons dried onion
2 chicken bouillon cubes
8 ounces chicken broth
1 tablespoon sugar
1 can cream of mushroom or cream of chicken soup
1/2 cup sour cream

Cook the tortellini according to package directions until just done. Drain and put into a baking dish. Top with half of the Monterey jack cheese.

Dredge the chicken in the flour and fry in the butter and olive oil in a skillet. When done, cut into bite size pieces and put on top of the cheese in the baking dish.

Put dry onion, bouillon cubes, chicken broth, cream soup and sugar in the skillet that you cooked the chicken in. Bring to a boil and turn off. Add the remaining cheese and stir in the sour cream and pour over the chicken in the baking dish. Bake at 350 degrees approximately 35 to 45 minutes.

CASHEW NUT SALAD

1/2-head of iceberg lettuce,
   torn into bite size pieces
1 cup cashew nuts coarsely chopped
1 cup Swiss cheese, cut into thin strips
1/2 cup vegetable oil
1/3 cup granulated sugar

2 tablespoons vinegar
1/2 teaspoon mustard
1/2 teaspoon poppy seeds
1/4 teaspoon salt
Pinch of pepper

Tear the lettuce and put into a salad bowl. Add the nuts and Swiss cheese. Combine the other ingredients to make a dressing and pour over the salad.

(menus continued on next page)

PARFAITS

6-ounce package gelatin dessert
3.4-ounce package instant vanilla pudding
1½ cups milk
Whipped topping

Prepare gelatin dessert of your choice according to package directions and let set till firm.

Prepare pudding using only 1½ cups milk.

In dessert dishes or short glasses, alternate layers of vanilla pudding, gelatin dessert and whipped topping, ending with whipped topping.

CHEESY CHICKEN SHELLS MEAL

(reduced calorie meal)

MENU

- ♥ *Cheesy Chicken Shells*
- ♥ *Fresh Cut Vegetables with Low-fat Dip*
- ♥ *Fat-Free Cookies with Fat-Free Frozen Yogurt*

CHEESY CHICKEN SHELLS

Oven temperature: 350 degrees

12 uncooked jumbo pasta shells
2 cups tomato sauce
2 egg whites, lightly beaten
1¾ cups part–skim ricotta cheese
1 boneless, skinless chicken breast, cooked and cut into cubes
 (approximately 4 ounces raw OR you can purchase cooked chicken
 ready to use)
3/4 cup frozen chopped spinach, thawed and drained well
1 teaspoon garlic powder
1 tablespoon oregano
1½ cups part-skim Mozzarella cheese, shredded
2/3 cup grated Parmesan cheese

Cook the jumbo shells in boiling water according to the package directions. Drain and rinse well with cold water to prevent them from cooking further and from sticking together. Set aside.

In a 9"x13" baking pan, spread 3/4 cup of the tomato sauce evenly over the bottom and set aside.

In a large bowl, combine the egg whites, ricotta cheese, chicken, spinach, garlic powder and oregano. Stir in 1/2 cup each of the Mozzarella cheese and Parmesan cheese.

To assemble, spoon the cheese mixture into the jumbo shells and place filled shells in a single layer in baking dish. Spread remaining sauce on top. Sprinkle with remaining cheese, cover and bake approximately 30 minutes.

FRESH CUT VEGETABLES with LOW-FAT DIP

Purchase your favorite variety of fresh vegetables such as celery, carrots, broccoli, cauliflower or whatever you like. Clean and cut into bite size pieces. Purchase a package of low-fat ranch dip. Arrange the vegetables on a plate with a bowl of the dip in the middle.

FAT-FREE COOKIES AND FROZEN YOGURT

Purchase a package of fat-free cookies of your choice. Purchase a container of fat-free frozen yogurt. Serve the yogurt with the cookies.

OLD FASHIONED PORK ROAST SLOW COOKER MEAL

MENU

- ♥ *Pork Roast and Gravy*
- ♥ *Mashed Redskin Potatoes*
- ♥ *Peas and Carrots*
- ♥ *Apple Pie*

When my children were growing up, we always ate our meals together. This was their favorite dinner.

PORK ROAST with GRAVY

Purchase a 3-pound pork butt roast. Season it with 1 teaspoon salt, 2 teaspoons sage, 1/2 teaspoon pepper, and 1 teaspoon garlic powder. Wrap the roast in foil and put it in the freezer. When ready to prepare, put the frozen roast into a slow cooker and cook on low for 8 hours.

When ready to serve, take the meat out and put on a plate and cover with foil. Turn the slow cooker to high and bring the remaining meat juices to a boil. Thicken with a small amount of cornstarch mixed with water. (The amount depends on the amount of juices in the slow cooker.) You also may add a jar of prepared pork gravy to the juices if you choose.

MASHED REDSKIN POTATOES

Wash approximately 16 small redskin potatoes and put into a saucepan and cover with cold water. Add 1 tablespoon salt to the water, cover and bring to a boil. Turn the heat down to simmer and cook until you can easily put a paring knife into a potato, about 20 to 25 minutes. Drain and put back into the pan.

Heat 1/2 cup whole or 2% milk in the microwave.

Add 1 stick of margarine or butter to the potatoes and mash until the butter is incorporated. Add the warm milk and continue to mash to the desired consistency.

PEAS and CARROTS

Purchase a bag of frozen peas and carrots from your grocery store and prepare according to directions.

APPLE PIE

Purchase a frozen pie and bake according to directions, or purchase a prepared apple pie from your bakery. Serve with ice cream or whipped topping.

CHRIS' PORK CHOP MEAL

MENU

- ♥ *Chris' Pork Chops*
- ♥ *Green Bean Casserole*
- ♥ *Minted Melon Dessert*

My daughter Chris called me one day, excited that she had prepared a delicious pork chop recipe and that I should try it. I agree with her! This is a great recipe and very easy.

CHRIS' PORK CHOPS

Grill turned to medium heat

2 tablespoons extra virgin olive oil
1 tablespoon lemon juice
1 tablespoon Worcestershire sauce
2 teaspoons oregano
1 teaspoon salt
1 teaspoon onion powder
1 teaspoon garlic powder
1 teaspoon pepper
1/2 teaspoon ground mustard
4 boneless pork loin chops

In a large resealable plastic bag, combine the first nine ingredients; add the pork chops. Seal the bag and turn to coat; refrigerate for eight hours or overnight.

Coat grill with cooking spray. Drain the pork chops and discard the marinade. Grill the pork, covered, over medium heat four to five minutes on each side or until a meat thermometer reads 150 degrees. Take off the grill and put on a plate and cover with foil. Let rest for at least 10 minutes before serving.

GREEN BEAN CASSEROLE

2 cans French style green beans, drained
1 can cream of mushroom soup
8-ounce package shredded Cheddar cheese
1 can Durkee French fried onions

Put the drained beans in a casserole dish and add the soup and cheese. Bake at 400 degrees for 25 minutes. Remove from the oven and sprinkle on the French fried onions and return to the oven and bake an additional 10 minutes.

MINTED MELON DESSERT

Purchase your favorite variety of melon or a combination of several different melons. Peel the melon and cut into bite size pieces. Chop 1 bunch of fresh mint and scatter pieces over the melon. Let sit for at least 30 minutes before serving. The mint gives the melon a wonderful taste.

APPLE PORK CHOP MEAL

MENU

- ♥ *Apple Pork Chops with Noodles*
- ♥ *Cheesy Carrots*
- ♥ *Ice Cream Crunch Dessert*

APPLE PORK CHOP
MEAL
grocery list
- ☐ Pork chops
- ☐ Apple pie filling
- ☐ Onions
- ☐ Noodles
- ☐ Barbecue sauce
- ☐ Carrots
- ☐ Velveeta cheese
- ☐ Butter
- ☐ Bread crumbs
- ☐ German chocolate cake mix
- ☐ Nuts
- ☐ Brown sugar
- ☐ Vanilla ice cream

APPLE PORK CHOPS

Oven temperature: 350 degrees

4 to 6 pork chops
1 can apple pie filling
1 medium onion sliced
20-ounce bottle barbecue sauce

Put the pie filling into a baking dish. Layer the sliced onion over the pie filling and pour 1 cup of the barbecue sauce over the onions. Top with the pork chops and the remaining barbecue sauce. Bake, covered, for 1 hour. Reduce heat to 300 degrees and bake for another hour till sauce is thickened and chops are tender. Serve with noodles of your choice, cooked according to package directions.

CHEESY CARROTS

Oven temperature: 350 degrees

6 cups sliced carrots (two 10-ounce bags frozen, or 2 pounds fresh)
1/2 cup onion, chopped
1/2 cup butter
1 cup (8 ounces) Velveeta cheese
Dry bread crumbs

Cook the carrots and onion in a saucepan in a small amount of water for approx 10 minutes. Drain and put into a casserole dish. Melt the butter and cheese and add to the carrots. Top with bread crumbs and bake uncovered for 30 to 40 minutes.

ICE CREAM CRUNCH DESSERT

Oven temperature: 350 degrees

1 German chocolate cake mix
3/4 cup softened butter or margarine
1/2 cup brown sugar
1/2 cup chopped nuts
1 quart softened vanilla ice cream

Mix dry ingredients together; cut in the butter or margarine until crumbly. Spread mixture in an 11"x14" baking sheet and bake at 350 degrees for approximately 15 minutes. Remove from the oven and stir to crumble. (For extra crunchy, return to the oven for 5 more minutes.) Stir this mixture into the softened ice cream and put into a dish and place in the freezer.

CATHY'S "MEAT THAT FALLS APART" MEAL

MENU

- ♥ *Pot Roast with Vegetables*
- ♥ *Blueberry Pie*

When my daughter Cathy was a teenager, she asked me to show her how to make "meat that falls apart." She was talking about pot roast. It became known in our house as "Cathy's meat that falls apart."

CATHY'S MEAT THAT FALLS APART MEAL

grocery list

- ☐ Blade chuck roast
- ☐ Garlic powder
- ☐ Lawry's seasoned salt
- ☐ Potatoes
- ☐ Carrots
- ☐ Onions
- ☐ Beef stock or bouillon
- ☐ Pie crusts
- ☐ Canned blueberry pie filling
- ☐ Granulated sugar
- ☐ Vanilla ice cream

POT ROAST with VEGETABLES

Oven temperature: 325 degrees

3½ to 4 pounds blade chuck roast
1 tablespoon kosher salt, divided
1 teaspoon pepper, divided
1 teaspoon garlic powder
1 teaspoon Lawry's seasoned salt
4 onions, peeled and cut into large chunks

8 to 9 medium potatoes cut in half (Peeling the potatoes is not necessary .It depends on your preference.)
8 medium carrots, cut in half
1 cup beef stock or beef broth (You can use 2 beef bouillon cubes and water if you don't have beef stock or beef broth.)

Place the beef stock or bouillon and the vegetables in a large Dutch oven. Sprinkle with 1½ teaspoons salt and ½ teaspoon pepper.

On a work surface, sprinkle the meat on both sides with the remaining 1½ teaspoons salt, 1/2 teaspoon pepper, garlic powder and Lawry's seasoned salt. Rub into both sides of the meat with your fingertips and put the meat on top of the vegetables. Cover with a tight-fitting lid and place in the.

Check the vegetables after two and a half hours. If they are done, remove and put into a baking dish and cover with foil. Return roast to over for another hour and a half to two hours. When the roast is almost done, put the pan with the vegetables back into the oven to warm before serving.

BLUEBERRY PIE

Oven temperature: 375 degrees

1 package prepared unbaked pie crusts (2 in a package)
1 large can blueberry pie filling

Granulated sugar
Vanilla ice cream

Unroll one pie crust and put into a 9" pie pan. Put the pie filling into the pie crust. Unroll the other pie crust and lay on a work surface. Make several slits in the pie crust approximately a half-inch long to let the steam escape. Pick the pie crust up and lay on top of the pie filling and press down all the way around the edge with your thumb to seal the pie edges. Sprinkle the pie with sugar and bake for approximately 40 minutes or until golden brown. Cool and serve with vanilla ice cream.

DON'S FAVORITE MEATLOAF MEAL

MENU

- ♥ *Don's Favorite Meatloaf*
- ♥ *Roasted Potatoes*
- ♥ *Easy Peach Pie*

My husband Don doesn't see any reason why anyone needs any meal other than meatloaf, which is his favorite thing to eat. This is his favorite recipe.

DON'S FAVORITE MEATLOAF

Oven temperature: 350 degrees

1½ pounds ground chuck
1/2 cup tomato sauce
1/2 cup evaporated milk
3/4 cup quick cooking oatmeal
1 egg

1/4 cup finely chopped onion
1 teaspoon salt
1/4 teaspoon pepper
1/4 teaspoon rubbed sage
3 strips raw bacon

Put the ground chuck in a large bowl. Add the other ingredients except for the bacon and mix well. Shape into a loaf and put into a baking pan that has been lined with foil. Place the strips of bacon over the meatloaf and cover loosely with foil. Bake one hour. Remove foil and bake a half-hour longer or until done in the middle.

ROASTED POTATOES

Oven temperature: 350 degrees

Place washed, small redskin potatoes in a bowl. Drizzle with extra virgin olive oil and kosher salt. Place on a baking pan and roast in the oven for an hour and a half.

GREEN BEANS

Prepare frozen green beans according to package directions.

EASY PEACH PIE

1 prepared graham cracker pie crust
18 large marshmallows
1/4 cup whole milk
.

8 ounces whipped topping
1 large can peaches, drained and cut into chunks OR
  6 fresh, ripe peaches peeled and cut into chunks

Place the marshmallows and milk in a microwave safe bowl and microwave until the marshmallows begin to melt. Stir well until they are incorporated into the milk. Cool.

Stir the diced peaches into the cooled marshmallow mixture. Fold in the whipped topping. Pour into the crust and refrigerate for at least FIVE hours before serving. Best if left to chill overnight.

PARTY CHICKEN MEAL

MENU

- ♥ *Party Chicken with Rice*
- ♥ *Zucchini Sauté*
- ♥ *Lemon Glaze Cake*

PARTY CHICKEN MEAL
grocery list

- ☐ Whole frying chicken or chicken parts
- ☐ Onion soup mix
- ☐ Apricot preserves
- ☐ Thousand Island dressing
- ☐ Butter
- ☐ Zucchini
- ☐ Green onions
- ☐ Dried basil
- ☐ Tomato
- ☐ Mozzarella cheese
- ☐ Parmesan cheese
- ☐ Lemon cake mix
- ☐ Lemon gelatin dessert
- ☐ Vegetable oil
- ☐ Powdered sugar
- ☐ Orange juice
- ☐ Eggs

PARTY CHICKEN

Oven temperature: 350 degrees

1 frying chicken or package of your favorite chicken pieces with skin on
1 envelope dry onion soup mix
8-ounce bottle of Thousand Island dressing
12-ounce jar of apricot jam

Place chicken pieces in a baking dish, skin side up. Sprinkle the dry onion soup mix over the chicken. Pour the Thousand Island dressing evenly over the soup. Spoon preserves over dressing. Cover and bake an hour and a half. (The sauce on the chicken is excellent served over rice or mashed potatoes.)

ZUCCHINI SAUTE

3 tablespoons butter
3 cups zucchini, sliced
1/4 cup green onion, sliced
1/2 teaspoon dried basil

1/3 teaspoon salt
1 medium tomato, cubed
1/4 cup shredded Mozzarella cheese
1/4 cup fresh grated Parmesan cheese

In a large skillet melt the butter over medium heat. Slice the zucchini and onion and put in the pan with the basil and salt. Cook until the zucchini is crispy tender, about 10 to 12 minutes. Stir in the tomato and cook 1 minute. Pour into a serving dish and top with the Mozzarella and Parmesan cheese.

LEMON GLAZE CAKE

CAKE:
3/4 cup water
6-ounce package lemon gelatin dessert
1 lemon cake mix
3/4 cup oil
4 eggs

Mix cake ingredients and put into 9"x13" baking pan. Bake 15 minutes at 350 degrees, then 30 minutes at 300 degrees. Take the cake out of the oven and poke holes all over the top using the end of a wooden spoon or a fork. Pour the following glaze over the surface of the cake.

GLAZE:
2 cups powdered sugar
2 tablespoons vegetable oil
1/3 cup orange juice

HAM LOAF MEAL

MENU

- ♥ *Ham Loaf with Horseradish Sauce*
- ♥ *Scalloped Potatoes*
- ♥ *Pound Cake and Berries*

HAM LOAF MEAL
grocery list
- ☐ Ground pork
- ☐ Ground ham
- ☐ Milk
- ☐ Bread crumbs
- ☐ Egg
- ☐ Brown sugar
- ☐ Mustard
- ☐ Vinegar
- ☐ Horseradish
- ☐ Cayenne pepper
- ☐ Paprika
- ☐ Whipping cream
- ☐ Potatoes
- ☐ Evaporated milk
- ☐ Flour
- ☐ Butter
- ☐ Mushroom soup
- ☐ Onion
- ☐ Pound cake
- ☐ Mixed berries
- ☐ Whipped topping
- ☐ Cornstarch

HAM LOAF

Oven temperature: 350 degrees

3/4 pound lean ground pork
1 pound ground smoked ham (Ask the butcher to grind it for you.)
1/2 cup whole or 2% milk
1/2 cup dry bread crumbs
1 egg

Mix the pork, ham, milk, bread crumbs, and egg. Shape into a loaf and place in a shallow baking pan. Bake for approximately one hour.

GLAZE:
6 tablespoons brown sugar
2 tablespoons water
2 tablespoons vinegar
1 teaspoon dry mustard OR 2 teaspoons regular mustard

Combine the brown sugar, water, vinegar and dry mustard. Spread on the ham loaf and put back into the oven to caramelize for approximately 15 minutes.

HORSERADISH SAUCE (optional):
2 tablespoons horseradish
2 teaspoons vinegar
1½ teaspoons mustard
1 teaspoon salt

1/4 teaspoon Worcestershire sauce
Dash of cayenne pepper
Dash of paprika
1/4 cup heavy cream, whipped

Combine the horseradish, vinegar, dry mustard, salt, Worcestershire sauce, cayenne, paprika and fold in the heavy whipped cream. Serve with the loaf.

SAUCY SCALLOPED POTATOES

4 cups peeled, thinly sliced potatoes
1 can cream of mushroom soup
12-ounce can evaporated milk
1 large onion sliced thin

2 tablespoons butter
1/2 teaspoon salt
Pinch of pepper

Mix all ingredients and put into slow cooker and cook on low approximately 6 to 8 hours.

POUND CAKE AND BERRIES

Buy a frozen pound cake and slice. Purchase a package of frozen mixed berries. Pour them into a saucepan with enough sugar just to sweeten and 1/4 cup water. Over medium heat, bring the juices to a boil and thicken with 2 teaspoons cornstarch mixed with1/4 cup cold water. Let cool before serving. Ladle the berries over the pound cake and top with whipped topping.

SALMON CHEESE CASSEROLE MEAL

MENU
- ♥ *Salmon Cheese Dish*
- ♥ *Mashed Potatoes Supreme*
- ♥ *Éclair Dessert*

SALMON CHEESE
CASEROLE MEAL
grocery list
- ☐ Salmon
- ☐ Bread crumbs
- ☐ Lemon juice
- ☐ Eggs
- ☐ Mushrooms
- ☐ Shredded cheese
- ☐ Minced onion
- ☐ Potatoes
- ☐ Sour cream
- ☐ Cream cheese
- ☐ Butter
- ☐ Garlic powder
- ☐ Vanilla pudding
- ☐ Graham crackers
- ☐ Whole or 2% milk
- ☐ Graham crackers
- ☐ Whipped topping
- ☐ Fudge topping

SALMON CHEESE CASSEROLE

Oven temperature: 350 degrees

14-ounce can salmon with liquid
4-ounce can mushrooms, drained
1½ cups dry bread crumbs
2 eggs, beaten
1 cup shredded cheese of your choice
1 tablespoon lemon juice
1 tablespoon minced onion

Break the salmon apart in a bowl and take out any pieces of bones and skin. Mix all ingredients together and pour into a casserole dish or baking pan. Cover loosely with foil and bake approximately 45 minutes. Take the cover off and continue to bake for another 10 minutes to brown.

MASHED POTATOES SUPREME

Oven temperature: 350 degrees

6 to 8 potatoes
8 ounces cream cheese
1 stick butter (1/2 cup)
1 cup sour cream

2 teaspoons garlic powder
1 teaspoon salt
1/4 teaspoon pepper

Peel potatoes and cook in water. Drain well. Mash cooked potatoes, then add remaining ingredients and mix together. Pour into a casserole dish or baking pan and cover. Bake until heated through, approximately 45 minutes. These are best if made the day before and baked when you bake the salmon.

ÉCLAIR DESSERT

2 packages (3.4 ounces each)
instant vanilla pudding mix
3 cups whole or 2% milk

2 (8-ounce) containers whipped topping, thawed
1 jar fudge ice cream topping
Graham crackers (about 36)

Make the pudding with the 3 cups milk and fold in one container thawed whipped topping.

Line a 9"x13" pan with graham crackers and spread half of the pudding mixture over the crackers. Top with another layer of graham crackers and spread with the remaining pudding mixture and cover with another layer of graham crackers. Cover with fudge topping, then whipped topping

SPECIAL

OCCASION

BREAKFASTS

CRESCENT ROLL EGG BAKE MEAL

MENU

- ♥ *Crescent Roll Egg Bake*
- ♥ *Monkey Bread*
- ♥ *Fresh Fruit*

CRESCENT ROLL
EGG BAKE MEAL
grocery list
- ☐ Eggs
- ☐ Whole milk
- ☐ Refrigerated crescent rolls
- ☐ Refrigerated biscuits
- ☐ Brown and serve sausages or smoked sausage links
- ☐ Shredded Mozzarella or Cheddar cheese
- ☐ Granulated sugar
- ☐ Cinnamon
- ☐ Walnuts
- ☐ Vanilla
- ☐ Bananas
- ☐ Fresh pineapple
- ☐ Fresh strawberries
- ☐ Fresh grapes
- ☐ Orange

CRESCENT ROLL EGG BAKE

Oven temperature: 350 degrees

8 eggs
1/4 cup whole milk *
1 can refrigerated crescent rolls
8 cooked sausage links
   (such as Swift's Brown and Serve links
    or Eckrich Smoky Links)
8 ounces shredded cheese (Mozzarella, Cheddar or a combination)
1/2 teaspoon salt
1/4 teaspoon pepper

(*To reduce fat, use skim milk, or a combination of skim milk and fat-free evaporated milk for richness.)

Mix the eggs, milk, salt and pepper together and set aside.

Unroll the refrigerated rolls and press dough into a 9"by 13" baking dish, flattening out the perforations to form a crust.

Cut the sausage links into bite size pieces and spread over the crust. Sprinkle the cheese over the sausage pieces. Pour the egg mixture over the cheese and bake for 45 minutes.

(recipes continued on next page)

MONKEY BREAD

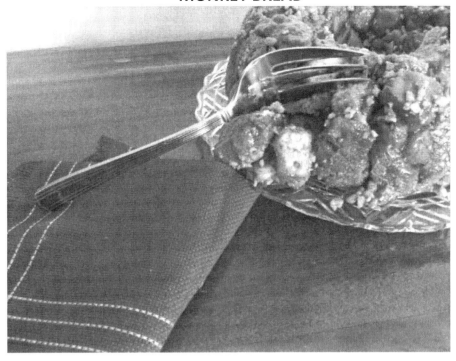

Oven temperature: 350 degrees

BREAD:

4 tubes refrigerated biscuits

3/4 cup granulated sugar

1½ teaspoons cinnamon

1/2 cup chopped walnuts (optional)

Separate the biscuits and cut into quarters.

Mix 3/4 cup of the sugar and 1½ teaspoons cinnamon in a plastic bag. Shake the biscuit pieces in the bag to coat, then put them into a greased tube pan. (You can use two bread tins or any deep casserole dish if you don't have a tube pan. However, if you are using bread tins, don't put more than two layers in each pan or they will overflow.)

SYRUP:

1½ sticks (12 tablespoons) butter or margarine

1 cup granulated sugar

1½ teaspoons cinnamon

1½ teaspoons vanilla

In a saucepan heat the butter or margarine, sugar, cinnamon and vanilla and bring to a boil. <u>Simmer slowly</u> for 5 minutes. Pour the mixture over the biscuit pieces in the pans and bake for 30 minutes. Remove from the oven and turn upside down on a plate.

FRUIT

Cut up fresh pineapple, fresh melon, fresh strawberries and fresh grapes into bite size pieces. Sprinkle with 1/4 cup fresh squeezed orange juice (optional) and serve.

HOLLY'S SAUSAGE PIE MEAL

MENU
- ♥ *Holly's Sausage Pie*
- ♥ *Baked Cheese Grits*
- ♥ *Sweet Potato Biscuits*

HOLLY'S SAUSAGE PIE

HOLLY'S SAUSAGE PIE MEAL
grocery list
- ☐ Frozen prepared pie crust
- ☐ Mild bulk sausage
- ☐ Butter
- ☐ Green onions
- ☐ Whole or 2% milk
- ☐ Cream cheese
- ☐ Eggs
- ☐ Shredded Cheddar cheese
- ☐ Worcestershire sauce
- ☐ Quick cooking grits
- ☐ Cayenne pepper
- ☐ Baking mix
- ☐ Sweet potatoes
- ☐ Cinnamon
- ☐ Sugar

Oven temperature: 375 degrees

9-inch deep dish frozen pie crust
1 pound mild bulk breakfast sausage
1 tablespoon butter
1/3 cup chopped green onions
3/4 cup whole or 2% milk
4 ounces cream cheese softened, cut into small pieces
4 eggs, slightly beaten
1 cup shredded sharp Cheddar cheese
1/2 teaspoon Worcestershire sauce
1 teaspoon salt
1/4 teaspoon pepper

Bake the pie crust until partially done, approximately 10 minutes. Take out of the oven and set aside to cool slightly.

Brown the sausage in a frying pan and drain off any grease. Take the sausage out and set it aside.

Melt the butter and sauté the onion for 5 minutes in the same pan used for the sausage. Add the milk to the pan with the green onions and heat just until it begins to steam. Remove from heat. Add cream cheese and stir well. Add beaten eggs, Cheddar cheese, Worcestershire sauce, salt and pepper. Pour mixture into the pie crust. Sprinkle the sausage on top of the egg mixture and bake in the 375 degree oven for 30 minutes.

BAKED CHEESE GRITS

Oven temperature: 350 degrees

4 cups whole or 2% milk
2 cups water
1½ cups quick cooking grits
1¼ sticks butter (10 tablespoons)

1 teaspoon kosher salt (table salt is all right)
½ teaspoon cayenne pepper
1 cup shredded Cheddar cheese
3 large eggs, slightly beaten

In a deep saucepan bring the water and milk to a boil. Add the grits, turn the heat to simmer and stir every few minutes for approximately two to five minutes. Remove the pan from the stove and stir in the remaining ingredients. Pour into an 8"x8" baking dish and bake for 30 to 40 minutes until the top is lightly browned. Serve hot.

(recipes continued on next page)

SWEET POTATO BISCUITS

Oven temperature: 450 degrees

2¼ cups prepared biscuit mix (such as Jiffy Mix or Bisquick)

1/2 cup whole or 2% milk

1/2 cup mashed sweet potatoes

1 teaspoon cinnamon

1/2 cup granulated sugar

Mix the biscuit mix, cinnamon and sugar together. Mix the milk and sweet potatoes together and add all at once to the dry mixture. Mix with a fork just until wet. Turn out onto a floured surface and pat down to about 1/2-inch thickness. Cut with a juice glass or a biscuit cutter and place on an ungreased baking sheet about one inch apart. Bake for 10 minutes.

OATMEAL COOKIE PANCAKE MEAL

MENU

- ♥ *Oatmeal Cookie Pancakes*
- ♥ *Turkey Sausages*
- ♥ *Fruit Kabobs*

OATMEAL COOKIE
PANCAKE MEAL
grocery list
☐ Old fashioned oatmeal
☐ Flour
☐ Brown sugar
☐ Baking powder
☐ Baking soda
☐ Cinnamon
☐ Nuts
☐ Sour cream
☐ Whole or 2% milk
☐ Eggs
☐ Vanilla
☐ Bananas
☐ Raisins (optional)
☐ Butter
☐ Syrup or honey
☐ Turkey sausages
☐ Chunk pineapple
☐ Maraschino cherries
☐ Bamboo skewers
☐ 7-up or Squirt if needed

OATMEAL COOKIE PANCAKES

MIX IN A BOWL:
1 cup old fashioned oatmeal
  (DO NOT substitute quick-cooking oats)
1 cup flour
1/2 cup brown sugar
2 teaspoons baking powder
1/2 teaspoon baking soda
1 teaspoon ground cinnamon
1/4 cup chopped walnuts

MIX IN A SEPARATE BOWL:
3/4 cup sour cream
3/4 cup whole or 2% milk
2 eggs
1 teaspoon vanilla

Whisk the wet ingredients into the dry ingredients until just combined.

2 very ripe bananas, mashed
3/4 cup raisins (optional)
2 tablespoons melted butter or margarine

Fold in the mashed bananas and the raisins. Stir in the melted butter.

Heat a griddle over medium heat and brush with some additional melted butter. Cook pancakes, using about 1/4 cup batter for each, until bubbles form on the top, then turn. Cook about two minutes on each side. Keep pancakes warm by layering between paper towels in a baking dish covered with foil in the oven with temperature set at 200 degrees. Serve with butter and syrup or honey.

TURKEY SAUSAGES

Lay pre-cooked turkey sausages on a baking sheet lined with foil. Heat in 325 degree oven approximately 15 minutes until heated through.

FRUIT KABOBS

1 can pineapple chunks, drained
1 bottle of large maraschino cherries, drained
3 bananas, cut into chunks

Thread fruit pieces on bamboo skewers. (Use any combination of fruit you like.)To keep bananas from turning brown, put the chunks into some lemon-lime carbonated soda, such as 7-up or Squirt until ready to assemble and serve.

GRILLED BREAKFAST SANDWICH MEAL

MENU
- ♥ *Grilled Breakfast Sandwich*
- ♥ *Blueberries & Cream*
- ♥ *Cocoa*

GRILLED BREAKFAST SANDWICH

For each sandwich:
2 slices sourdough, English muffin bread
  (OR other dense sliced bread
1 fried egg
1 slice cheddar cheese
2-ouncesausage patty, cooked and drained
  (OR use ham, bacon or Canadian bacon)
1 slice tomato
1 teaspoon basil pesto
Extra virgin olive oil

If you have a tabletop grill, such as a Foreman, plug it in to heat while you assemble the sandwich. Brush each slice of bread lightly with the olive oil on one side. Assemble the sandwich with the basil pesto, tomato, fried egg, sausage patty and cheese on unoiled side of bread. Top with second slice of bread. Put sandwich into the tabletop grill or put on a griddle or non-stick frying pan on the stove on medium heat and cover. Let sandwich cook until cheese begins to melt. Turn to brown other side.

BLUEBERRIES and CREAM

1 cup blueberries   2 tablespoons powdered sugar
1/4 cup heavy cream   Few drops of vanilla

Mix the cream, powdered sugar and vanilla and pour over the berries and serve. Makes two 3/4-cup servings.

HOT COCOA

1/2 cup granulated sugar   1/4 cup hot water
1/4 cup unsweetened cocoa powder   4 cups milk
Pinch of salt   1 teaspoon vanilla

Mix sugar, cocoa and salt in a saucepan; stir in water. Cook and stir over medium heat until mixture boils; boil and stir two minutes. Stir in milk and heat. DO NOT BOIL. Remove from heat and add vanilla. Top with whipped topping if desired.

BREAKFAST BURRITO MEAL

MENU

- ♥ *Southwest Breakfast Burrito*
- ♥ *Breakfast Salad*
- ♥ *Tube Donuts*

SOUTHWEST BREAKFAST BURRITO

9 eggs
1 pound chorizo sausage (or bulk pork sausage)
1 teaspoon salt
1/4 teaspoon pepper
4 tablespoons butter, divided
1 green bell pepper, chopped
1/2 medium onion, chopped
1½ cups Colby jack cheese
6 (10-inch) flour tortillas

Break eggs into a bowl and add the salt and pepper. Whisk well to combine. Melt 3 tablespoons butter in a non-stick pan. Cook eggs in the butter, then remove from skillet and set aside. Brown the sausage in the same skillet. Drain meat and set aside.

In the same skillet, melt one tablespoon of butter. Add the onions and bell pepper and sauté on medium heat until softened and lightly browned, about 10 minutes. Combine vegetables, sausage and eggs.

Lay out a flour tortilla and put 1/6 of the egg sausage mixture on the tortilla. Put 1/4 cup Colby jack cheese on top of the egg mixture and roll the tortilla up. Roll burritos in foil to keep warm until serving time. Serve with salsa and jalapenos.

BREAKFAST SALAD

1 can (16 ounces) peach pie filling
1 can (16 ounces) pineapple tidbits drained
10-ounce can mandarin oranges, drained

2 cups miniature marshmallows (colored ones are nice to use)
1 cup maraschino cherries

Mix all ingredients and chill.

TUBE DONUTS

1 can refrigerated buttermilk biscuits
Granulated sugar
Vegetable oil

Open the biscuits and lay each one out on a work surface. Cut a small hole in the center of each using a donut cutter or simply poke your finger in the middle and work it around to make a small hole.

Place approximately 3 cups oil in a saucepan to heat. (To test, drop a small piece of bread in the oil. If the bread floats, the oil is hot enough.) Place each biscuit donut into the oil. Fry about one minute and turn. Take out and drain on paper towels. Place some granulated sugar in a paper bag. Put the donuts into the bag and shake to coat with sugar.

FRENCH TOAST BREAKFAST MEAL

MENU

- ♥ *Cinnamon French Toast*
- ♥ *Turkey Bacon*
- ♥ *Citrus Quick Bread*

CINNAMON FRENCH TOAST

1 large loaf French bread
4 eggs
1/2 cup heavy cream OR whole milk
1 teaspoon cinnamon
1/8 teaspoon nutmeg
Butter and syrup

Cut the French bread into diagonal slices about two inches thick. Set aside.

Mix the eggs, cream, cinnamon, and nutmeg together with a whisk.

Over medium heat, melt enough butter in a non-stick frying pan or griddle to cover the bottom of the pan. Dip each piece of bread into the egg mixture and lay in the pan. Cook on each side until browned and egg mixture is set. Serve with butter and syrup.

TURKEY BACON

Purchase turkey bacon and fry according to package directions.

CITRUS QUICK BREAD

Oven temperature: 350 degrees

18.5-ounce lemon or orange cake mix
2 tablespoons brown sugar
1 teaspoon cinnamon
1 tablespoon cold butter
1/2 cup chopped pecans or walnuts

3.4-ounce package instant vanilla pudding
4 eggs
1 cup sour cream
1/3 cup oil

In a bowl, mix 2 tablespoons cake mix, brown sugar and cinnamon. Cut the butter into the mix until it is crumbly. Stir in pecans or walnuts and set aside.

Mix the pudding mix, eggs, sour cream, oil and cake mix. Pour into two greased 8"x 4" bread tins. Sprinkle with brown sugar and dry cake mix mixture and bake at 350 degrees for 45 minutes.

HEART HEALTHY BREAKFAST MEAL

MENU

- ♥ *Heart Healthy Breakfast Casserole*
- ♥ *Bran Muffins*
- ♥ *Fresh Melon*

HEART HEALTHY BREAKFAST CASSEROLE

Oven temperature: 350 degrees

1 cup 2% milk
2 cartons Egg Beaters (8 ounces each)
3/4 teaspoon dry mustard (OR substitute 1 teaspoon regular salad mustard)
1/4 teaspoon salt
1/8 teaspoon pepper
1 cup shredded part skim Mozzarella cheese
1/2 pound turkey sausage
6 slices stale French bread cut into cubes

Brown turkey sausage in non-stick skillet sprayed with food release spray.

Mix the milk, Egg Beaters, cheese and seasonings together. Add crumbled sausage and bread. Mix well and pour into an 11"x2" baking dish or 9" pie plate, sprayed with food release spray. Bake uncovered 40 minutes.

HIGH FIBER BRAN MUFFINS

Oven temperature: 400 degrees

1½ cups flour
1/2 cup sugar
1 tablespoon baking powder
1/4 teaspoon salt
2 cups bran cereal (not flakes)
1¼ cups fat-free milk
1/4 cup Egg Beaters
1/4 cup vegetable oil

Stir together flour, sugar, baking powder and salt. Set aside.

In a large mixing bowl, combine the bran cereal and milk. Let stand approximately 2 minutes or until cereal softens. Add the Egg Beaters and oil. Beat well. Add flour mixture stirring only until combined. (You may add raisins or nuts to the batter before baking if you like.) Using a medium size ice cream scoop, scoop batter into muffin pans and bake for 20 minutes.

MELON

Purchase melon of your choice and cut into bite-size pieces to serve.

SNACK
MEALS

CHIPS & CHEESE SNACK MEAL

MENU
- ♥ *Chips and Cheese*
- ♥ *Blueberry Salad*

CHIPS & CHEESE SNACK MEAL
grocery list
- ☐ Tortilla chips
- ☐ Ground beef
- ☐ Colby jack cheese
- ☐ Green onions
- ☐ Onion
- ☐ Jarred jalapenos
- ☐ Tomato
- ☐ Taco seasoning mix
- ☐ Blueberry (or cherry) pie filling
- ☐ Gelatin dessert mix
- ☐ Sour cream

CHIPS & CHEESE
(Makes two large plates)

Large bag tortilla chips of your choice
1 pound ground beef
1/2 medium onion, chopped
1/2 teaspoon salt
1/4 teaspoon pepper
1 package taco seasoning
2 pounds shredded Colby jack cheese
1 medium tomato, diced
1/2 cup sliced pickled jalapenos
2 green onions, chopped

In a skillet, brown the ground beef with the chopped onion, salt and pepper. Add taco seasoning following directions on the package. Set beef aside and keep warm.

Spray two large microwaveable dinner plates (10 or 11 inches) with food release spray. Cover the plates with a single layer of tortilla chips.

Sprinkle one pound of cheese evenly between the two plates on top of chips. Top with another layer of tortilla chips and sprinkle the rest of the cheese between the two plates. Cover with film and microwave approximately 1 minute on high. Check after 30 seconds, since microwaves vary.

Take out of the microwave and top each plate with half of the ground beef mixture, green onions, tomatoes and jalapenos.

BLUEBERRY SALAD

1 can blueberry pie filling (or use cherry)
6-ounce package red gelatin dessert
2 cups boiling water
2 cups sour cream

Bring water to boiling and mix all ingredients together. Pour into a 9"x13" pan and let set until firm.

ANTIPASTO SALAD SNACK MEAL

MENU

- ♥ *Antipasto Salad*
- ♥ *Swiss Cheese Bread*
- ♥ *Packaged Cookies*

ANTIPASTO SALAD

1 pound rotini pasta, cooked and drained
3½-ounce package pepperoni slices, cut into halves
2½-ounce can sliced ripe olives, drained
1/2 cup diced sweet red pepper
1/2 cup diced green bell pepper
4 medium mushrooms, sliced
15-ounce can garbanzo beans
1 clove garlic, crushed or minced (OR 1/2 teaspoon garlic powder)
2 tablespoons chopped fresh basil, (OR 2 teaspoons dried basil)
2 teaspoons salt
1/2 teaspoon dried oregano
1/8 teaspoon pepper
1/4 teaspoon cayenne pepper
1 bottle Italian dressing of your choice

Cook the pasta, rinse with cold water and drain. Add the remaining ingredients and mix well. (Use as much dressing as your taste dictates.)

SWISS CHEESE BREAD

Oven temperature: 350 degrees

1 large loaf of French bread	1 teaspoon mustard
12 slices Swiss cheese	2 teaspoons lemon juice
1½ sticks butter (12 tablespoons)	1 tablespoon poppy seeds
2 tablespoons dried onion	1 teaspoon beau monde seasoning

(Beau monde seasoning is not always easy to find but can be purchased in most larger grocery stores, gourmet stores or stores that specialize in spices. It can be left out, but it does add a particular taste to the bread.)

Mix the softened butter, onion, mustard, lemon juice, poppy seed and beau monde together. Set aside.

Make slashes almost all the way through the bread from the top to the bottom at approximately two-inch intervals. Spread butter mixture generously on slices between cuts. (Using your hands works well.) Rub any remaining butter over the top and sides of the bread. Tuck cheese slices into each cut. Fold cheese in half if it fits better. Wrap the loaf in foil and place on a baking sheet. Bake approximately 45 minutes. Serve warm.

HOLLY'S MEATBALL SNACK MEAL

MENU

- ♥ *Holly's Meatballs*
- ♥ *Hot Ranch Potatoes*
- ♥ *Fresh Cut Vegetables*

HOLLY'S MEATBALL
SNACK MEAL
grocery list
- ☐ Ground chuck
- ☐ Eggs
- ☐ Quick oatmeal
- ☐ Garlic powder
- ☐ Rubbed sage
- ☐ Onion
- ☐ Whole, 2% or fat-free milk
- ☐ Tomato sauce
- ☐ White vinegar
- ☐ Brown sugar
- ☐ Worcestershire sauce
- ☐ Redskin potatoes
- ☐ Green onions
- ☐ Hormel bacon pieces
- ☐ Hidden Valley Ranch with Bacon dressing
- ☐ Assorted fresh vegetables

HOLLY'S MEATBALLS

Oven temperature: 400 degrees

MEATBALLS:
1½ pounds ground chuck
1 egg
3/4 cup quick cooking oatmeal
1 teaspoon salt
1/4 teaspoon pepper
1 teaspoon garlic powder
1/2 teaspoon ground sage
1/2 cup very finely minced onion
2 tablespoons milk
1 tablespoon horseradish

Mix all ingredients and make into tablespoon-size meatballs. Place on a baking sheet lined with foil and bake 10 minutes. Turn each meatball and bake another 10 minutes. Put into a Dutch oven or baking pan and add the sauce.

SAUCE:
10-ounce can tomato sauce
2 tablespoons white vinegar
6 tablespoons brown sugar
2 tablespoons Worcestershire sauce

Simmer meatballs and sauce on low on top of the stove or bake uncovered for approximately 45 minutes, or cook in slow cooker several hours on low heat.

HOT RANCH POTATOES

3 to 4 pounds bite-size redskin potatoes, or larger redskin potatoes cut into wedges.
2 bunches green onions, chopped
1 jar Hormel bacon pieces
1 large bottle Hidden Valley Ranch with Bacon Dressing

Wash and dry potatoes; cut into wedges if necessary. Bake on a baking sheet or boil in water until tender. Put the potatoes into a 9"x13" baking dish. Add the chopped green onion and bacon pieces and put into the oven to cook for 10 minutes. Remove from the oven and add the ranch dressing. Serve hot.

VEGETABLE TRAY

Cut cleaned carrots, celery, cauliflower, broccoli, mushrooms, cherry tomatoes and any other vegetables you like and arrange pieces on a tray and chill.

ARTICHOKE DIP MEAL

MENU

- ♥ *Hot Artichoke and Genoa Dip*
- ♥ *Karen's No-bake Cookies*

HOT ARTICHOKE & GENOA DIP

13½-ounce can artichoke hearts, drained and chopped
2/3 cup Hormel Genoa salami
   (OR substitute ham, bacon or pepperoni)
1 cup shredded Cheddar cheese
1/2 cup fresh grated Parmesan cheese
1/2 cup mayonnaise (DO NOT substitute salad dressing)
1/4 cup sliced green onions

Mix the artichoke hearts, meat, ½ cup Cheddar, Parmesan, mayonnaise and ¼ cup green onion. Spoon the mixture into a 9-inch pie plate that has been sprayed with food release spray. Sprinkle with the remaining cheese and green onion. Bake for 20 to 25 minutes or until light brown. Serve with pita chips, crackers or bagel chips.

KAREN'S NO-BAKE COOKIES

2 cups sugar
1 stick (8 tablespoons) butter or margarine
1/2 cup unsweetened cocoa powder
1/2 cup whole or 2% milk
1/2 cup peanut butter
3 cups quick cooking oatmeal
1 teaspoon vanilla
Pinch of salt

In a deep saucepan, bring the sugar, butter, cocoa powder and milk to a boil, stirring frequently. Once it starts to boil, time it for exactly two minutes, then remove from heat. Add peanut butter and vanilla and stir. Add the oatmeal. Drop mixture by spoonfuls onto waxed paper or parchment paper. Let set until cool and firm.

TUNA SPREAD & CRACKERS SNACK MEAL

MENU

- ♥ *Tuna Spread/Assorted Crackers*
- ♥ *Quick Peanut Butter Cookies*

TUNA SPREAD &
CRACKERS
SNACK MEAL
grocery list

☐ Albacore tuna
☐ Celery
☐ Onion
☐ Mustard
☐ Horseradish
☐ Dill weed
☐ Eggs
☐ Mayonnaise or salad dressing
☐ Chunky peanut butter
☐ Granulated sugar
☐ Assorted crackers

TUNA SPREAD with ASSORTED CRACKERS

12-ounce can albacore tuna, drained and flaked
3 stalks celery, finely chopped
1 teaspoon grated onion
1/2 teaspoon mustard
1 teaspoon horseradish
1/4 teaspoon dill weed
2 boiled eggs, chopped
1/2 cup mayonnaise or salad dressing, depending on your taste

Mix all ingredients together and chill. When ready to serve, put into a serving bowl and set in the center of a large serving platter or tray and surround with assorted crackers.

QUICK PEANUT BUTTER COOKIES

Oven temperature: 350 degrees

1 cup chunky peanut butter
1 cup sugar
1 egg
Pinch of salt

Mix well and roll into small balls. Press down slightly with a fork dipped in water. Bake for 10 minutes. Watch closely so they don't burn since ovens vary. These make a soft and chewy cookie!

BLT PIZZA
SNACK MEAL

MENU

- ♥ *BLT Pizza*
- ♥ *Peanut Butter Cocoas*

BLT PIZZA
SNACK MEAL
grocery list

☐ Prepared pizza crust
☐ Olive oil
☐ Shredded Mozzarella cheese
☐ Bacon
☐ Mayonnaise
☐ Lettuce
☐ Tomatoes
☐ Butter or margarine
☐ Miniature marshmallows
☐ Peanut butter
☐ Cocoa Krispies cereal
☐ Rice Krispies cereal

BLT PIZZA

My husband and I retired – briefly – and cooked at our church-supported camp for young people. This was the meal the kids asked for most often.

Oven temperature: 500 degrees

Purchase a prepared pizza crust and brush with olive oil. Cover with shredded Mozzarella cheese. Top with cooked crumbled bacon. Bake until cheese is melted and starts to brown in a few spots.

Remove pizza from oven. Spread with mayonnaise (Don't substitute salad dressing.)Top with shredded lettuce and diced tomatoes. (These can also be made as individual pizzas using the small prepared crusts.)

PEANUT BUTTER COCOAS

6 tablespoons butter or margarine
16 ounces miniature marshmallows
3/4 cup peanut butter
5 cups Cocoa Krispies cereal
4 cups Rice Krispies cereal

Melt the butter in a saucepan and add the marshmallows. Heat the mixture on low until the marshmallows are almost melted. Take off the heat and stir in the peanut butter. Add the cereals and stir well. Press into a 9"x13" pan that has been sprayed with food release spray, or into a baking sheet. To serve, cut into squares.

GREEK
LAYERED DIP MEAL

MENU

- ♥ *Greek Layered Dip*
- ♥ *Emily's Fruit Punch Bars*

GREEK LAYERED
DIP SNACK MEAL
grocery list
- ☐ Cream cheese with chives and onions
- ☐ Hummus
- ☐ Cucumber
- ☐ Italian plum or Roma tomatoes
- ☐ Sliced ripe olives
- ☐ Feta cheese
- ☐ Green onions
- ☐ Dried oregano
- ☐ Eggs
- ☐ Granulated sugar
- ☐ Crushed pineapple
- ☐ Flour
- ☐ Baking soda
- ☐ Vanilla
- ☐ Walnuts
- ☐ Coconut
- ☐ Evaporated milk
- ☐ Butter or margarine

GREEK LAYERED DIP

8 ounces cream cheese with chives and onions, softened
8 ounces plain hummus
1 cucumber, peeled, seeded and chopped
  *(To seed a cucumber, cut in half lengthwise and
  scoop out the center with a teaspoon.)*
3 Italian plum tomatoes (or Roma tomatoes), seeded and chopped
  *(To seed a tomato, cut in quarters and run your thumb
  along under the seeds.)*
2.5-ounce can sliced ripe olives, drained
4 ounces feta cheese, crumbled
1/4 cup chopped green onion
1 teaspoon dried oregano

Spread cream cheese in bottom of a 10-inch pie plate. Drop the hummus by small spoonfuls evenly over the cream cheese and spread out on the entire surface. Top with the remaining ingredients in order listed. Serve with pita chips or bagel chips.

FRUIT PUNCH BARS

Emily, the wife of one of our pastors, brought these unbelievably rich bars to Sunday school one week. Everyone loved them. The recipe uses no shortening.

2 eggs
1½ cups sugar
20-ounce can crushed pineapple with juice
2¼ cups flour
1½ teaspoons baking soda

1/2 teaspoon salt
1 teaspoon vanilla
1/2 cup chopped walnuts
1½ cups coconut

Beat eggs with the sugar. Add the pineapple with the juice and stir in dry ingredients, vanilla, walnuts and coconut. Pour into an 11"x14" baking sheet. Bake at 350 degrees for 25 minutes or until set in the middle. Drizzle with glaze.

GLAZE:
¼ cup sugar
¾ cup evaporated milk
½ cup butter or margarine
1 teaspoon vanilla

Pour all ingredients into a saucepan and bring to a boil. Boil for two minutes, stirring constantly.

WING DINGER SNACK MEAL

MENU

- ♥ *Wing Dingers*
- ♥ *Seven Layer Salad*

WING DINGERS

Oven temperature: 400 degrees

1 packet dry onion soup mix
1/2 cup unsulphured molasses
1/4 cup soy sauce
1/4 cup bottled taco sauce
1/2 cup lemon juice
18 chicken wings

Combine all ingredients and refrigerate overnight. Place in a 9"x13" baking pan and bake at 400 degrees for 45 minutes to 1 hour.

SEVEN LAYER SALAD

1/2 head of lettuce, chopped
1 cup frozen peas (Do not thaw.)
1 cup mayonnaise (Don't substitute salad dressing.)
3 tablespoons sugar
6 hard boiled eggs, chopped
1 cup Hormel bacon pieces
2 cups shredded Cheddar cheese
8-ounce can sliced water chestnuts, drained

Cut the lettuce and put into a 9"x13" baking dish. Top with the water chestnuts. Cover with the bacon bits, chopped eggs and peas. Sprinkle on half of the cheese.

Mix the mayonnaise and sugar together and spread over the cheese. Sprinkle the remaining cheese over the mayonnaise mixture. Chill for at least five hours or overnight.

PIZZA BUBBLE SNACK MEAL

MENU

- ♥ *Pizza Bubbles*
- ♥ *Lemonade Stand Pie*

**PIZZA BUBBLE
SNACK MEAL**
grocery list

- ☐ Frozen lemonade concentrate
- ☐ Sweetened condensed milk
- ☐ Whipped topping
- ☐ Graham cracker pie crust
- ☐ Refrigerated biscuits
- ☐ Pizza sauce
- ☐ Mushrooms
- ☐ Onion
- ☐ Green pepper
- ☐ Shredded Mozzarella cheese
- ☐ Pepperoni
- ☐ Ground chuck
- ☐ Garlic powder

PIZZA BUBBLES

Oven temperature: 350 degrees.

1 tube refrigerated biscuits
15-ounce can pizza sauce
1 cup mushrooms, chopped
1 cup onion, finely chopped
1 cup green pepper, chopped
1 cup shredded Mozzarella cheese at room temperature
1½ ounces pepperoni, cut into small pieces
1 pound ground chuck
1 teaspoon salt
1/4 teaspoon pepper
1 teaspoon garlic powder

Brown the ground chuck with the salt, pepper and garlic powder. Drain and set aside.

Cut the biscuits into fourths; place in a 9"x13" baking pan and bake for 10 minutes.
Break the biscuits apart but leave in the pan. Combine the remaining ingredients and mix with the baked biscuits. Return to the oven for an additional 25 to 30 minutes.

LEMONADE STAND PIE

6-ounce can frozen lemonade concentrate, thawed
1 can sweetened condensed milk (not evaporated)
16-ounce container of whipped topping, thawed (reserve approximately 1 cup for topping)
1 ready-made graham cracker pie crust

Fold sweetened condensed milk and the lemonade together. Fold in the whipped topping. Pour into the graham cracker crust and top with reserved whipped topping. Freeze until firm.

VEGETABLE PIZZA SNACK MEAL

MENU

- ♥ *Mini-bagel Vegetable Pizza*
- ♥ *Ice Cream and Chocolate Cake*

VEGETABLE PIZZA
SNACK MEAL
grocery list

☐ Cream cheese
☐ Mayonnaise (not salad dressing)
☐ Hidden Valley dry ranch
   dressing mix
☐ Broccoli
☐ Cauliflower
☐ Sweet red pepper
☐ Sweet yellow pepper
☐ Shredded Cheddar cheese
☐ Mini bagels
☐ Pepperidge Farm
   frozen chocolate cake
☐ Ice Cream

MINI-BAGEL VEGETABLE PIZZA

16 ounces cream cheese, softened
3/4 cup mayonnaise
1/2 envelope Hidden Valley Ranch dry dressing mix
1 cup broccoli, finely chopped
1 cup cauliflower, finely chopped
1 sweet red pepper, finely chopped
1 sweet yellow pepper, finely chopped
Shredded Cheddar cheese
12 mini-bagels

Combine the cream cheese, mayonnaise and ranch dressing mix. Set aside.

Separate the mini bagels and spread each half with the cream cheese mixture. Press the spread side of each bagel half in the shredded Cheddar cheese. Lay bagel, cheese side up, on a baking sheet. Top each bagel with some of each of the chopped vegetables. Refrigerate the bagels until time to serve.

ICE CREAM and CHOCOLATE CAKE

Purchase a Pepperidge Farm Fudge Cake and thaw. Cut into slices and top with ice cream.

TORTILLA ROLLS SNACK MEAL

MENU

- ♥ *Tortilla Rolls*
- ♥ *Fresh Strawberries with Fruit Dip*

TORTILLA ROLLS

12 flour tortillas (8-inch)
2 packages cream cheese (8 ounces each), softened
3 green onions, chopped
12 slices deli-sliced boiled ham
1/2 cup chunky salsa
1/4 cup mayonnaise
1/2 teaspoon salt
Pinch of pepper

Mix the cream cheese, chopped green onions, chunky salsa, mayonnaise, salt and pepper.Spread evenly on each flour tortilla and lay a slice of ham on the tortilla. Roll up and cut into four equal pieces.

FRESH STRAWBERRIES with FRUIT DIP

1 quart fresh strawberries, washed and stems removed.
8 ounces cream cheese
1 cup powdered sugar
7-ounce jar marshmallow cream

Combine the cream cheese, powdered sugar and marshmallow cream and serve with the berries.

SPINACH DIP SNACK MEAL

MENU

- ♥ *Spinach Dip in a Bread Bowl*
- ♥ *Rocky Road Fudge*

SPINACH DIP in a BREAD BOWL

10-ounce package frozen chopped spinach, thawed and well drained
1 cup mayonnaise (DO NOT substitute salad dressing)
1 cup sour cream
8-ounce package Knorr dry vegetable soup mix
4 green onions, chopped
8-ounce can sliced water chestnuts, drained and chopped
Round loaf of bread such as sourdough or rye, unsliced

Cut the top off of the loaf of bread. Pull out bite-size pieces and arrange on a platter around the remaining bread shell. Combine the remaining ingredients and place in the center of the bread shell.

ROCKY ROAD FUDGE

12-ounce package semi-sweet chocolate chips
14-ounce can sweetened condensed milk
2 tablespoons butter or margarine
2 cups chopped nuts
10½-ounce package miniature marshmallows

In a microwave safe bowl, mix the chocolate chips and butter and microwave until the chocolate chips are melted. Immediately stir in the sweetened condensed milk, marshmallows and nuts. Pour into an 8"x8" buttered dish and cool.

SEVEN LAYER DIP SNACK MEAL

MENU

- ♥ *Seven Layer Bean Dip*
- ♥ *Lime Dessert*

SEVEN LAYER DIP
SNACK MEAL
grocery list

- ☐ Graham cracker pie crust
- ☐ Vanilla ice cream
- ☐ Lime sherbet
- ☐ Lemon juice
- ☐ Granulated sugar
- ☐ Butter
- ☐ Eggs
- ☐ Refried beans
- ☐ Avocados
- ☐ Mayonnaise
- ☐ Tomatoes
- ☐ Green onions
- ☐ Shredded Colby jack cheese
- ☐ Sliced ripe olives

SEVEN LAYER BEAN DIP

2 avocados, peeled and mashed
1 teaspoon lemon or lime juice
1 cup mayonnaise
1 cup sour cream
1-pound can refried beans
1 package taco seasoning
2 ripe tomatoes, chopped
4 green onions, chopped
1 pound shredded Colby jack cheese
1 cup ripe olives, sliced

Mash avocados and mix with lime juice. Mix the mayonnaise, sour cream and taco seasoning in a bowl and set aside.

Spread the refried beans out evenly on a serving platter, round pizza pan, cookie sheet or large meat platter. Spread the mashed avocados over the beans. Spread the mayonnaise mixture over the avocados. Top with the tomatoes, onions, olives and Colby jack cheese. Serve with tortilla chips for dipping.

LIME DESSERT

1 prepared graham cracker pie crust
1 quart of vanilla ice cream
2 cups lime sherbet
2 tablespoons lemon juice
1/2 cup sugar
3 tablespoons butter or margarine
1 egg, beaten well

Soften the ice cream and sherbet and mix together. Put the mixture in the pie crust and freeze firm.

In a saucepan, cook the lemon juice, sugar, butter and egg. Cook in a double boiler or in a bowl over hot water until it begins to thicken. Let cool and spread over the ice cream. Freeze until all is firm.

SOUP MEALS

HEARTY ALPHABET SOUP MEAL

MENU

- ♥ *Hearty Alphabet Soup*
- ♥ *Rolls*
- ♥ *Fruit with Sherbet*

HEARTY ALPHABET SOUP

1/2 pound beef (Use round steak, stew beef or ground chuck.)
14.5-ounce can stewed tomatoes
8-ounce can tomato sauce
1 cup water or beef broth
1 envelope dry onion soup mix
10-ounce package frozen mixed vegetables
1/2 cup uncooked alphabet pasta

Mix the meat, tomatoes, tomato sauce, water and soup mix in a slow cooker. Cover and cook on low 6 to 8 hours.

Turn slow cooker to high. Stir in the vegetables and pasta. Add more water or broth if mixture seems too dry and thick. Cover and cook on high approximately 30 minutes or until pasta is done.

ROLLS

Purchase a package of frozen yeast rolls from your grocery store. Thaw, let rise and bake according to package directions. These usually take approximately 6 hours or more.

FRUIT with SHERBET

Purchase canned pears, peaches, pineapple or a combination of several fruits. Serve in bowls with a scoop of sherbet on top.

TACO SOUP MEAL

MENU

- ♥ *Taco Soup*
- ♥ *Crackers/Tortilla Strips*
- ♥ *Pudding*

TACO SOUP

15-ounce can whole kernel Mexican style corn
15-ounce can black beans, rinsed and drained
2 cans chicken broth (14 ounces each)
1½ cups chunky mild salsa
2 cups chopped cooked chicken
1 teaspoon cumin
1 tablespoon chili powder

Purchase canned chicken, use deli rotisserie chicken, or cook fresh chicken at home. (This also can be made without meat.)

Mix all ingredients in a slow cooker and put on low for 3 hours. Serve with crackers and colored tortilla strips (found in the produce section of the store).

;

PUDDING

6-ounce box instant pudding of your choice
3 cups half and half
Half of an 8-ounce container of whipped topping

Make the pudding with the 3 cups of half and half. Fold in the whipped topping. Serve in dishes with more topping if you like.

JANET'S "DOG BONE" SOUP MEAL

MENU

- ♥ *Split Pea Soup*
- ♥ *Pumpkin Muffins*
- ♥ *Gelatin with Fruit Dessert*

SPLIT PEA SOUP with SMOKED PORK

2 smoked pork hocks (found with the ham
  in meat department)
1-pound bag of dried split peas
2 onions, diced
4 carrots, diced
3 quarts of water or chicken broth
1 teaspoon Lawry's seasoned salt
1/2 teaspoon black pepper
1/8 teaspoon cayenne pepper
8 ounces dry lentils

Combine all ingredients in a Dutch oven and cover. Let come to a
boil and turn down heat to simmer. Simmer for at least one hour
and test for seasoning. Remove ham hock bones before eating.
(This can also be made in a slow cooker.)

PUMPKIN MUFFINS

Oven temperature: 400 degrees

4 eggs
2 cups sugar
3/4 cup Miracle Whip salad dressing (You may use a
  house brand if you like)
16-ounce can pumpkin

1 cup chopped nuts
2¾ cups flour
2 teaspoons baking soda
1/2 teaspoon salt
1 teaspoon cinnamon

Beat eggs and sugar. Stir in salad dressing. Add pumpkin and nuts. Mix well.

Mix together the flour, baking soda, salt and cinnamon. Stir the flour mixture into the pumpkin mixture.
Spoon the batter into paper-lined muffin tins, filling almost full. Sprinkle the batter with sugar if you like.
Bake 15 to 20 minutes.

GELATIN with FRUIT DESSERT

6 ounce package of your favorite gelatin dessert
15-ounce can crushed pineapple or fruit cocktail
3.4-ounce package instant vanilla pudding mix

1 cup whole or 2% milk
8 ounces whipped topping

Prepare the gelatin according to package directions. Drain the fruit and use the liquid for part of the liquid
called for in the gelatin directions. Put into a serving dish. When the gelatin has set, mix the vanilla
pudding and milk. Spread over the top of the gelatin. Spread whipped topping over the pudding.

WHITE CHICKEN CHILI MEAL

MENU

- ♥ *White Chicken Chili*
- ♥ *Garlic Bread*
- ♥ *Dump Cake*

WHITE CHICKEN CHILI

1½ onions, chopped
1 garlic clove, minced, or 1 teaspoon garlic powder
3 tablespoons olive oil
4 cups chicken stock (you can use canned)
4-ounce can green chilies, chopped
1 teaspoon cumin
1/2 teaspoon oregano
1/2 teaspoon basil
1/2 teaspoon cayenne pepper
1/2 teaspoon salt
1/2 teaspoon black pepper
22-ounce jar Great Northern beans
2 chicken breasts
8 ounces sour cream
1 cup Monterey jack cheese, shredded

Simmer chicken breasts in water or chicken broth until cooked. Cut meat into cubes. Sauté onion and garlic in olive oil until soft. Add chicken stock, chilies, cumin, oregano, basil, cayenne pepper, salt, black pepper, beans and chicken. Simmer 30 minutes. Add sour cream and cheese. Heat through but DO NOT BOIL as sour cream may curdle.

GARLIC BREAD

Purchase prepared garlic bread from your grocery store frozen food section and prepare according to the directions on the box.

DUMP CAKE

Oven temperature: 350 degrees

8-ounce can crushed pineapple, drained
1 can cherry pie filling
1 yellow cake mix
1 cup walnuts
1 stick butter or margarine

Dump pineapple in 9"x13" baking pan and spread over the bottom. Dump the cherry pie filling over the pineapple and spread out. Sprinkle cake mix on top, leveling with a fork. Sprinkle with walnuts and dot with the butter. Bake 45 minutes to one hour. Cake should be light brown.

SANTA FE SOUP MEAL

MENU

- ♥ *Stacy's Santa Fe Soup*
- ♥ *Grace's Rolls*
- ♥ *Angel Food Cake with Coconut Cream*

SANTA FE
SOUP MEAL
grocery list

- ☐ *Round steak*
- ☐ *Green pepper*
- ☐ *Onion*
- ☐ *Ginger*
- ☐ *Soy sauce*
- ☐ *Garlic powder or cloves*
- ☐ *Mushrooms*
- ☐ *Crushed red pepper, cayenne or Tabasco sauce*
- ☐ *Chocolate graham cracker pie crust*
- ☐ *Coffee flavored ice cream*
- ☐ *Fudge topping*
- ☐ *Pecans*
- ☐ *Whipped topping*

STACY'S SANTA FE SOUP

My good friend Stacy brought me this soup just as a love gift one day when she knew I had been quite busy. It was such a great treat and easy to make.

2 chicken breasts (approximately 1 pound total)
1 teaspoon onion powder
1 teaspoon garlic powder
3 tablespoons olive oil
1/4 teaspoon black pepper
1 onion, chopped
4-ounce can green chilies
15-ounce can Progresso Santa Fe Chicken Soup

12 ounces canned turkey or chicken, drained
15-ounce can corn kernels with liquid
15-ounce can black beans, rinsed and drained
4 cups chicken stock
2 tablespoons taco seasoning
1 cup brown rice
15-ounce can diced roasted tomatoes with garlic and onion

Season the chicken breasts with the onion powder, garlic powder and pepper and brown in olive oil on each side for approximately three to four minutes. Remove from heat and cut into bite-size pieces.

Mix all ingredients except rice in a large saucepan and bring to a boil .Add the rice, stir well, and simmer until rice is done. (Add more chicken stock as needed.)

GRACE'S ROLLS

This recipe was given to me by my neighbor, Grace, whose recipe for Dutch Meatball Soup is also in this book.

Oven temperature: 350 degrees

2 packages dry yeast
2¼ cups warm water
1/2 cup sugar
1 teaspoon salt

3 eggs
1/3 cup vegetable oil
7 cups flour

Add sugar and salt to warm water. Add half of the flour to the water mixture and sprinkle in the yeast. Beat thoroughly; add eggs and oil and beat again. Add remaining flour. Let rise till double in bulk. Shape into rolls and let rise again for 30 minutes. Bake at 350 degrees for approximately 15 minutes.

ANGEL FOOD CAKE with COCONUT CREAM

Prepared angel food cake
  purchased from your bakery
8 ounces whipped topping
1 cup milk
2/3 cup sugar
3 tablespoons cornstarch
1/4 teaspoon salt

2 eggs
2 cups whipping cream, divided
1 teaspoon coconut extract
1/2 teaspoon vanilla extract
2 tablespoons butter
2 cups coconut

Prepare some ice water in a large pan or the sink to use later.

Whisk together the sugar, cornstarch and salt and set aside.

Heat the milk over low heat until it is simmering. Add the sugar mixture and whisk well. Add the eggs and 1 cup of the cream. Continue to whisk and cook over low heat until the mixture is bubbling. Add the butter, vanilla extract and coconut extract and stir well. Set pan in ice water and cover tightly with plastic wrap. Cool completely. Meanwhile, whip the remaining cream until stiff. Fold into the cooled cooked mixture.

Cut the angel food cake into two layers. Spread the coconut cream on each layer. Frost the outside with whipped topping and sprinkle all over with the coconut. Chill before serving.

BEEF STEW
SOUP MEAL

MENU
- ♥ *Beef Stew*
- ♥ *Pudding Dessert*
- ♥ *Joan's Rolls (recipe page 157)*

This stew recipe is one I made when I was first married and still make today. The recipe for rolls is from a long-time friend in my church.

(recipe page 157)

BEEF STEW SOUP MEAL
grocery list

- ☐ Potatoes
- ☐ Onion
- ☐ Cloves
- ☐ Lemon juice
- ☐ Carrots
- ☐ Stew beef
- ☐ Cornstarch
- ☐ Garlic powder
- ☐ Paprika
- ☐ Whole milk
- ☐ Instant chocolate pudding
- ☐ Fudge ice cream topping
- ☐ Whipped topping

BEEF STEW

2 pounds stew meat cubes
2 tablespoons olive oil
2 quarts cold water
1/4 teaspoon paprika
1 teaspoon sugar
3 cups diced, peeled potatoes
1 onion, chopped
2 cups peeled, sliced carrots
1/2 teaspoon garlic powder
1/4 teaspoon cloves
1/2 teaspoon lemon juice
2 teaspoons salt
1/2 teaspoon pepper

Brown the meat in olive oil in a Dutch oven or other heavy pan until the juices have caramelized. When all the meat is completely browned add the 2 quarts water, onion, garlic powder, paprika, cloves, sugar, lemon juice, salt and pepper. Let simmer for approximately 30 minutes. Add the vegetables. Let simmer another 45 minutes or until the meat is tender.

TO THICKEN:
3 tablespoons cornstarch
1/2 cup water

Dissolve the cornstarch in the water and stir into the hot stew mixture. Let come to a boil and turn off heat when stew has thickened.

PUDDING DESSERT

1 box chocolate flavored graham crackers
2 (3.4 ounce) packages instant chocolate pudding mix
1 large can evaporated milk
1 1/3 cups whole milk
8 ounces whipped topping mix
1 jar fudge ice cream topping

Mix the pudding with the evaporated milk and whole milk in a bowl. Fold in the whipped topping.

Put a layer of chocolate graham crackers in the bottom of a 9"x13" dish. Spread with half of the pudding mixture. Top with another layer of graham crackers and the rest of the pudding mixture. Top with more graham crackers and spread them with the fudge topping. Chill overnight. Cut into squares to serve.

POTATO SOUP WITH A TWIST

MENU

♥ *Potato Soup with a Twist*
♥ *Rose's Bran Muffins*
   (recipe page 156)
♥ *Cherry Dessert*

I invented this simple Potato Soup with a Twist recipe one day when I didn't have enough milk to make my normal recipe. I took some to a friend who had given me the home-grown potatoes and it was much appreciated.

POTATO SOUP
with a TWIST MEAL
grocery list
☐ Potatoes
☐ Onion
☐ Celery
☐ Kosher salt
☐ Chicken broth
☐ Evaporated milk
☐ Ranch dressing
☐ Sour cream
☐ Parmesan or Swiss cheese
☐ Cherry pie filling
☐ Yellow cake mix
☐ Butter
☐ Walnuts
☐ Almond flavoring
☐ Whipped topping or ice cream

POTATO SOUP WITH A TWIST

8 cups cubed potatoes
1 large onion, chopped
3 stalks celery, diced
1 tablespoon kosher salt
Approximately 4 cups chicken broth
   OR water (enough to cover the potatoes)

Bring potatoes to a boil and boil until very well done. Mash slightly with a potato masher until cubes are just broken up.

ADD:
1/2 cup ranch dressing
1/2 cup sour cream
1/2 cup evaporated milk
1 cup shredded Parmesan or Swiss cheese

Heat until hot through, but don't boil.

CHERRY DESSERT

Oven temperature: 350 degrees

1 large can cherry pie filling
1 teaspoon almond flavoring
1 regular size package yellow cake mix
1/2 cup butter
1 cup chopped walnuts
Whipped topping or ice cream

Grease a 9"x13" baking pan.

Pour the cherry pie filling into a bowl. Add the almond flavoring and stir. Pour into the baking pan. Sprinkle the dry cake mix over the pie filling. Melt the butter and pour evenly over the cake mix. Sprinkle the walnuts over all and bake for approximately 45 minutes until browned evenly. Serve with whipped topping or ice cream.

BROCCOLI CHEESE SOUP MEAL

MENU
- ♥ *Broccoli Cheese Soup*
- ♥ *Mark's Parmesan Bread*
  (recipe page 158)
- ♥ *Peanut Butter Cookies*

BROCCOLI CHEESE SOUP

grocery list

- ☐ Potatoes
- ☐ Celery
- ☐ Broccoli
- ☐ Onion
- ☐ Velveeta cheese
- ☐ Evaporated milk
- ☐ Sausage
- ☐ Peanut butter
- ☐ Vegetable shortening
- ☐ Brown sugar
- ☐ Milk
- ☐ Vanilla
- ☐ Eggs
- ☐ Flour
- ☐ Baking soda

BROCCOLI CHEESE SOUP

Approximately 8 cups peeled, cubed potatoes
2 (10-ounce) bags frozen broccoli
   (OR substitute broccoli and cauliflower mix
   or California blend)
1 large onion, chopped
2 stalks celery, chopped
2 pounds Velveeta cheese, cubed
1/2 cup evaporated milk
1 tablespoon salt
1 pound smoked sausage, polish sausage or ham (optional)

Put the potatoes, onions, celery and salt in a large pot. Add just enough water to cover. Bring to a boil and boil until the potatoes are very well done. Mash slightly with a potato masher until potatoes are in bite size chunks.

Add the broccoli and cook until tender. Add the evaporated milk and Velveeta cheese and heat until cheese is melted but don't boil. Add more milk if soup seems too thick.

PEANUT BUTTER COOKIES

Oven temperature: 350 degrees

1 cup peanut butter
1/2 cup vegetable shortening
1¼ cups packed brown sugar
3 tablespoons milk
1 teaspoon vanilla

1 egg
1¾ cups flour
1 teaspoon salt
1 teaspoon baking soda

Cream peanut butter, shortening, brown sugar, milk, vanilla and egg in a mixing bowl. Add the dry ingredients. Using a small ice cream scoop or a tablespoon, make dough into balls and place on a greased baking sheet. Press down with a fork dipped in water to make a criss-cross design. Bake approximately 10 minutes at 350 degrees.

NEW YEAR'S DAY CHILI MEAL

MENU

- ♥ *New Year's Day Chili*
- ♥ *Cathy's Buttermilk Biscuits*
- ♥ *Aunt Leah's Peach Pinwheels*

My husband Don would never eat chili until he tried this recipe that my sister entered in a local chili cook-off. Her buttermilk biscuits are the best I've ever had! These peach pinwheels were a favorite of my Aunt Leah and she made them often.

NEW YEAR'SDAY CHILI

NEW YEAR'S DAY
CHILI MEAL
<u>grocery list</u>
- ☐ Ground beef
- ☐ Tomato paste
- ☐ Onion
- ☐ Paprika
- ☐ Chili powder
- ☐ Tomatoes
- ☐ Chili beans
- ☐ Self rising flour
- ☐ Butter
- ☐ Baking soda
- ☐ Sugar
- ☐ Buttermilk
- ☐ Bisquick
- ☐ Cream or evaporated milk
- ☐ Nuts
- ☐ Tapioca
- ☐ Cinnamon
- ☐ Sliced peaches
- ☐ Lemon juice

2 cups cold water
1 pound ground beef
6-ounce can tomato paste
1 small onion, chopped fine
2 tablespoons paprika
1 tablespoon chili powder
14-ounce can chili beans with liquid
32 ounces tomatoes
Salt and pepper to taste

Put ground beef and water in a saucepan. Heat gradually to boiling, stirring occasionally. Add tomato paste, onion paprika and chili powder. Reduce heat and simmer uncovered for 90 minutes. Add remaining ingredients and simmer 30 minutes.

SISTER CATHY'S BUTTERMILK BISCUITS

Oven temperature: 450 degrees

Mix in a flat-bottom bowl:

2 cups <u>self-rising</u> flour
1/8 teaspoon baking soda
2 teaspoons sugar

5 tablespoons margarine
1 scant cup buttermilk

Cut margarine into dry ingredients with a pastry blender until particles are fine. Gradually add buttermilk, mixing with a fork until all flour mixture is moistened. Dump onto a floured surface and knead lightly three or four strokes. Pat dough out into a circle, about an inch thick, and cut with round cutter (a drinking glass or soup can with ends cut out works well.) Push extra pieces together and cut last biscuit, or pat into round shape. Place on shiny baking sheet with no sides, with biscuits just touching. Bake just until biscuits are lightly brown on edges, about 8 to 10 minutes. Eat piping hot with homemade strawberry jam.

AUNT LEAH'S PEACH PINWHEELS

CRUST:

1 ½ cup Bisquick baking mix
1/3 cup cream or evaporated milk
1 tablespoon sugar

Stir to make a soft dough. On a lightly floured surface, roll dough out into a rectangle about twelve inches long by eight inches wide. Spread dough with the following mixture:

2 tablespoons butter
2 tablespoons sugar
3 tablespoons nuts

Starting with the long side, roll up the dough. Cut the roll into 1-inch pieces.

FILLING:

1 cup sugar
2 tablespoons tapioca
1/2 teaspoon cinnamon
1/4 teaspoon salt
4 cups sliced peaches
1 cup water
1 tablespoon lemon juice

Mix all ingredients and cook over low heat just until it starts to bubble. Pour into a 9"x13" baking pan and top with the biscuit rolls, laying them cut-side down. Bake approximately 30 minutes or until biscuits are browned.

COMBINATION MUSHROOM SOUP MEAL

MENU

- ♥ *Combination Mushroom Soup*
- ♥ *Assorted Crackers*
- ♥ *Stewed Fruit Crumble*

Most people think of mushroom soup as a canned ingredient to add to a casserole-style dish to make it creamy. This is much different! It's a special favorite of friends who come for game night and soup.

COMBINATION MUSHROOM SOUP MEAL
grocery list
- ☐ Dried porcini mushrooms
- ☐ Assorted mushrooms
- ☐ Extra virgin olive oil
- ☐ Garlic
- ☐ Red onion
- ☐ Butter
- ☐ Thyme
- ☐ Chicken stock
- ☐ Flat leaf parsley
- ☐ Mascarpone or cream cheese
- ☐ Lemon
- ☐ Assorted crackers
- ☐ Sugar
- ☐ Cloves
- ☐ Cinnamon
- ☐ Nutmeg
- ☐ Orange
- ☐ Pears
- ☐ Peaches
- ☐ Plums
- ☐ Rhubarb
- ☐ Berries
- ☐ Apples
- ☐ Vanilla
- ☐ Flour
- ☐ Butter

COMBINATION MUSHROOM SOUP

1/2 cup dried porcini mushrooms
2 tablespoons extra virgin olive oil
1½ pounds mixed fresh mushrooms, wiped clean and sliced
  (Use a combination of wild mushrooms, baby
  portabellas, button or whatever kind you like)
2 cloves garlic, peeled and finely chopped
1 medium red onion, chopped
1 tablespoon butter
2 teaspoons chopped fresh thyme leaves
  or 1 teaspoon dried thyme
1 teaspoon kosher salt
1/4 teaspoon black pepper
5 cups chicken stock
3 tablespoons chopped fresh flat leaf parsley
2 tablespoons cream cheese or mascarpone
1 lemon

Place the porcini in a small dish, add boiling water just to cover, and leave to soak.

In a large pan heat the olive oil and add the fresh mushrooms. Add the crushed garlic, onions, butter, thyme, salt and pepper. Cook approximately one minute until you see the moisture coming out of the mushrooms. Remove pan from the heat.

Drain the porcini mushrooms and reserve the liquid. Chop half of the porcini and leave the other half whole. Strain the liquid to remove any sandy particles or grit. (Use a fine mesh strainer, cheesecloth, or paper coffee filter.) Add liquid to the porcini, onion and fresh mushroom mixture and put it back on the heat. Cook until most of the liquid has evaporated. Season to taste and add the chicken stock. Bring to a boil and simmer for approximately half an hour.

Take half of the mixture from the pan and puree it in a food processor, blender, or if you don't have either of these, use an electric mixer to break it up. Add back into the soup. Add the chopped parsley and cream cheese or mascarpone. Place the juice and zest of the lemon in a small dish with a dash of salt and pepper. Add to the soup just before serving. Serve with a basket of assorted buttery crackers, such as Town House or Ritz.

(recipes continued on next page)

STEWED FRUIT CRUMBLE

Oven temperature: 375 degrees

1½ cups sugar
1 cup boiling water
1/8 teaspoon cloves
1/2 teaspoon cinnamon
1/8 teaspoon ground nutmeg
Zest of half an orange
2 pears, peeled and cut into pieces
4 peaches, peeled and cut into pieces
4 purple plums, halved

2 cups diced rhubarb
1 cup berries of your choice
2 sweet apples, peeled and cut into pieces
1 teaspoon vanilla
1½ cups flour
1 stick (8 ounces) butter
1/2 cup sugar

Put 1½ cups sugar in a large saucepan and add 1 cup boiling water. Add the cloves, cinnamon, nutmeg, and orange zest. Boil until the liquid becomes clear and the sugar has dissolved. Turn down to a simmer and add the rhubarb and apple. Cook for approximately two minutes then add the peaches, pears and plums. Continue to cook for three or four minutes and add the berries and vanilla. Remove pan from heat.

Mix the flour, butter and 1/2 cup sugar together until mixture is crumbly. Put the fruit into individual oven-proof dishes or into a shallow casserole dish and top with the crumb mixture.
Bake approximately 20 minutes or until browned.

SIMPLE ONION SOUP MEAL

MENU

- ♥ *Simple Onion Soup*
- ♥ *Summer Garden Salad*
- ♥ *Caramel Apple Pie*

SIMPLE ONION
SOUP MEAL
grocery list
- ☐ Onions
- ☐ Thyme
- ☐ Garlic
- ☐ Bay leaf
- ☐ Olive oil
- ☐ Butter
- ☐ Beef stock
- ☐ Baguette or ciabatta
- ☐ Gruyere or Swiss cheese
- ☐ Iceberg lettuce
- ☐ Summer squash
- ☐ Zucchini
- ☐ Green bell pepper
- ☐ Red onion
- ☐ Dijon mustard
- ☐ Extra virgin olive oil
- ☐ Lemon
- ☐ Sweetened condensed milk
- ☐ Powdered sugar
- ☐ Eggs
- ☐ Flour
- ☐ Apples
- ☐ Cream
- ☐ Vanilla ice cream (optional)

SIMPLE ONION SOUP

2½ pounds onions, peeled and sliced thin
2 teaspoons fresh thyme, chopped
3 cloves garlic, finely chopped
1 bay leaf
3 tablespoons extra virgin olive oil
1 tablespoon butter
6 cups beef stock
Salt and pepper
1 baguette or ciabatta loaf
4 ounces Gruyere or Swiss cheese

Slowly fry the onions in a thick-bottomed pan with the olive oil, butter, thyme, garlic, and bay leaf. Place a lid on the pan to be able to cook them slowly without caramelizing them for approximately 15 minutes. Stir several times to keep them from sticking. Remove the lid and continue to cook until slightly caramelized. Add the beef stock, turn the heat down and simmer for approximately 20 minutes.

To serve, put into a bowl and top with some of the cheese, then a slice of the baguette. Drizzle the bread with a little olive oil, place on a baking sheet and put into the oven under the broiler to lightly toast the bread.

SUMMER GARDEN SALAD

1 head of iceberg lettuce, torn into bite-size pieces
1 yellow summer squash
1 zucchini
1 cup fresh peas
1 bell pepper cut into thin strips
1/2 red onion cut into thin strips
2 cups cherry tomatoes

1/2 cup extra virgin olive oil
1/2 teaspoon Dijon mustard
1/4 teaspoon salt
Pinch of black pepper
1 teaspoon lemon juice
1/4 teaspoon lemon zest

Cut zucchini and yellow squash into slices, then cut slices in half. Tear the lettuce into pieces and put it into a salad bowl. Add the vegetables and toss. Pour the extra virgin olive oil into a small dish and add the mustard, salt, pepper, lemon juice and lemon zest. Mix well with a small whisk and pour over the salad.

(recipes continued on next page)

CARAMEL APPLE PIE

My son-in-law, Sean, misses some of the dishes he knew as a child growing up in Great Britain. I learned to make this typically British dessert just for him.

Oven temperature: 350 degrees

CRUST:
5 tablespoons butter
1 cup powdered sugar
1/4 teaspoon kosher salt
2 cups flour
Zest of half a lemon
2 egg yolks
2 tablespoons cold heavy cream

Cream the butter, powdered sugar and salt, then work in the flour, lemon zest and egg yolks by hand or in a food processor. Divide dough into two balls. Wrap each piece in plastic wrap and refrigerate for at least one hour.

To form bottom crust, turn a 10-inch pie plate upside down on a flat surface. Press one ball of chilled dough over the upturned plate. Place a second plate over the dough and press to finish shaping crust, then invert both plates together. Remove the inside plate, leaving the bottom crust in the second plate. Trim edge of crust. Place in freezer.

FILLING:
2 (14 ounce) cans sweetened condensed milk. <u>Do not open cans.</u>
2 heaping tablespoons powdered sugar
Six cups peeled, sliced cooking apples
Vanilla ice cream

To make the caramel, put the <u>unopened </u>cans of condensed milk in a deep pan and cover with water. Bring to a boil, then reduce the heat. Cover pan and simmer constantly for approximately three hours. Check the pan often to make sure there is enough water to keep cans covered. When done, set aside to cool.

Peel and slice the apples and toss with the powdered sugar.

Remove the bottom crust from the freezer and spread one can of caramel over it. Place the apples on top and pour any remaining juice over them. Top with the second can of caramel. On a lightly floured surface, press out second ball of chilled dough and place on top of filling. Seal pastry edges and bake near the bottom of the oven for approximately 40 minutes. Serve with vanilla ice cream.

THE DINER MEATBALL SOUP MEAL

MENU

- ♥ *The Diner Meatball Soup*
- ♥ *Mandarin Cheese Salad*
- ♥ *My Mom's Three-grain Bread*

THE DINER
MEATBALL SOUP
MEAL
grocery list
- ☐ Ground beef
- ☐ Bread crumbs
- ☐ Eggs
- ☐ Parsley
- ☐ Garlic
- ☐ Paprika
- ☐ Chicken broth
- ☐ Spinach
- ☐ Frozen mixed vegetables
- ☐ Parmesan cheese
- ☐ Pimento cheese
- ☐ Cream cheese
- ☐ Mayonnaise
- ☐ Peach pie filling
- ☐ Pineapple tidbits
- ☐ Mandarin oranges
- ☐ Marshmallows
- ☐ White flour
- ☐ Wheat flour
- ☐ Oats
- ☐ Wheat germ
- ☐ Yeast
- ☐ Butter
- ☐ Yellow corn meal
- ☐ Evaporated milk
- ☐ Honey

THE DINER
MEATBALL SOUP

We owned a small diner for a short time and this was one of the popular soups we offered.

1 pound ground beef
1/2 cup dry bread crumbs
1 egg
1 tablespoon flat leaf parsley, chopped
1/2 clove garlic, minced
1/2 teaspoon paprika
1/2 teaspoon salt
1/2 teaspoon pepper
4 cups chicken broth
2 cups fresh spinach
2 cups frozen mixed vegetables
1/4 cup Parmesan cheese

Mix the ground beef, bread crumbs, egg, parsley, garlic, paprika,
salt and pepper and form into meatballs using a small ice cream scoop or a tablespoon.

Pour the chicken broth into a pot and heat to boiling. Add the meatballs to the broth a couple at a time and simmer approximately 15 minutes. Add the mixed vegetables and spinach and continue to simmer until vegetables are done. Add salt and pepper to taste and serve with the Parmesan cheese.

MANDARIN CHEESE SALAD

15-ounce jar pimento cheese spread
8 ounces cream cheese
1/2 cup mayonnaise
22-ounce can peach pie filling

22-ounce can drained pineapple tidbits
11-ounce can mandarin oranges, drained
1 cup miniature marshmallows

Combine the cheese and mayonnaise; fold in the fruit and marshmallows and chill.

(recipes continued on next page)

MY MOM'S THREE-GRAIN BREAD

Mom made this bread often, and always sent a loaf home with us when we visited.

Oven temperature: 375 degrees

STIR TOGETHER:

1 cup white flour

2 cups whole wheat flour

1 cup rolled oats

1/2 cup wheat germ

1/2 cup yellow corn meal

2 teaspoons salt

2 tablespoons (2 packages) dry yeast

Set aside.

COMBINE:

1 cup hot water

1/4 cup butter

Large can evaporated milk

1/4 cup honey

Add the dry ingredients and beat two minutes.

BEAT IN:

2 eggs

Gradually add 2½ to 3 cups white flour

On floured surface, knead dough by hand approximately six or seven minutes until elastic. Let rise until double. Divide into two loaves and put into greased bread pans. Let rise again until double. Bake at 375 degrees approximately 20 minutes, then lower oven temperature to 350 degrees and bake approximately 30 minutes until the loaf sounds hollow when tapped.

ROASTED VEGETABLE SOUP MEAL

MENU

- ♥ *Roasted Vegetable Soup*
- ♥ *Sassy Cornbread*
- ♥ *Chris' Fruit Pie*

ROASTED VEGETABLE SOUP MEAL

grocery list

- ☐ Chicken
- ☐ Sweet potatoes
- ☐ Squash
- ☐ Carrots
- ☐ Onion
- ☐ Garlic
- ☐ Fennel
- ☐ Chicken stock
- ☐ Lemon
- ☐ Rosemary
- ☐ Olive oil
- ☐ Flour
- ☐ Cornmeal
- ☐ Baking powder
- ☐ Buttermilk
- ☐ Butter
- ☐ Creamed corn
- ☐ Green chilies
- ☐ Cheddar cheese
- ☐ Graham cracker crust
- ☐ Sweetened condensed milk
- ☐ Crushed pineapple
- ☐ Peaches
- ☐ Whipped topping
- ☐ Maraschino cherries
- ☐ Pecans

ROASTED VEGETABLE SOUP

I made this roasted vegetable soup one day when I had leftover vegetables from dinner the night before. I thought I had invented a great new soup until I happened to see a similar recipe in a magazine the next day.

Oven temperature: 425 degrees

1 whole chicken
2 large sweet potatoes
1 butternut squash
4 large carrots
2 large onions
1 whole head garlic
4 cloves garlic
1 fennel bulb
4 cups chicken stock
1 lemon
2 sprigs fresh rosemary
Extra virgin olive oil
Kosher salt
Black pepper

Place the peeled and cleaned vegetables plus 4 cloves of the garlic in a large shallow roasting pan and drizzle with extra virgin olive oil. Sprinkle with kosher salt and black pepper.

Rinse the chicken and pat dry. Cut the lemon in half and place inside the chicken along with the rosemary sprigs. Cut the top off the head of garlic and place inside the chicken. Bend the wing tips backward and drizzle olive oil over the chicken and rub until skin is thoroughly covered. Sprinkle with kosher salt and pepper. Place the chicken on top of the vegetables. Bake approximately 1 hour and 15 minutes. Use a thermometer to test chicken. When done, cool the chicken and vegetables.

Pull the chicken off the bones and place in a container to be used for other purposes.

Take the pan juices as well as the caramelized pieces in the roasting pan and place in a soup pot. Add the chicken broth. Add the roasted vegetables and bring to a boil. Simmer approximately 15 minutes. Puree part of the soup and add back to the batch. If desired, add some of the chicken to the soup.

(recipes continued on next page)

SASSY CORNBREAD

Oven temperature: 400 degrees

1 cup flour
1 cup cornmeal
1 teaspoon salt
4 teaspoons baking powder
1 cup buttermilk

2 eggs
1/4 cup butter, melted
8 ounces creamed corn
4 ounces canned, chopped green chilies
1 cup grated Cheddar cheese

In a bowl, combine the dry ingredients.

In a separate bowl, whisk together buttermilk, eggs and butter. Stir into the dry ingredients.
Stir in remaining ingredients and turn into a greased 9"x9" baking pan. Bake 20 to 25 minutes.

CHRIS' FRUIT PIE

1 can sweetened condensed milk
1/3 cup lemon juice
1 large can crushed pineapple, drained
1 can peaches, drained and diced

1/2 cup sliced maraschino cherries
1/2 cup toasted pecans
16-ounce container whipped topping
10-inch graham cracker pie crust

Drain fruit very dry. Mix first six ingredients and fold in the whipped topping. Turn into the graham cracker crust and chill. For easier slicing, freeze for about 30 minutes before serving time.

STEAK SOUP MEAL

MENU

- ♥ *Steak Soup*
- ♥ *Cheesy Bread Sticks*
- ♥ *Pear and Gorgonzola*
  Cheese Salad

STEAK SOUP

I was introduced to this Steak Soup and the Pear and Gorgonzola Salad when we took a trip to Kentucky and visited what used to be the Shaker community. We ate in an authentic Shaker restaurant and were treated to some delicious food and wonderful service.

1½ pounds round steak
3 tablespoons butter
4 cups water
14 ounces beef broth
16 ounces chopped tomatoes
1 cup chopped carrots
1 cup chopped celery
1 cup chopped onion
10 ounces frozen mixed vegetables
Salt and pepper to taste

Cut round steak into bite-size pieces. Melt butter in soup pot and brown the meat. Add water, broth, tomatoes and salt. Bring to a boil, reduce heat and simmer 40 minutes. Add the next three ingredients and simmer 30 minutes. Add frozen mixed vegetables and simmer 10 minutes.

CHEESY BREAD STICKS

Oven temperature: 350 degrees

1 loaf frozen bread dough
4 tablespoons butter
8 ounces Mozzarella cheese, shredded
1 teaspoon extra virgin olive oil

1/2 teaspoon minced garlic
Cornmeal
Pizza sauce (optional)

Thaw the bread dough in the refrigerator overnight. Roll thawed dough to approximately 8"x12". Lightly dust a greased cookie sheet with cornmeal. Place the rolled dough on the cookie sheet.

Melt the butter. Add the olive oil and garlic and brush mixture onto dough. Cover with the Mozzarella and bake about 20 to 25 minutes. Cut into strips. Serve with warmed pizza sauce for dipping if desired.

PEAR AND GORGONZOLA SALAD

1/3 cup Gorgonzola cheese
2/3 cup softened cream cheese
1 tablespoon cream
4 fresh pears, cut in half lengthwise and core removed

Crush the Gorgonzola cheese. Add softened cream cheese and cream. Beat until smooth. Fill the hollow of a pear half with a small ball of the cheese mixture. Serve round-side-up on a leaf of lettuce.

GRACE'S DUTCH MEATBALL SOUP MEAL

MENU

- ♥ *Grace's Dutch Meatball Soup*
- ♥ *English Muffin Bread*
- ♥ *Snickerdoodles (recipe page 164)*

GRACE'S DUTCH
MEATBALL SOUP
MEAL
grocery list
☐ Ground beef
☐ Chicken broth
☐ Dry vegetable soup
☐ Egg noodles
☐ Carrots
☐ Celery
☐ Onion
☐ Cabbage
☐ Garlic powder
☐ Lawry's seasoned salt
☐ Flour
☐ Yeast
☐ Baking soda
☐ Milk
☐ Honey
☐ Cornmeal

GRACE'S DUTCH MEATBALL SOUP

My sweet next door neighbor, Grace, brought this delicious soup to me soon after I returned from the hospital after having some minor surgery. It's easy but very tasty.

1 pound ground beef
1 teaspoon salt
1½ cups chopped onion
1½ cups chopped celery
1½ cups diced carrots
1½ cups diced potatoes
1½ cups broccoli florets
1½ cups green beans
1½ cups cabbage
Half of a-pound bag of wide egg noodles
Salt and pepper as desired

Mix the meat with the salt and shape into small balls.

In a saucepan, put 2 quarts cold water and bring to a boil. Drop the meatballs in and cook for 5 minutes. Add the vegetables and cook until tender. Add the wide egg noodles and cook until done. Season to taste with salt and pepper. If more liquid is needed, add canned chicken stock to make desired consistency.

ENGLISH MUFFIN BREAD

Oven temperature: 400 degrees

5 to 6 cups flour, divided
2 tablespoons yeast
2 teaspoons salt
1/2 teaspoon baking soda
2 tablespoons soft butter

2 cups milk
1/2 cup water
1 tablespoon honey
1/4 cup cornmeal

Mix 3 cups flour, yeast, salt and baking soda. Set aside. Heat the milk, water, butter and honey together to very warm. Add liquids to dry ingredients and add 2 to 3 more cups of flour. Spoon into two greased loaf pans that have been dusted with the cornmeal. Sprinkle loaves lightly with more cornmeal. Cover and let rise 45 minutes, or until up to the top of the pans. Bake 40 minutes. Remove from the pans and cool.

RICH
BEEF NOODLE
SOUP MEAL

MENU

- ♥ *Rich Beef Noodle Soup*
- ♥ *Lettuce Salad Deluxe*
- ♥ *Brownie Pudding*

RICH BEEF NOODLE
SOUP MEAL
grocery list
- ☐ Ground beef
- ☐ Onions
- ☐ Garlic powder
- ☐ Lawry's seasoned salt
- ☐ Beef broth
- ☐ Bouillon cubes
- ☐ Canned mushrooms
- ☐ Egg noodles
- ☐ Head lettuce
- ☐ Red onion
- ☐ Muenster
- ☐ Genoa salami
- ☐ Ripe olives
- ☐ Italian dressing
- ☐ Butter
- ☐ Powdered sugar
- ☐ Vanilla
- ☐ Eggs
- ☐ Flour
- ☐ Granulated sugar
- ☐ Lemons
- ☐ Pecans
- ☐ Cream cheese

RICH BEEF NOODLE SOUP WITH MUSHROOMS

2 pounds ground beef
1 cup chopped onions
2 teaspoons garlic powder
2 teaspoons Lawry's seasoned salt
1/2 teaspoon pepper
2 teaspoons salt
4 quarts beef broth
2 beef bouillon cubes
8 ounces canned mushrooms (don't drain)
½-pound wide egg noodles

Brown the ground beef with the chopped onions, garlic powder, seasoning salt, pepper, and salt. When thoroughly browned, add the beef broth, bouillon cubes, and mushrooms. Bring to a boil and add the egg noodles and cook until the noodles are tender. Season to taste. Add more beef broth if needed.

LETTUCE SALAD DELUXE

1 head lettuce
1 small red onion, chopped
8 ounces Muenster cheese

4 ounces sliced ripe olives
1/3 pound Genoa salami, unsliced
1 bottle Italian salad dressing

Tear lettuce into bite-sized pieces. Cut cheese and salami into bite-size pieces. Drain olives. Combine lettuce, onion, cheese, olives and salami. Toss with desired amount of Italian dressing.

(recipes continued on next page)

CATHY'S CREAMY LEMON PECAN BARS

My daughter Cathy brought these delicious Lemon Pecan Bars to our family crab boil and they were so good I had to ask her for the recipe. They taste like a fresh lemon pie.

Oven temperature: 350 degrees

1/2 cup butter
1/3 cup powdered sugar
2 teaspoons vanilla
1¼ cups flour
1/3 cup pecans, toasted and chopped
8 ounces cream cheese, softened
2 cups granulated sugar
3 eggs
1/4 cup flour
1/2 cup fresh lemon juice (approximately 3 lemons)
Zest of one lemon
1 tablespoon powdered sugar

Mix the butter, powdered sugar and vanilla in a bowl. Gradually stir in 1¼ cups flour and the pecans. Mix till it holds together. Press onto the bottom of a greased a 9"x13" baking pan. Bake 15 minutes.

Meanwhile, beat cream cheese and granulated sugar in a bowl and add the remaining ¼ cup flour and eggs. Beat well. Stir in the lemon juice and lemon zest. Pour over the crust and bake 30 minutes or until set. Remove from oven and cool completely. Then sprinkle with the 1 tablespoon powdered sugar.

SOUP SUPPER POT MEAL

MENU

- ♥ *Soup Supper Pot*
- ♥ *Apple Pecan Salad*
- ♥ *Tomato Basil Bread*

SOUP SUPPER POT
MEAL
grocery list

- ☐ Garlic
- ☐ Olive oil
- ☐ Assorted vegetables
- ☐ Tomato sauce
- ☐ Tomato paste
- ☐ Beef broth
- ☐ Tomatoes
- ☐ White beans
- ☐ Oregano
- ☐ Basil
- ☐ Small pasta
- ☐ Parmesan cheese
- ☐ Apples
- ☐ Celery
- ☐ Pecans
- ☐ Lemon juice
- ☐ Olive oil
- ☐ Poppy seeds
- ☐ Greens
- ☐ Cheddar cheese
- ☐ Whole wheat flour
- ☐ Baking soda
- ☐ Gingerroot
- ☐ Basil
- ☐ Scallions
- ☐ Fresh tomatoes
- ☐ Sugar
- ☐ Eggs

SOUP SUPPER POT

Many people remember having soup suppers at social gatherings. This is a great tradition and the following soup is one that would be great to share with friends and family.

1 clove garlic, minced
2 tablespoons extra virgin olive oil
7 cups assorted chopped vegetables such as
    cabbage, carrots, onions, celery, corn, zucchini or peas
1 cup tomato sauce
1 tablespoon tomato paste
5 cups beef broth
16 ounces cooked white beans such as great northern or pea beans
1/2 teaspoon oregano
1/2 teaspoon basil
1/2 teaspoon kosher salt
1/2 teaspoon pepper
1/3 cup uncooked small pasta of your choice such as
    alphabet, tubetti, or ditalini
Fresh grated Parmesan cheese

Sauté the vegetables briefly in olive oil in a large cooking pot. Add the tomato sauce, tomato paste, beef broth, beans, oregano, basil, salt and pepper. Simmer uncovered for 15 minutes. Sprinkle the pasta over the soup. Simmer for about 15 minutes, or until the pasta is tender. Serve with the fresh Parmesan cheese.

(recipes continued on next page)

APPLE PECAN SALAD

1 cup chopped apple
1 cup chopped celery
8 ounces Cheddar cheese, cut into strips
4 cups torn assorted greens
1 cup chopped toasted pecans
1 tablespoon fresh lemon juice
2 tablespoons fresh orange juice
1 tablespoon extra virgin olive oil
1 tablespoon toasted poppy seeds

Combine the apple, celery, cheese, assorted greens and pecans in a bowl and mix well.

Combine the lemon juice, orange juice, oil and poppy seeds and whisk until blended. Blend other ingredients and pour over the mixture. Serve chilled.

BASIL TOMATO BREAD

Oven temperature: 350 degrees

5 cups whole wheat flour (OR use half heat and half white)
1 teaspoon baking soda
1 teaspoon baking powder
1 teaspoon kosher salt
1 small piece of gingerroot OR 1/2 teaspoon ground ginger
1/2 cup chopped fresh basil leaves or 1/4 cup dried basil leaves
1 scallion, cut into 1" pieces
3 tomatoes, seeded and quartered
1½ cups sugar
3 eggs
1/2 cup extra virgin olive oil

Combine the flour, baking soda, baking powder and salt in a food processor and mix well. Remove from the processor and set aside.

Place the piece of gingerroot, basil and scallion in the food processor and process for 10 seconds. Add the sugar and process for 10 seconds until smooth. Add the eggs and process for one minute. Add the olive oil and process briefly until blended. Add the flour mixture and pulse 6 times until the flour disappears. Spread the dough in a 2 greased loaf pans. Bake for 40 minutes or until bread tests done.

GOLDEN CAULIFLOWER SOUP MEAL

MENU

- ♥ *Golden Cauliflower Soup*
- ♥ *Apple Salad*
- ♥ *Easy Raisin Bread*
  (recipe page 161)

GOLDEN
CAULIFLOWER
SOUP MEAL
grocery list

- ☐ *Cauliflower*
- ☐ *Onion*
- ☐ *Butter*
- ☐ *Milk*
- ☐ *Flour*
- ☐ *Chicken bouillon*
- ☐ *Cheddar cheese*
- ☐ *Nutmeg*
- ☐ *Granny Smith apples*
- ☐ *Fuji or Red Delicious apples*
- ☐ *Snickers bars*
- ☐ *Whipped topping or whipping cream*

GOLDEN CAULIFLOWER SOUP

I like the tangy cheese taste in this Cauliflower Soup and I especially like it with this Apple Salad accompaniment

2 (10-ounce) packages frozen cauliflower OR
   1 small head fresh cauliflower, separated into small florets
2 cups water
1/2 cup chopped onion
1/3 cup butter
1/2 cup flour
2 cups whole milk
2 tablespoons chicken flavored bouillon
1 cup sharp shredded cheddar cheese OR
   1 cup cubed Velveeta
1/4 teaspoon grated nutmeg

In a saucepan, cook the cauliflower in 1 cup of the water until tender. Reserve 1 cup cooked florets. In blender or food processor, blend remaining cauliflower and liquid. Set aside.

In a large saucepan, cook onion in butter until tender. Stir in flour. Gradually add the remaining 1 cup water, milk and bouillon, stirring over medium heat until well blended and thickened. Add cheese, pureed cauliflower, reserved florets and nutmeg. Cook and stir until cheese melts and mixture is hot. **DO NOT BOIL.**

APPLE SALAD

3 Granny Smith apples, cut into bite size pieces (don't peel)
3 Fuji or Red Delicious apples, cut into bite size pieces (don't peel)
16 ounces whipped topping or
2 cups whipping cream, whipped with 1/4 cup sugar and 1 teaspoon vanilla
1 bag of Snickers fun-size candy bars, or 5 large Snickers candy bars

Cut the candy into small pieces. Mix the apples, candy bars and whipped topping. Do not mix too far ahead of serving time. This will not hold overnight.

ALPHABET CHICKEN SOUP MEAL

MENU

- ♥ *Alphabet Chicken Soup*
- ♥ *Peanut Apple Crisp*
- ♥ *Corn Muffins*

ALPHABET
CHICKEN SOUP
MEAL
grocery list

- ☐ Garlic
- ☐ Stewing chicken
- ☐ Peppercorns
- ☐ Poultry seasoning
- ☐ Alphabet pasta
- ☐ Carrots
- ☐ Celery
- ☐ Onion
- ☐ Apples
- ☐ Flour
- ☐ Sugar
- ☐ Cinnamon
- ☐ Peanut butter
- ☐ Peanuts
- ☐ Butter
- ☐ Cornmeal
- ☐ Baking powder
- ☐ Whole milk
- ☐ Eggs

ALPHABET CHICKEN SOUP

If you have children or grandchildren, they can make a game of finding their name in the alphabet pasta in this soup. The Peanut Apple Crisp is a variation of apple crisp that I've made for years.

3- to 4-pound stewing chicken, cut into pieces
3 quarts water
1 tablespoon salt
6 peppercorns
1/2 teaspoon poultry seasoning
2/3 cup alphabet pasta
1½ cups carrots, frozen or fresh cut up
1 cup finely chopped celery
1/2 cup chopped onion
Salt
Pepper

In a large Dutch oven or soup pan, combine the chicken, water, salt, peppercorns and poultry seasoning. Bring to a boil. Cover and cook over low heat one hour or until chicken is tender. Remove chicken and peppercorns. Skim off fat from broth.

Cut meat from bones and return to the soup. Add the pasta, carrots, celery and onion. Cook, covered, 20 to 30 minutes or until pasta is tender. Season with salt and pepper. If more chicken flavor is desired, add chicken bouillon to broth.

(recipes continued on next page)

PEANUT APPLE CRISP

Oven temperature: 350 degrees

6 medium sized cooking apples such as
Ida Red or Granny Smith
2/3 cup sugar
1 teaspoon cinnamon
1/2 cup peanut butter
1/2 teaspoon salt
1/4 cup flour

Peel the apples and toss with the other ingredients. Put into a 9"x13" baking pan.

TOPPING:
1 cup sugar
1/2 cup butter
1/2 cup flour
1/4 teaspoon salt
1 cup dry roasted peanuts

Mix all ingredients together until crumbly and put on top of the apples. Bake for approximately 45 minutes.

CORN MUFFINS

Oven temperature: 350 degrees

3 cups flour
1 cup sugar
1 cup medium cornmeal
2 tablespoons baking powder
1½ teaspoons salt
1½ cups whole milk
½ pound butter, melted and cooled
2 eggs

Line a 12-cup muffin pan or 24-cup mini-muffin pan with paper liners.

Mix the flour, sugar, cornmeal, baking powder and salt together in a bowl. In another bowl, mix the milk, melted butter, and eggs and add to the dry ingredients. Stir just until moistened.

Pour into the muffin pans and bake 30 minutes for large muffins, 25 minutes for smaller muffins or until a toothpick inserted in the top comes out clean.
(An easy way to make uniform muffins is to purchase an ice cream scoop that holds slightly less than your muffin pans and use it to scoop out the batter.)

SIMPLE THANKSGIVING SOUP MEAL

MENU

- ♥ *Simple Thanksgiving Soup*
- ♥ *Bean and Bacon Slaw*
- ♥ *Cheesy Biscuits (recipe page 160)*

(recipe page 160)

SIMPLE THANKSGIVING SOUP grocery list

- ☐ Turkey carcass
- ☐ Celery
- ☐ Onion
- ☐ Bay leaf
- ☐ Dry chicken soup mix
- ☐ Other vegetables as desired
- ☐ Kidney beans
- ☐ Bacon
- ☐ Mayonnaise
- ☐ Vinegar
- ☐ Cabbage
- ☐ Celery
- ☐ Parsley
- ☐ Sugar
- ☐ Flour
- ☐ Nuts
- ☐ Butter
- ☐ Canned chocolate pudding
- ☐ Whipped topping
- ☐ Cream cheese
- ☐ Powdered sugar

SIMPLE THANKSGIVING SOUP

You always have to do something with the turkey carcass after Thanksgiving dinner. This is a simple, tasty soup that makes good use of the deceased bird!

Carcass from a large turkey
3 stalks celery with tops, coarsely chopped
1 onion, sliced
1 tablespoon salt
1 bay leaf
12 cups water
13.4-ounce package dry chicken, onion or vegetable soup mix

Simmer turkey carcass, celery, onion, salt and bay leaf in water about 2 hours. Turn turkey if necessary during cooking to cook all parts evenly.

Remove carcass. Strip meat from bones and add it to the broth. Bring soup to a boil and add soup mix. Simmer about 10 minutes. This soup is even better if made the day before it is served. Also good with other vegetables such as peas, corn and green beans added to the broth.

BEAN AND BACON SLAW

15-ounce can kidney beans
1½ cups cabbage
1/2 cup celery
1/2 cup chopped onion
2 tablespoons chopped flat leaf parsley
5 strips of bacon, fried and crumbled
Dash of salt
2 tablespoons vinegar
1 tablespoon sugar
1/2 cup mayonnaise

Drain and rinse the kidney beans. Put in a large bowl with all other ingredients. Mix and chill.

RAINY DAY SOUP MEAL

MENU

- ♥ *Rainy Day Soup*
- ♥ *Lemon or Lime Dessert*
- ♥ *Cheesy French Bread*

RAINY DAY SOUP

This soup is so quick to make but has such great flavor. It's suitable for any rainy day, hence the name.

10-ounce can beef broth
10-ounce can vegetable soup
   (OR use 1 bag frozen mixed vegetables
   and increase the beef broth to 2 cans)
2 cans water
2 cups chopped cabbage
1 pound roasted sausage cut into bite size pieces
Small can tomatoes (approximately 1 cup)
1/2 cup uncooked small pasta, such as ditalini or tubetti
1 medium onion, sliced
2 tablespoons Parmesan cheese
1 small clove garlic, minced
1/2 teaspoon caraway seed

Combine all ingredients in a saucepan and bring to a boil. Simmer for 30 minutes or until done.

LEMON OR LIME DESSERT

One prepared angel food cake
1 bottle of lime or lemon curd (purchased in the ethnic food section in the English or Dutch section)
16-ounce container of whipped topping

Slice the angel food cake in half and spread with a little of the lemon or lime curd. Fold the rest of the lemon or lime curd into the whipped topping and frost the cake all the way around, on top and inside the middle hole. Slice and serve.

CHEESY FRENCH BREAD

Oven temperature: 400 degrees

2 sticks butter, softened
1 teaspoon garlic powder
1 teaspoon dried minced onion
1 teaspoon lemon juice

4 ounces cream cheese
2 cups shredded hard Cheddar cheese
1 loaf of French bread

Mix first six ingredients together until smooth.

Cut French bread loaf in half lengthwise. Spread each half with the butter and cheese mixture. Place on a baking sheet and bake five minutes, or until the cheese is bubbly and has started to brown slightly.

CHUNKY ITALIAN SOUP MEAL

MENU
- ♥ *Chunky Italian Soup*
- ♥ *Chocolate Mousse*
- ♥ *Onion Herb Bread*

CHUNKY ITALIAN SOUP

The Italian sausage in this soup gives it a rich flavor that you don't always find in vegetable-type soups.

2 pounds bulk or link sweet Italian
   OR hot Italian sausage
1 large onion, chopped
1 clove garlic, minced
2 (15-ounce) cans beef broth
1 (15-ounce) jar spaghetti sauce
1 (15-ounce) can garbanzo beans
1 (15-ounce) can kidney beans
1 medium zucchini, sliced
4 cups water
1 cup celery, diced
1 cup carrots, sliced
1½ teaspoons basil
Salt/pepper
1½ cups dry macaroni, cooked and drained
Grated Parmesan cheese

In a large Dutch oven, brown the sausage well and add the onion and garlic. Sauté until the onion is translucent; drain off the fat. Add the remaining ingredients, except pasta and cheese. Simmer for 30 minutes then add the pasta and simmer another 10 minutes. Serve soup with the Parmesan cheese.

CHOCOLATE MOUSSE

6 ounces semi-sweet chocolate
1/2 cup water
6 eggs, separated
1/2 cup granulated super fine sugar

2 teaspoons vanilla
1 cup heavy cream, whipped
Dash of salt
1/4 cup granulated super fine sugar

Melt chocolate and water over low heat in a small saucepan; cool a few minutes. In a medium bowl beat egg yolks with 1/2 cup sugar until thick and pale. Blend chocolate and vanilla into egg yolks. Fold in whipped cream. Beat egg whites with salt and sugar until stiff peaks form. Fold into chocolate mixture. Chill at least 6 hours before serving.

(recipes continued on next page)

ONION HERB BREAD

Oven temperature: 375 degrees

3¼ cups whole wheat flour
2 tablespoons yeast
  or 2 packages yeast
2 tablespoons sugar
1 teaspoon kosher salt
1/2 teaspoon sage

1/2 teaspoon crushed dried rosemary
1/4 teaspoon thyme
1 cup finely chopped onion
1/2 cup extra virgin olive oil
1¼ cups warm water
1 egg

Combine 1/2 cup flour, yeast, sugar, salt, sage, rosemary and thyme in a large mixing bowl. Mix well.

Sauté the onion in hot olive oil in a saucepan for five minutes or until golden. Add to the flour mixture.

Add the water and egg to the flour mixture and blend at low speed until moistened. Beat at medium speed for 3 minutes longer. Gradually stir in the remaining flour by hand to make a stiff batter.

Spoon the batter into a greased 2-quart baking dish. Let rise, covered, in a warm place until light and doubled in bulk. Bake 35 to 40 minutes or until golden brown.

ZUPPA PASTA FAGIOLA SOUP MEAL

MENU

- ♥ *Zuppa Pasta Fagiola*
- ♥ *Herbed Garlic Bread*
- ♥ *Easy Chocolate Cream Roll*

ZUPPA PASTA FAGIOLA

When I was small, my dad made what we called "spasta vasholi." What he was actually making was this delicious Italian soup.

3/4 pound dried white kidney or lima beans
Water
Ham shank (approximately 2 pounds) or a meaty ham bone
2 cloves garlic, minced
4 medium firm tomatoes, peeled and chopped
1/2 teaspoon pepper
1/4 teaspoon rubbed sage
1/4 teaspoon thyme leaves
6 cups water
1/4 cup olive oil
1 cup dry white wine
1 teaspoon salt
1/4 teaspoon pepper
2 ounces (1 cup) twist-shaped pasta such as rotini

Soak the beans in water overnight; drain. Remove skin and excess fat from the ham shank. In a large kettle, combine the beans, ham shank, garlic, 1/2 of the chopped tomatoes, 1/2 teaspoon pepper, sage, thyme and 6 cups water. Bring to a boil. Cover and simmer gently two hours or until beans are tender. Remove shank from kettle. Dice meat and return to kettle. While beans are cooking, combine olive oil, the remaining chopped tomatoes, wine, salt and 1/4 teaspoon pepper in medium saucepan. Simmer, uncovered, 20 minutes. Pour into the bean mixture and bring to a boil. Add macaroni and continue to cook 9 to 12 minutes or until pasta is tender.

HERBED GARLIC BREAD

1 loaf frozen bread dough,
   thawed according to package directions
1/4 cup melted butter
1/4 teaspoon garlic powder

1 tablespoon finely chopped
   fresh or dried parsley flakes
1 teaspoon dried chives
1 tablespoon beaten egg

Slice thawed dough into 16 pieces forming each into a ball. Melt the butter in a small saucepan. Remove from the heat and stir in the egg, parsley, chives and garlic powder. Dip each ball of dough into the butter mixture, coating completely. Arrange in a single layer in a buttered 9"x 5" loaf pan. Pour over any remaining butter mixture. Let rise in warm place until dough just reaches top of pan, approximately 2½ hours. Preheat oven to 350 degrees and bake until top is golden brown, approximately 25 minutes.

EASY CHOCOLATE ICE CREAM ROLL

Oven temperature: 375 degrees

3 eggs, separated
1/2 cup sugar
1/2 cup flour
1/3 cup cocoa powder
1/4 cup sugar
1/2 teaspoon baking soda
1/4 teaspoon salt
1/3 cup water
1 teaspoon vanilla
1 tablespoon sugar
1 quart peppermint stick, vanilla, or chocolate ice cream

Line a 15½"x 10½"x1" jelly roll pan with aluminum foil. Generously grease the foil.

Beat egg yolks three minutes and gradually add the 1/2 cup sugar. Continue to beat two more minutes.

Combine the flour, cocoa, 1/4 cup sugar, baking soda and salt. Add alternately with the water on low speed just until batter is smooth. Add vanilla and set aside.

Beat egg whites until foamy, then add 1 tablespoon sugar and beat until stiff peaks form. Carefully fold into the chocolate mixture. Spread the batter evenly into prepared pan. Bake at 375 degrees for 14 to 16 minutes or until it springs back when touched lightly.

Invert cake onto a slightly dampened towel. Carefully remove the foil. Immediately roll the cake and towel together from narrow end. Let stand 1 minute. Unroll, remove the towel, then re-roll the cake. Cool completely on wire rack. Unroll cake and spread with softened ice cream, then re-roll. Cover with foil and freeze immediately. Serve with ice cream.

SALAMI &
CHEESE SOUP MEAL

MENU
- ♥ *Salami and Cheese Soup*
- ♥ *Green Bean Salad*
- ♥ *Madeline Cake*
  (recipe page 166)

SALAMI & CHEESE SOUP

This hearty soup calls for a lighter dessert and this Madeline Cake is light as air. There's no leavening except the air you beat into it.

1 cup hard salami cut into small cubes
2 cups peeled, diced potatoes
1/2 cup diced celery
1 large onion, chopped
1 tablespoon butter
3 cups chicken broth
1 cup half-and-half
3 eggs
Salt and pepper to taste
1 cup shredded Gruyere or Swiss cheese
1/2 cup finely chopped flat leaf parsley
1 red bell pepper, seeded and diced (optional)

Pour the broth into a large saucepan along with the potatoes and celery. Bring to a boil and simmer for approximately 15 minutes.

Sauté the onion in the butter in a frying pan. Add to the broth mixture, and put all into a blender or food processer and process slightly. This can also be done with a potato masher. Return half of the mixture to the soup pan and add the half-and-half and eggs to the remaining half in the food processor or blender. Process until smooth, then add to the broth and vegetables. Cook over low heat until heated and thickened, but don't bring to a boil. Add the cheese and salami.

Serve garnished with parsley and pass bowls of salami pieces, red peppers, cheese and parsley.

GREEN BEAN SALAD

1/3 cup extra virgin olive oil
1¼ teaspoons oregano leaves, crushed
1/2 teaspoon garlic powder
1½ teaspoons salt, divided
2 tablespoons red wine vinegar

1/2 cup red wine vinegar
4 cups water
1 pound fresh green beans, trimmed and washed
 OR 1 (9 ounce) package frozen whole green beans
1/2 cup sliced small onion rings

In a small bowl combine the oil, oregano, garlic powder and 1 teaspoon of the salt; set aside for 10 minutes for flavors to blend. Mix in 2 tablespoons red wine vinegar.

In a large skillet, combine 1/2 cup red wine vinegar, water and remaining 1/2 teaspoon salt; bring to a boil. Add green beans and onions; reduce heat and simmer, covered, until beans are crisp-tender, about 8 minutes. Drain and place in a bowl. Pour seasoned vinegar mixture over beans and onions; toss well to coat. Cover and refrigerate at least two hours or overnight.

BREAKFAST
SOUP MEAL

MENU
- ♥ *Breakfast Soup*
- ♥ *Breakfast Fruit Salad*
- ♥ *Waffles or toast*

BREAKFAST SOUP

Soup for breakfast? I think your family will enjoy this nice surprise some day when you want to do something special for them in the morning.

1/2 pound bacon
1 pound bulk breakfast sausage, crumbled
2 cups whole milk
2 tablespoons flour
1 teaspoon salt
1 tablespoon butter (don't substitute margarine)
1 tablespoon bacon grease
1 cup shredded Swiss cheese
1 cup chicken broth
2 cups herb flavored croutons
Frozen waffles, butter and syrup or buttered toast

Fry the sausage and drain and set aside. Fry the bacon and drain, reserving 2 tablespoons of the bacon drippings.

Pour the bacon drippings into a saucepan. Add the butter and melt over medium heat. Add the flour and stir until thickened, about two minutes. Add the milk and chicken broth and cook and stir until it just comes to a boil. Add the sausage, crumbled bacon, cheese and butter and heat through. Add the croutons just before serving. Serve in bowls with waffles hot from the toaster and butter and syrup, or slices of buttered toast.

BREAKFAST FRUIT SALAD

1-pound can peach pie filling
2 medium bananas, cut into slices
1-pound can pineapple chunks, drained
10-ounce can mandarin oranges, drained
1/2 cup maraschino cherries, drained and chopped

Mix all ingredients together and chill for one hour.

SALMON CHOWDER SOUP MEAL

MENU

- ♥ *Salmon Chowder*
- ♥ *Dill Bread*
- ♥ *Easy Coconut Macaroons*
  (recipe page 162)

I'm not a big fan of fish or seafood but this rich Salmon Chowder is absolutely delicious and reminds me of the "Salmon Soup" my mom used to make. It goes great with the Dill Bread.

SALMON CHOWDER

7¾-ounce can salmon
1/2 cup chopped onion
1/3 cup chopped celery
1/4 cup chopped green pepper
3 tablespoons butter
1 cup diced potatoes
1 cup diced carrots
2 cups chicken broth
1½ teaspoons salt
3/4 teaspoon pepper
1/2 teaspoon dill seed
1/2 cup diced zucchini or green beans
13-ounce can evaporated milk
8¾-ounce can cream style corn

Remove skin and bones from salmon, if you prefer.

Sauté the onion, celery and green pepper in butter until translucent. Add potatoes, carrots, chicken broth and seasonings. Cover and simmer 30 minutes. Add the zucchini, salmon, corn and milk. Heat through but do not boil. (It's best to break up the salmon into smaller chunks before adding it to the mixture.)

SALMON CHOWDER
SOUP MEAL
grocery list
- ☐ Canned salmon
- ☐ Onion
- ☐ Celery
- ☐ Green pepper
- ☐ Butter
- ☐ Potatoes
- ☐ Carrots
- ☐ Chicken broth
- ☐ Zucchini or green beans
- ☐ Dill seed
- ☐ Cream corn
- ☐ Evaporated milk
- ☐ Flour
- ☐ Sugar
- ☐ Instant dry onion
- ☐ Soda
- ☐ Small curd cottage cheese
- ☐ Yeast

DILL BREAD

Oven temperature: 350 degrees

2¼ cups flour
2 tablespoons sugar
1 teaspoon salt
1 tablespoon instant minced onion
2 teaspoons dill seed
1/4 teaspoon soda

1 egg
1 tablespoon soft butter
1/4 cup hot tap water
1 cup small curd cottage cheese
at room temperature
1 package dry yeast or 1 tablespoon yeast

Mix 1/4 cup flour, sugar, salt, onion, dill seed, soda and yeast. Add soft butter and hot water. Beat 2 minutes at high speed. Stir in additional flour by hand to make stiff batter. Cover and let rise 75 minutes. Punch down.

Line casserole dish with foil and grease the foil. Place batter in dish. Let rise 50 minutes. Bake 30 to 40 minutes at 350 degrees. (It's done when you tap the loaf on the top and it sounds hollow.)

HEARTY MICHIGAN CHOWDER SOUP MEAL

MENU

- ♥ *Hearty Michigan Chowder*
- ♥ *Pumpkin Cream Muffins*
- ♥ *Blueberry Pie*

This Hearty Michigan Chowder with the Pumpkin Cream Muffins and Blueberry Pie speak of the heart of the Michigan countryside where I grew up. This is definitely a comfort food meal.

HEARTY MICHIGAN CHOWDER

2 cups boiling water
2 cups chopped potatoes
1/2 cup carrot slices
1/2 cup chopped onion
1½ teaspoons salt
1/4 teaspoon pepper
1/4 cup butter
1/4 cup flour
2 cups whole milk
3 cups shredded sharp Cheddar cheese
17-ounce can cream corn
1 pound roasted sausage, sliced (optional)

Combine water, vegetables, sausage if you choose, and seasonings. Cover, simmer ten minutes. Do not drain.

Make a white sauce with the butter, flour and milk. Add the cheese and stir until melted. Add corn and undrained vegetables. Heat but do not boil. (I think this is equally as good without meat.)

PUMPKIN CREAM MUFFINS

Oven temperature: 350 degrees

1 egg
2 eggs
1 cup sugar
1/3 cup sugar
1¼ cups flour
2 teaspoons cinnamon
1/4 cup oil

1/4 teaspoon ground cloves
1/8 teaspoon grated nutmeg
1 cup canned pumpkin
1 teaspoon baking soda
1/2 teaspoon salt
8 ounces cream cheese, softened

Combine 2 of the eggs, 1 cup sugar, cinnamon, oil and pumpkin. In separate bowl mix the flour, baking soda, and salt. Add to pumpkin mixture. *(Continued on next page)*

In another bowl, blend together cream cheese, 1 egg and 1/3 cup sugar.

Fill muffin liners to half- full with the pumpkin mixture. Top each muffin with 1 tablespoon of the cream cheese mixture.

CRUMB TOPPING:

1/4 cup sugar	½ teaspoon cinnamon
3 tablespoons flour	2 tablespoons softened butter

Mix the topping ingredients until crumbly and top each muffin with approximately 1 tablespoon of the mixture. Bake 15 to 18 minutes.

BLUEBERRY PIE

Oven temperature: 375 degrees

PIE CRUST:
(This is easily made in a food processor if you have one)

2 cups flour	1/3 cup cold vegetable shortening
1 teaspoon salt	1/4 teaspoon salt
1/3 cup cold butter	Ice water

Mix dry ingredients until crumbly. Add 7 tablespoons ice water and stir just until pastry holds together. Divide into two pieces and wrap in plastic wrap and refrigerate for at least one hour.

FILLING:

1 cup sugar	1 tablespoon butter or margarine
1/3 cup flour	5 cups blueberries
1/2 teaspoon lemon zest	or 1 (20-ounce) package frozen
Dash salt	blueberries, thawed
2 teaspoons lemon juice	

In a large mixing bowl combine the sugar, flour, lemon zest and salt. Add berries to sugar mixture and toss berries to coat. Put filling into pie crust.

Remove dough from refrigerator and roll out one ball into a circle to fit a 9" pie plate. Add filling. Drizzle berries with the lemon juice and dot with the butter.

Roll out second ball of dough and cut a couple of slits to allow steam to escape. Adjust the top crust over the blueberries. Seal the edges. Cover lightly with foil and bake for 20 minutes. Remove foil and bake for 20 to 25 minutes or until crust is golden.

TUNA AU GRATIN POTATOES SOUP MEAL

MENU

- ♥ *Tuna Au Gratin Potatoes Soup*
- ♥ *Lemon Pudding Cake*
- ♥ *Beer Cheese Triangles*
  (recipe page 105)

This Tuna and Au Gratin Potatoes soup is a real hit with kids who like tuna sandwiches. The cheesy flavor from the potatoes mixed with the hearty tuna make a filling soup, and the Lemon Pudding Cake and Beer Cheese Triangles are perfect accompaniments.

TUNA AU GRATIN
POTATOES SOUP
MEAL
grocery list

☐ Chicken broth (optional)
☐ Au Gratin Potato mix
☐ Tuna
☐ Broccoli
☐ Whole milk
☐ Evaporated milk
☐ Cheddar cheese
☐ Sugar
☐ Flour
☐ Butter
☐ Lemons
☐ Eggs
☐ Bisquick or other baking mix
☐ Beer

TUNA AU GRATIN POTATOES SOUP

4 cups water or chicken broth
1 package Au Gratin potatoes mix
6.5-ounce can tuna packed in oil, drained
10-ounce package frozen chopped broccoli, partially thawed
1 cup whole milk
1 cup shredded cheddar cheese
1/2 cup evaporated milk
1/2 teaspoon salt

In a saucepan, combine the water and contents of the potato package, including the seasoning mix. Cover and simmer 20 to 25 minutes. Stir occasionally. Add tuna, broccoli, whole milk, evaporated milk, cheese and salt. Heat until hot through.

LEMON PUDDING CAKE

Oven temperature: 350 degrees

3/4 cup sugar
1/4 cup flour
1/4 teaspoon salt
3 tablespoons butter, melted
1½ teaspoons lemon zest

1/4 cup fresh lemon juice
3 beaten egg yolks
1½ cups whole milk
3 egg whites

In a large mixing bowl combine the sugar, flour and salt. Stir in the melted butter, lemon zest and lemon juice. In a small bowl, mix the egg yolks and milk. Add to flour mixture.

In a mixer bowl beat egg whites to stiff peaks. Gently fold egg whites into lemon batter. Turn into an ungreased 8"x8"x2" baking pan. Place in a larger pan on oven rack. Pour hot water into the large pan to a depth of one inch. Bake 35 to 40 minutes or until top is golden and springs back when touched. Serve warm or chilled in individual dessert dishes.

VEGETABLE MACARONI SOUP MEAL

MENU

- ♥ *Vegetable Macaroni Soup*
- ♥ *Apple Dumplings*
- ♥ *Onion Bread*

VEGETABLE
MACARONI
SOUP MEAL
grocery list

- ☐ Carrots
- ☐ Onion
- ☐ Brown sugar
- ☐ Marjoram
- ☐ Thyme
- ☐ Garlic
- ☐ Stewed tomatoes
- ☐ Celery
- ☐ Lentils
- ☐ Dried basil
- ☐ Chicken broth
- ☐ Italian seasoning
- ☐ Oregano
- ☐ Pepper
- ☐ Bay leaves
- ☐ Tomato paste
- ☐ Green beans
- ☐ White wine vinegar
- ☐ Parmesan cheese
- ☐ Apples
- ☐ Sugar
- ☐ Cinnamon
- ☐ Nutmeg
- ☐ Red food coloring
- ☐ Butter
- ☐ Flour
- ☐ Baking powder
- ☐ Vegetable shortening
- ☐ Milk
- ☐ Yeast
- ☐ Chives
- ☐ Poppy seed
- ☐ Dehydrated onion

VEGETABLE MACARONI SOUP

This recipe for Vegetable Pasta Soup came out of an old cookbook dated 1940 that gave all kinds of recipes for using garden produce. It's delicious and the Apple Dumplings and Onion Bread go great with it.

6 cups water, divided
2 cups sliced carrots
1½ cups chopped onion
1 tablespoon brown sugar
1/2 teaspoon marjoram
1/2 teaspoon thyme
3 cloves garlic, crushed
28-ounce can chopped stewed tomatoes
1 cup celery, diced
1 cup dried lentils
1 teaspoon each: Italian seasoning, oregano and dried basil
6 cups chicken broth
1 teaspoon pepper
2 bay leaves
6-ounce can tomato paste
5 cups green beans, whole or cut
1/4 cup white wine vinegar
1 cup pasta of your choice (macaroni, twists, or broken spaghetti are all good)
Parmesan cheese

Combine all ingredients except 2 cups of the water, vinegar and pasta in a large stock pot and bring to a boil. Cover and reduce heat to simmer for 45 minutes. Add reserved water, vinegar and pasta and cook for approximately 10 minutes. Remove bay leaves and serve topped with Parmesan cheese.

(recipes continued on next page)

APPLE DUMPLINGS

Oven temperature: 375 degrees

6 medium-size apples
1½ cups sugar
1½ cups water
1/2 teaspoon cinnamon
1/4 teaspoon grated nutmeg
8 drops red food coloring
3 tablespoons butter
2 cups flour
1 teaspoon baking powder
1 teaspoon salt
2/3 cup shortening
1/2 cup milk

Peel and core apples.

Prepare syrup by mixing sugar, water, cinnamon, nutmeg and food coloring in a saucepan and bring to a boil. Remove from heat and add butter. Set aside.

To make pastry, cut shortening into dry ingredients. Add milk and stir until flour is moistened. Roll out dough on a lightly floured surface into a rectangle approximately 18"x12". Cut into six 6-inch squares and place an apple on each square. Sprinkle generously with additional sugar, nutmeg and cinnamon; dot with butter. Moisten edges of pastry, bring edges to center and pinch together. Place in an ungreased pan and pour syrup over dumplings. Bake for 35 minutes.

ONION BREAD

Oven temperature: 425 degrees

1 package dry yeast or 1 tablespoon bulk dry yeast
1¼ cups warm water
1 cup milk, scalded
2 tablespoons butter
2 tablespoons sugar
1 tablespoon salt
1/2 cup fresh snipped chives
1/4 cup poppy seeds
1 tablespoon minced, dehydrated onion
6 cups flour

Dissolve yeast in 1/4 cup of the warm water and allow to stand 10 minutes. In a small bowl, combine the milk, remaining water, butter, sugar and salt, mixing well. Add to the yeast mixture. Add the chives, poppy seeds, onion and one cup flour. Add flour a half-cup at a time until the dough is stiff and begins to pull away from the sides, approximately 2½ cups total.

Turn dough onto a floured board and knead in 2 more cups of flour. Shape dough into a ball. Place in an oiled mixing bowl, turning the ball to oil all surfaces. Allow to rise until doubled. Punch down and form into two loaves. Place loaves in oiled 9"x5" loaf pans and bake at 425 degrees for 15 minutes. Reduce heat to 350 degrees and bake for an additional 25 to 30 minutes.

CORN & SHRIMP CHOWDER MEAL

MENU

- ♥ *Corn and Shrimp Chowder*
- ♥ *Boston Bean Bread*
- ♥ *Rhubarb Cake*

CORN & SHRIMP CHOWDER

This easy-to-make chowder is from a restaurant we went to in Florida one winter when we were vacationing and the owner was kind enough to give me the recipe.

8 ounces sliced bacon
3 tablespoons green pepper, chopped
1/2 cup celery
3 tablespoons carrot, diced
2 medium onions, chopped
1 small bay leaf
2 tablespoons flour
4 cups water
3 cups potatoes, diced
7-ounce can creamed corn
1 cup fresh or frozen corn kernels
2 cups evaporated milk
Salt and pepper
1 pound shrimp, cooked and cleaned

In a large soup pot, cook bacon until crisp, stirring frequently.
Remove meat and pour off all but 3 tablespoons of the fat. Add the next five ingredients and sauté for five minutes. Blend in flour. Add water and potatoes. Cover and simmer 15 minutes. Add the remaining ingredients and heat through. Remove the bay leaf. Sprinkle with salt and pepper.

RHUBARB CAKE

Oven temperature: 350 degrees

6 cubs rhubarb, coarsely chopped (If frozen, let thaw and drain well.)
1 cup sugar
1 tablespoon butter
1 white cake mix plus ingredients to prepare according to directions
Whipped topping

Place the rhubarb in a 9"x13" baking pan. Sprinkle with the sugar and stir slightly. Top with dots of the butter.

Prepare the white cake mix according to box directions and pour over the rhubarb. Bake until cake tests done, about 30 minutes. (Cake is done when toothpick inserted in the middle is dry when removed.) Remove pan to a rack to cool. When ready to serve, cut squares and turn each piece fruit-side-up and top with whipped topping.

CORN & SHRIMP CHOWDER MEAL
grocery list

- ☐ Bacon
- ☐ Green pepper
- ☐ Celery
- ☐ Carrot
- ☐ Onion
- ☐ Bay leaf
- ☐ Flour
- ☐ Potatoes
- ☐ Cream corn
- ☐ Fresh or frozen corn
- ☐ Evaporated milk
- ☐ Shrimp
- ☐ Flour
- ☐ Yeast
- ☐ Brown sugar
- ☐ Bean and bacon soup
- ☐ Large Shredded Wheat biscuits
- ☐ Molasses
- ☐ Butter
- ☐ Eggs
- ☐ White cake mix
- ☐ Rhubarb
- ☐ Sugar
- ☐ Whipped topping
- ☐ Oil

BOSTON BEAN BREAD

Oven temperature: 375 degrees

5 to 6 cups flour
2 packages dry yeast or 5 teaspoons bulk yeast
2 teaspoons salt
1½ cups water
11-ounce can bean and bacon soup,
  undiluted
2 large shredded wheat biscuits, crumbled
1/4 cup molasses
2 tablespoons brown sugar
2 tablespoons butter
3 eggs

In a mixing bowl, combine 1 cup of the flour, the yeast, brown sugar, and salt.

In a saucepan, mix the water and soup with the crumbled shredded wheat biscuits, molasses and butter. Heat just till warm (butter does not need to be melted).

Add the liquid mixture to the flour mixture. Add the eggs and blend at low speed with a mixer until moistened, then beat three minutes at low speed. Gradually add in as much of the remaining flour as you need to make a stiff batter. (It should be hard to beat with a spoon.) Continue to beat the mixture on low with an electric mixer for 5 minutes.

Cover the dough and let it rise till double, approximately 1 hour. Stir the dough after it has risen and divide into two 9"x5"loaf pans. Cover and let rise again until the dough comes up to the top of the pan.

For a shiny crust, beat together 1 egg and 1 tablespoon water. Brush on top of the loaves. Bake approximately 40 minutes. Turn loaves out onto a cooling rack to cool.

CREAMY CHICKEN SOUP MEAL

MENU

- ♥ *Creamy Chicken Soup*
- ♥ *Broccoli Salad*
- ♥ *Granny's Buns (recipe page 156)*

CREAMY CHICKEN
SOUP MEAL
grocery list

- ☐ Butter
- ☐ Flour
- ☐ Milk
- ☐ Light cream
- ☐ Chicken broth
- ☐ Cooked chicken
- ☐ Broccoli
- ☐ Bacon
- ☐ Red onion
- ☐ Shredded Cheddar cheese
- ☐ Vinegar
- ☐ Mayonnaise
- ☐ Sugar

CREAMY CHICKEN SOUP

This soup may be the first one you want to teach your children or grandchildren to make since it is so simple and tasty.

6 tablespoons butter
6 tablespoons flour
1/2 cup whole milk
1/2 cup light cream
3 cups chicken broth
1 cup cooked white meat chicken, chopped
Dash of salt and pepper

In a saucepan, melt the butter. Blend in flour. Stir in milk, cream and chicken broth. Cook over low heat, stirring occasionally, until mixture thickens and comes to a boil. Reduce heat and stir in chicken and pepper. Return soup to boiling and serve immediately. Add more chicken broth if soup seems too thick.

BROCCOLI SALAD

1 large bunch broccoli
1 pound bacon
1/2 red onion, diced
1 cup shredded Cheddar cheese
1 cup mayonnaise
1/2 cup sugar
2 tablespoons vinegar

Separate broccoli into florets and trim stems. Fry bacon until crisp. Drain and crumble the slices. Mix the broccoli florets, crumbled bacon and red onion together. Mix the mayonnaise, sugar and vinegar together until well blended and add to the salad. Add shredded cheese and mix.

SUPER SPICY TEXAS CHOWDER SOUP MEAL

MENU

- ♥ *Super Spicy Texas Chowder*
- ♥ *Fiesta Biscuits (recipe page 158)*

These recipes came from Texas where my daughter and son-in-law lived right after they were married. I love the spicy flavors of the southwest!

SUPER SPICY TEXAS CHOWDER

14-ounce can chopped tomatoes
8 ounces frozen corn
10-ounce can chicken broth
15-ounce can black beans, drained and rinsed
4-ounce can green chilies
1 pound ground beef
3/4 cup hot salsa
2 tablespoons lime juice
1 teaspoon ground cumin
1/2 teaspoon garlic powder
1/4 teaspoon pepper
1 medium onion, chopped
1 cup sour cream
1 cup shredded Monterey jack cheese
1 tablespoon hot pepper sauce, according to taste
1 teaspoon salt
1/2 teaspoon pepper

Brown the ground beef in a saucepan with the chopped onion. Add all other ingredients except sour cream, cheese and hot sauce, and heat to boiling. Turn down and simmer for 15 minutes. Turn off the heat and add sour cream and cheese. Stir to melt. Add hot pepper sauce to taste.

PEACHY PIZZA

1 roll refrigerated sugar cookie dough
15-ounce can sliced peaches, drained
   (reserve 1/3 cup juice)
8-ounce package cream cheese, softened

1/3 cup sugar
1 teaspoon almond extract
Fresh raspberries, blueberries or strawberries

Roll the cookie dough into a 12-inch circle and put on a 12" pizza pan. Bake as directed and cool. In a bowl stir together the cream cheese, sugar, almond extract and reserved peach syrup until creamy and smooth. Spread filling over crust. Arrange peach slices and berries on top of cream cheese filling. Cover and chill 2 to 24 hours. Serve with whipped dessert topping if desired.

BOUNTY
BEAN SOUP MEAL

MENU

- ♥ *Bounty Bean Soup*
- ♥ *Bell Pepper Bread*
- ♥ *Black Forest Cake*

There are hundreds of recipes for Bean Soup as well as Black Forest Cake, but both of these are slightly different, and delicious.

**BOUNTY
BEAN SOUP**

15-ounce package mixed beans for soup
  (about 3 cups assorted beans)
1/4 cup millet
2 tablespoons salt
1 large green pepper, chopped
28-ounce can tomatoes
1 fresh lemon, squeezed
1 clove garlic, minced
1 smoked ham hock or a meaty ham bone
1 large onion, chopped
2 teaspoons chili powder
Salt and pepper to taste

Wash beans and place in pan or kettle. Cover with water and add salt. Soak overnight, drain, and add 2 quarts water. Add millet, ham hock or ham bone. Bring to a boil and simmer slowly two hours. Add onion, tomatoes, green pepper, chili powder, lemon, salt and pepper. Simmer another 30 minutes. Add salt and pepper to taste.

BLACK FOREST CAKE

Oven temperature: 350 degrees

2 (15-ounce) cans tart cherries
2 tablespoons cornstarch
4 tablespoons water
1 tablespoon almond flavoring
1 package chocolate cake mix

3 squares semi-sweet chocolate
2 cups whipping cream
1/4 cup powdered sugar
1 teaspoon vanilla
14 maraschino cherries

In a medium bowl, combine the tart cherries and 1/3 of the reserved cherry juice. Set aside. Mix the cornstarch and water in a small bowl.

Drain off 1/3 cup of cherry juice from the tart cherries and mix with the almond flavoring. Set aside, and pour the cherries and the rest of the juice into a saucepan. Heat the cherries to boiling and thicken with as much of the cornstarch and water mixture as needed to make a sauce that can still be poured. Set aside to cool. *(Continued on next page.)*

**BOUNTY BEAN SOUP
MEAL**
<u>grocery list</u>

- ☐ Mixed beans for soup
- ☐ Millet
- ☐ Green pepper
- ☐ Canned tomatoes
- ☐ Lemon
- ☐ Garlic
- ☐ Green pepper
- ☐ Ham hock
- ☐ Tomatoes
- ☐ Chili powder
- ☐ Red bell pepper
- ☐ Yellow bell pepper
- ☐ Sun dried tomatoes
- ☐ Yeast
- ☐ Sugar
- ☐ Flour
- ☐ Rosemary
- ☐ Low-fat plain yogurt
- ☐ Tomato paste
- ☐ Olive oil
- ☐ Tart cherries
- ☐ Almond flavoring
- ☐ Chocolate cake mix
- ☐ Cornstarch
- ☐ Semi-sweet chocolate
- ☐ Whipping cream
- ☐ Powdered sugar
- ☐ Vanilla
- ☐ Maraschino cherries
- ☐ Oil
- ☐ Eggs

114

(Black Forest Cake, cont.)

Prepare the cake mix according to package directions. Meanwhile, with a vegetable peeler, shave a few curls from the chocolate for garnish. Grate the remaining chocolate.

Remove cake from oven and cool 15miutes, then prick the top of the cake all over with a fork. Pour the flavored cherry juice all over the top of the cake. Pour the tart cherries and sauce over the top of the cake.

Whip the cream, vanilla and powdered sugar together till stiff and spread on top of the cherries. Top with the maraschino cherries, grated chocolate and chocolate curls for garnish.

BELL PEPPER BREAD

Oven temperature: 425 degrees

1 small red bell pepper
1 small green bell pepper
1 small yellow bell pepper
2 ounces dry pack sun-dried tomatoes
1/4 cup boiling water
1 tablespoon dry yeast
1 teaspoon superfine sugar
2/3 cup tepid water
4 cups flour
2 teaspoons dried rosemary
2 tablespoons tomato paste
2/3 cup low-fat natural unsweetened yogurt
1 tablespoon kosher salt
1 tablespoon olive oil

Preheat oven to 425 degrees.

Cut the peppers in half and take out the seeds. Arrange on a broiler rack. Roast until the skin is charred. Let cool for 10 minutes. Peel off the skin and chop the flesh. Slice the tomatoes into strips. Place in a bowl and pour on boiling water. Leave to soak.

Mix the yeast and sugar in a small dish, pour over the tepid water, and leave for 10 to 15 minutes until frothy. Mix the flour and 1 teaspoon dried rosemary. Make a well in the center and pour in the yeast mixture. Add the tomato paste, tomatoes with soaking liquid, bell peppers, yogurt and half the salt. Mix to form a soft dough.

Turn out onto a lightly floured surface and knead for three to four minutes. Place in a lightly floured bowl. Cover and leave in a warm room for 40 minutes, until dough doubles in size. Knead dough again and place in a lightly greased round spring form pan. Using a wooden spoon, form dimples in the surface. Cover and leave for 30 minutes. Brush with oil and sprinkle with rosemary and salt. Bake for 35 to 40 minutes.

CHEESE BURGER POTATO SOUP MEAL

MENU

- ♥ *Cheese Burger Potato Soup*
- ♥ *Zesty Butter Sticks*
- ♥ *Banana Squares*

POTATO BURGER
with CHEESE
SOUP MEAL
grocery list

- ☐ Ground chuck
- ☐ Bacon
- ☐ Carrots
- ☐ Celery
- ☐ Onion
- ☐ Italian seasoning
- ☐ Potatoes
- ☐ Beef broth
- ☐ Cheez Whiz or Velveeta
- ☐ Flour
- ☐ Milk
- ☐ Sour cream
- ☐ French bread
- ☐ Butter
- ☐ Chervil
- ☐ Basil
- ☐ Garlic powder
- ☐ Onion powder
- ☐ Sugar
- ☐ Baking soda
- ☐ Bananas
- ☐ Mayonnaise
- ☐ Vanilla
- ☐ Nuts
- ☐ Powdered sugar

CHEESE BURGER POTATO SOUP

This is a hearty soup good after football games, especially when served with these unusual bread sticks.

1 pound ground chuck
6 slices bacon, fried till almost done
1/4 cup bacon grease
1 medium chopped onion
1 cup chopped carrots
3/4 cup diced celery
1 tablespoon Italian seasoning
4 cups beef broth
4 cups cubed potatoes (peeled or unpeeled)
1/4 cup flour
2 cups Cheez Whiz or Velveeta cheese cubes
1½ cups milk
1 teaspoon salt
1/2 teaspoon pepper
1/2 cup sour cream

Brown the ground chuck in a Dutch oven. Remove the meat from the pan and set aside.

Fry the bacon in the Dutch oven till almost done. Remove and put with the ground chuck. Drain off all but 1/4 cup of the fat.

Sauté the onion, carrots and celery in the meat drippings for approximately ten minutes on medium heat. Add the broth, potatoes and meat. Turn heat to high and bring to a boil, then reduce heat and simmer, covered, for approximately ten to twelve minutes, or until vegetables are tender.

In a small saucepan, melt the butter and add the flour. Cook approximately one minute then add to the soup, stirring constantly. Raise heat and bring to a boil. Cook and stir for approximately two minutes. Reduce heat to low and add the cheese, milk, salt, pepper and Italian seasoning. Remove from the heat and add the sour cream.

(recipes continued on next page)

ZESTY BUTTER STICKS

Oven temperatures: 425 degrees

1/2 loaf French or Italian bread (approximately 10"x 4")
1/2 cup butter, softened
1/2 teaspoon <u>each</u> chervil and basil leaves
1/4 teaspoon <u>each</u> garlic powder and onion powder

Cut bread in half lengthwise, then cut each half lengthwise into three wedges. In a small bowl combine the remaining ingredients. Blend well. Spread herbed butter on cut surfaces of bread wedges. Bake on ungreased baking sheet for 7 to 9 minutes or until golden brown.

BANANA SQUARES

Oven temperature: 350 degrees

2 cups flour
1 cup sugar
1 teaspoon baking soda
1/2 teaspoon salt
1 cup mashed ripe bananas

2/3 cup mayonnaise
1/4 cup water
1 teaspoon vanilla
1/2 cup chopped nuts
powdered sugar

Grease an8" x 8" pan.

In a large bowl, stir together first four ingredients, then add the next four ingredients. With a mixer on medium speed, beat at least two minutes or until smooth. Stir in nuts. Pour into the prepared pan. Bake for 35 to 40 minutes or until a toothpick inserted in the enter comes out clean. Cool and dust with powdered sugar.

CREAMY BROCCOLI SOUP MEAL

MENU

- ♥ *Creamy Broccoli Soup*
- ♥ *Pear Salad*
- ♥ *Almond Sandies*

CREAMY BROCCOLI CHEESE SOUP

This Broccoli Soup calls for an unusual ingredient. I learned this from a cook we employed years ago who made many delicious soups.

1 bunch fresh broccoli OR a 1-pound bag of frozen broccoli
1 quart chicken stock or water
2 heaping tablespoons chicken bouillon granules OR
    1 Maggi brand chicken bouillon cube
1 cup dry coffee creamer (preferably Creamora)
3 heaping tablespoons flour
3 tablespoons butter
2 cups chicken stock or broth

Cut fresh broccoli into small pieces. Cook broccoli in the chicken stock or water until tender. Add bouillon and dry creamer to the cooking liquid, stir until dissolved.

Melt the butter in a small pan and add the flour. Cook about 2 minutes and stir in the 2 cups chicken stock or broth. Add the broth mixture to the broccoli mixture and heat and stir until thickened. Add salt and pepper to taste.

PEAR SALAD

28-ounce can pears, drained, reserving 1 cup juice
3-ounce package lime gelatin
8-ounce package cream cheese
2 tablespoons cream
1 cup whipping cream, whipped with 1 teaspoon vanilla

Mash pears. Heat reserved pear juice to boiling and pour over the dry lime gelatin. Mash the cream cheese with 2 tablespoons cream until smooth. Mix in gelatin and cool. Add the mashed pears and fold in the 1 cup whipped cream. Refrigerate until set.

ALMOND SANDIES

Oven temperature: 300 degrees

3/4 cup sugar
1/2 cup margarine
1/2 cup butter
1/4 teaspoon baking powder

1/4 teaspoon baking soda
1/4 teaspoon salt
1¾ cups flour
2 teaspoons almond extract

Cream butter, margarine and sugar. Add dry ingredients. Add almond extract. Drop by teaspoonful on ungreased cookie sheet. Bake for 17 to 22 minutes.

UPPER PENINSULA BEAN SOUP MEAL

MENU
- ♥ *Upper Peninsula Bean soup*
- ♥ *Vienna Bread (recipe page 157)*
- ♥ *Mint Dessert*

Vienna Bread (recipe page 157)

UPPER PENINSULA BEAN SOUP MEAL
grocery list
- ☐ White beans
- ☐ Ham hocks
- ☐ Dry onionsoup mix
- ☐ Carrot
- ☐ Celery
- ☐ Ketchup
- ☐ Thyme
- ☐ Oreos
- ☐ Big marshmallows
- ☐ Evaporated milk
- ☐ Mint flavoring
- ☐ Green food coloring
- ☐ Whipping cream or whipped topping

UPPER PENINSULA BEAN SOUP

My husband and his life-long friend, Lee, spend time in the Upper Peninsula of Michigan most every year and this recipe for bean soup is one he brought back from one of those visits.

2 cups dried white beans
8 cups boiling water
3 ham hocks
1 package dry onion soup mix
1/2 cup ketchup
1 teaspoon salt
1/2 teaspoon thyme
3 stalks celery, chopped
1 large carrot, diced
1/2 teaspoon pepper

Wash and sort the beans. Place in a large kettle and cover with the boiling water. Simmer until beans are plump. Add the ham hocks, dry onion soup mix, ketchup, salt, thyme, pepper, celery and carrot. Simmer until vegetables and beans are tender.

(You will need to add more water or chicken broth as you simmer this mixture, sometimes as much as 5 cups, but add it 1 cup at a time as it is needed. Chicken broth adds more flavor.)

MINT DESSERT

26 Oreo cookies or house brand chocolate sandwich cookies
32 large marshmallows
1 cup evaporated milk
1/8 teaspoon salt
1/2 teaspoon peppermint flavoring
Few drops of green food coloring
1 pint whipping cream or 8 ounces thawed whipped topping

Melt marshmallows and milk in double boiler or in the microwave and add the salt, flavoring and coloring. Let cool.

Whip cream until very stiff or use the whipped topping and fold into cooled marshmallow mixture. Crush cookies and put half of the crumbs on bottom of a 9"x13"pan.Add the filling and top with the rest of the crumbs. Let stand overnight. Cut into squares.

SUE'S DILLED POTATO SOUP MEAL

MENU

- ♥ *Sue's Potato-Dill Soup*
- ♥ *Bread Machine Whole Wheat Rolls (recipe p.157)*
- ♥ *Peach Torte*

Bread Machine Whole Wheat Rolls (recipe p.157)

SUE'S POTATO SOUP MEAL
grocery list
- ☐ Potatoes
- ☐ Onions
- ☐ Chicken bouillon
- ☐ Onion powder
- ☐ Thyme
- ☐ Sage
- ☐ Dill weed
- ☐ Coconut milk
- ☐ Peaches
- ☐ Cake mix
- ☐ Butter
- ☐ Nuts
- ☐ Coconut
- ☐ Brown sugar

DILLED POTATO SOUP

5 cups diced potatoes (red potatoes are best)
1 cup chopped onion
1 Maggi brand chicken bouillon cube OR
   other chicken bouillon to measure 1 tablespoon
2 cups water
1 teaspoon salt
1 teaspoon onion powder
1 teaspoon dried thyme
1 teaspoon rubbed sage
1 teaspoon dill weed
15-ounce can coconut milk

Put the potatoes, onions, onion powder and salt iin a saucepan. Add 2 cups water. Boil gently until vegetables are tender. Remove from heat.

With a slotted mixing spoon, take out two big spoonfuls of the mixture and put it into a blender or small bowl. Pulse in a blender until slightly smooth, or mash with a potato masher, then return them to the saucepan.

Add the coconut milk, thyme, sage and dill, and reheat. Check for seasoning and add more salt if needed. This soup is best if made a day ahead to let the seasonings flavor the whole batch of soup.

PEACH TORTE

Oven temperatures: 350 degrees

1 quart sliced peaches, undrained
1 butter brickle cake mix *
3/4 cup butter melted

1 cup chopped nuts
1 cup coconut
1 cup brown sugar

Put peaches and juice in a 9"x13" baking pan. Spread the dry cake mix over the peaches. Drizzle the melted butter over the cake mix. Sprinkle on the nuts, coconut and brown sugar. Bake 50 to 60 minutes.

You may substitute yellow or white cake mix and add 1 teaspoon butter extract flavoring to the peach juice.

FAMILY FAVORITES

The recipes in this portion of the book are all family favorites and are mostly very simple recipes. These were the things my children loved to eat when they were growing up and recipes they still use.

Beef

KIM'S ITALIAN BAKE

Oven temperature: 350 degrees

1 tube refrigerated biscuits
1 medium size jar spaghetti sauce
1 pound ground chuck
1 onion, chopped
1½ cups frozen mixed vegetables
2 cups shredded Mozzarella cheese
1 tablespoon Italian seasoning
1 teaspoon salt
1/4 teaspoon pepper

Brown the ground chuck with the onion and seasonings.

Put the frozen mixed vegetables into a strainer and run hot water over them for one or two minutes. Drain well and add to the ground chuck mixture. Add the spaghetti sauce to the meat and vegetable mixture and stir well. Pour into a 7"x11" casserole dish or baking pan. Top with the refrigerated biscuits. Bake uncovered 30 minutes. (The biscuits can be cut in half and placed cut-side-down on top of the mixture for a different look.)

KIM'S ITALIAN BAKE
grocery list
☐ Refrigerated biscuits
☐ Spaghetti sauce
☐ Ground chuck
☐ Onion
☐ Frozen mixed vegetables
☐ Mozzarella cheese
☐ Italian seasoning

SWISS STEAK

Oven temperature: 350 degrees

3 pounds sirloin steak (Ask butcher to run the meat
   through the cuber machine.)
1/4 cup extra virgin olive oil
2 tablespoons butter
1 small can pureed tomatoes
8 ounces shredded Cheddar cheese
1/2 cup flour
1 teaspoon salt
1/4 teaspoon pepper

SWISS STEAK
grocery list

- ☐ Sirloin steak
- ☐ Olive oil
- ☐ Butter
- ☐ Pureed tomatoes
- ☐ Cheddar cheese
- ☐ flour

Cut tenderized steak into six pieces. In a skillet, melt the butter on medium heat. Mix the flour and seasoning in a pie plate. Dredge the sirloin steak pieces in the flour and brown in the butter. When completely browned, pour the tomatoes over the meat, cover and bake in the oven for approximately two hours. Remove cover and top with the shredded Cheddar. Put the cover back on for 5 minutes to melt the cheese.

JIM'S
BEEF STROGANOFF

2 pounds ground chuck
1 medium onion, chopped
2 cans cream of mushroom soup
1 pint sour cream
1 can mushrooms, drained (optional)
1 teaspoon garlic powder
1 teaspoon salt
1/4 teaspoon pepper
1-pound package egg noodles, cooked and drained

JIM'S BEEF STROGANOFF
grocery list

- ☐ Ground chuck
- ☐ Onion
- ☐ Cream soup
- ☐ Mushrooms (optional)
- ☐ Sour cream
- ☐ Garlic powder
- ☐ Egg noodles
- ☐ Onion

Brown the ground chuck, onion and seasonings in a skillet. Drain
off any grease. Add the cream soup, mushrooms and sour cream. Heat through, but DO NOT BOIL. Boiling the mixture will cause it to curdle. Serve over the cooked noodles.

YOU GUYS
SPAGHETTI

2 large cans Franco American prepared spaghetti
1/2 medium onion, chopped
1½ pounds ground chuck
1 teaspoon salt
1/4 teaspoon pepper
1 teaspoon garlic powder
1 small green pepper, chopped

YOU GUYS SPAGHETTI
grocery list

- ☐ Franco American spaghetti
- ☐ Onion
- ☐ Ground chuck
- ☐ Garlic powder
- ☐ Green pepper

Brown ground chuck with seasonings in a Dutch oven or large
skillet. Add the green pepper and continue to cook two or three
minutes. Add the spaghetti and cover. Simmer on low about 30 minutes and serve.

MISS BEA'S GOULASH

When my children were all little (7 children under 6 years old, including twins) a sweet lady from our church named Bea would come unexpectedly every now and then with a meal for our dinner and a big box of groceries and other treats for the children. We always appreciated her thoughtfulness. The following recipe is one she often brought and we all loved it.

MISS BEA'S
GOULASH
<u>grocery list</u>
- ☐ Ground chuck
- ☐ Onion
- ☐ Macaroni
- ☐ Stewed tomatoes
- ☐ Tomato soup
- ☐ Garlic powder

2 pounds ground chuck
1 medium onion, chopped
2 cups dry macaroni, cooked and drained
1 28-ounce can stewed tomatoes (chop the tomatoes
    before adding to the mixture)
1 can condensed tomato soup
1 teaspoon salt
1/4 teaspoon pepper
1 teaspoon garlic powder

Brown the ground chuck with the onion and seasoning. Add the cooked macaroni, stewed tomatoes and tomato soup. Cover and simmer about 15 minutes on top of the stove. Stir several times.

NO PEEK BEEF TIPS

NO PEEK BEEF TIPS
<u>grocery list</u>
- ☐ Stew beef
- ☐ Mushrooms
- ☐ Ginger ale
- ☐ Cream of mushroom soup
- ☐ Dry onion soup mix

2 pounds stew beef chunks
1 can mushrooms with juice
1 cup ginger ale
1 can cream of mushroom soup
1 package dry onion soup mix

Layer ingredients in a slow cooker and cook on low 6 to 8 hours.

MY KIDS' BEANS & HAMBURGER

MY KIDS' BEANS &
HAMBURGER
<u>grocery list</u>
- ☐ Onion
- ☐ Pork and beans
- ☐ Ground beef or ground chuck
- ☐ Garlic powder
- ☐ Lawry's seasoned salt
- ☐ Worcestershire sauce

1½ pounds ground beef or ground chuck
1 medium sized onion, chopped
1 tablespoon Worcestershire sauce
2 cans (28 ounces each) pork and beans
1 teaspoon garlic powder
1 teaspoon Lawry's seasoned salt
1/4 teaspoon pepper
1 teaspoon salt

Brown the meat with the chopped onion and seasonings. Add the beans and Worcestershire sauce and simmer on low heat for approximately 30 minutes .Great with garlic bread.

PLUMB GOOD CHILI

This chili was introduced to our family by my son Jim' Bolt's friend, Chris Plumb. He came with Jim to our cottage one year to hunt deer and, thoughtful person that he was, he brought an enamel canner full of chili made from his own recipe. Sometime later Chris and his wife had a child with severe health problems and they had no health insurance at the time. I told him if he would give me his chili recipe, I would give him and his wife all the proceeds from our food business sale of his chili for one week to help with his son's medical bills. He agreed, and it became one of the most popular items we sold over the years. That's Chris on the left, and Jim at right.

PLUMB GOOD CHILI
grocery list
- ☐ Stewed tomatoes
- ☐ Ground chuck
- ☐ Onions
- ☐ Lawry's seasoned salt
- ☐ Garlic powder
- ☐ Chili powder
- ☐ Cumin
- ☐ Picanti sauce
- ☐ Mild pepper rings
- ☐ Kidney beans

(This is a large quantity recipe so you will have some to freeze.)

10 pounds ground chuck
5 large onions, chopped
1 tablespoon salt
1 tablespoon Lawry's seasoned salt
1 teaspoon pepper
1 tablespoon garlic powder

2/3 cup chili powder
4 teaspoons cumin
4 cups picanti sauce
4 cups mild pepper rings, chopped slightly
2 No.10 cans kidney beans
2 No.10 cans stewed tomatoes

Brown the ground chuck with the seasonings and chopped onion. Drain slightly.

Chop the tomatoes until they are in small pieces and add to the ground chuck. Add the rest of the ingredients and simmer for approximately 30 to 45 minutes.

125

Chicken & Turkey

BEST BAKED CHICKEN

Oven temperature: 325 degrees

1 cut-up frying chicken or your favorite
pieces of chicken (about 3 pounds), skin on

MIX TOGETHER:
3 tablespoons Lawry's seasoned salt
2 teaspoons garlic powder
2 teaspoons onion powder
1 teaspoon salt
1/2 teaspoon pepper

Lay the chicken on a baking sheet that has been lined with foil. Sprinkle the seasoning mixture over the chicken. Put 1/2 cup water on the bottom of the pan around the chicken pieces and bake approximately 45 minutes or until tender.

CHRIS' CHICKEN OR TURKEY ENCHILADAS

Oven temperature: 350 degrees

3 tablespoons onion, diced fine
8 ounces cream cheese, softened
4 cups cooked turkey or chicken
Flour tortillas
1 can cream of chicken soup
1 cup whole milk
8 ounces sour cream
1 cup Monterey jack cheese, shredded

Mix the onion and cream cheese until soft. Add cooked meat.
Divide among 6 flour tortillas and roll up. Place in a baking dish.

Mix the soup, sour cream and milk and pour over the enchiladas. Top with the Monterey jack cheese. Cover and bake approximately 45 minutes.

SHERRI'S SIMPLE BARBECUE CHICKEN

Oven temperature: 350 degrees

6 to 8 chicken pieces with skin, selection of your choice
1 bottle Hunt's barbecue sauce
Garlic powder
Pepper

SHERRI'S SIMPLE BARBECUE CHICKEN
grocery list
☐ Chicken pieces
☐ Hunts barbecue sauce
☐ Garlic powder

Put the chicken in baking dish and pour barbecue sauce over all. Sprinkle with garlic powder and pepper. Cover with foil and bake two and a half to three hours. Uncover and cook another hour and a half.

KAREN'S CHICKEN & NOODLES OR DUMPLINGS

KAREN'S CHICKEN & NOODLES or DUMPLINGS
grocery list
☐ Chicken
☐ Carrots
☐ Celery
☐ Onion
☐ Chicken stock
☐ Noodles, refrigerated biscuits, or baking mix

CHICKEN AND BROTH:
1 frying chicken
1 large carrot
1 large stalk celery
1 onion cut into chunks
1 teaspoon salt
1/4 teaspoon pepper
1 quart chicken stock

Purchase a frying chicken, remove the giblets and discard. Freeze the rest of the chicken. When you're ready to make this dish, put the frozen chicken into a crock pot with all the other ingredients. Cook on low for 8 hours.

Remove the chicken from the slow cooker. Take the chicken off the bones and discard the skin and bones. Remove vegetables from the broth and discard. Place the chicken back into the crock pot and turn on high.

IF USING NOODLES:
As soon as the stock begins to boil, add a 1-pound package of egg noodles and cook until tender.
IF USING DUMPLINGS:
Follow the recipe on the baking mix box for dumplings. Turn crock pot on high until broth boils. Drop dumplings into the boiling broth to cook. (You may also use a tube of raw refrigerated biscuits and drop into the stock.)

CATHY'S CALIFORNIA CHICKEN

Oven temperature: 350 degrees

1/3 cup flour
1/2 teaspoon salt
1/4 teaspoon ground nutmeg
1 pound boneless, skinless chicken breasts
3 tablespoons butter
1 large can pineapple, drained, reserve the juice
1 cup pineapple juice (use the juice from the can of pineapple and add water if necessary to make 1 cup)
1/3 cup soy sauce
1 tablespoon granulated sugar

Mix the flour and seasonings and dredge the chicken.

Melt the butter in a skillet. Brown the chicken in the butter. Place chicken in a baking dish. Combine the remaining ingredients and pour over the chicken and bake uncovered for 45 minutes. Add reserved pineapple. Continue cooking 15 more minutes.

CATHY'S CALIFORNIA CHICKEN
grocery list
- [ ] Flour
- [ ] Nutmeg
- [ ] Boneless skinless chicken
- [ ] Butter
- [ ] Pineapple
- [ ] Soy sauce
- [ ] Granulated sugar

HOLLY'S CHICKEN PIE

Oven temperature: 375 degrees

3 cups cooked chicken
1 (10 ounce) package peas and carrots
1 can cubed potatoes
1 tablespoon dried, minced onion
8 ounces Velveeta cheese, cubed, or jar of Cheez Whiz
1 can cream of chicken soup
1 teaspoon salt
1/4 teaspoon pepper
8-ounce can refrigerated crescent rolls OR
1 can refrigerated pizza dough

Mix the chicken, peas and carrots, potatoes and onion with the salt and pepper.

Mix the cream of chicken soup with the cubed cheese and stir into the other ingredients. Put mixture into a 9"x13" baking pan.

Unroll the refrigerated dough and stretch to cover the mixture. Bake approximately 25 minutes until golden brown.

HOLLY'S CHICKEN PIE
grocery list
- [ ] Cooked chicken
- [ ] Frozen peas and carrots
- [ ] Potatoes
- [ ] Velveeta or Cheez Whiz
- [ ] Cream of chicken soup
- [ ] Dried minced onion
- [ ] Refrigerated crescent rolls or pizza dough

HOLLY'S BUFFALO CHICKEN WRAPS

Oven ready spicy chicken tenders (25-ounce package)
4 flour tortillas
1 cup Buffalo wing sauce, flavor of your choice
4 tablespoons melted butter
2 cups Cheddar cheese
Shredded lettuce
Chopped tomato

HOLLY'S BUFFALO CHICKEN WRAPS
grocery list
- [ ] Oven ready spicy chicken tenders
- [ ] Buffalo wing sauce
- [ ] Butter
- [ ] Cheddar cheese
- [ ] Lettuce
- [ ] Tomato

Prepare the Buffalo tenders according to the package directions. Mix approximately 1/4 cup wing sauce with 1 tablespoon melted butter and spread on the flour tortilla. Top with the prepared chicken tenders, Cheddar cheese, lettuce and tomato. Form into a roll and cut in half.

CHICKEN CLUB WRAP

4 slices smoked chicken
8 slices cooked bacon
1/2 cup shredded lettuce
2 tablespoons diced tomato
1 tablespoon mayonnaise
1 tablespoon shredded Parmesan cheese
4 tomato basil flour tortillas

CHICKEN CLUB WRAP
grocery list
- [ ] Oven ready spicy chicken tenders
- [ ] Sliced smoked chicken
- [ ] Cooked bacon
- [ ] Shredded lettuce
- [ ] Tomato
- [ ] Mayonnaise
- [ ] Parmesan
- [ ] Tomato basil flour tortillas

Spread mayonnaise on tortillas. Top with the lettuce, tomato, shredded Parmesan, chicken and bacon. Form into a roll. Cut each roll in half.

CHICKEN & RICE

Oven temperature: 350 degrees

1 cup raw rice (not instant)
1 package dry onion soup mix
1 chicken, cut up (or your favorite pieces)
1 can cream of chicken soup
1 can cream of mushroom or celery soup
1 can water
1 teaspoon salt
1/4 teaspoon pepper

CHICKEN & RICE
grocery list
- [ ] Rice
- [ ] Onion soup mix
- [ ] Chicken
- [ ] Cream of chicken soup
- [ ] Cream of mushroom or celery soup

Place rice in a 9"x13" baking pan. Lay the chicken pieces on top of the rice and sprinkle with the dry onion soup mix. Mix the soup and water together and add the salt and pepper. Pour over the chicken and cover with foil. Bake covered approximately an hour and a half.

Pork, Ham & Sausage

JANET'S SIMPLE PORK CHOPS

Oven: 350 degrees

6 rib pork chops
2 tablespoons olive oil
1 can cream of mushroom soup

Brown the chops in a skillet in the olive oil. Pour the mushroom soup over all the chops and cover, put into the oven to bake for approximately one hour. This makes a good sauce and fall-apart chops.

JANET'S SIMPLE
PORK CHOPS
☐ Rib pork chops
☐ Olive oil
☐ Cream of mushroom soup

HOLLY'S ROASTIE CASSEROLE

Oven temperature: 350 degrees

6 to 8 medium potatoes boiled, drained and cut into cubes (or substitute canned potato cubes)
1 package smoked sausage links, 12 ounces
15-ounce can corn, drained
1 can cream of chicken soup
1 teaspoon salt
1/4 teaspoon pepper

HOLLY'S ROASTIE
CASSEROLE
grocery list
☐ Potatoes, raw or canned
☐ Smoked sausage links
☐ Corn
☐ Cream soup

Prepare the potatoes and put into a casserole or baking dish. Cut sausage links into fourths and add to potatoes. Add the other ingredients and cover. Bake approximately 45 minutes. Remove cover. Bake 15 more minutes.

SCALLOPED PINEAPPLE & HAM

Oven temperature: 350 degrees

1/2 cup butter, melted
3 eggs, beaten slightly
1/4 cup granulated sugar
1/2 cup brown sugar
4 cups dry bread cubes
2 tablespoons flour
2 large cans crushed pineapple with the juice
1 teaspoon vanilla
3 cups cubed, smoked ham

SCALLOPED
PINEAPPLE & HAM
grocery list
☐ Butter
☐ Eggs
☐ Granulated sugar
☐ Brown sugar
☐ Flour
☐ Bread cubes
☐ Crushed pineapple
☐ Vanilla
☐ Smoked ham

Cream butter, sugar and eggs. Add bread cubes and mix in remaining ingredients. Pour into a 9"x13" baking dish and cover loosely with foil. Bake for 45 minutes and remove foil. Continue to bake until set in the middle.

JANET'S SAUSAGE SKILLET

2 pounds Oscar Meyer miniature cheese cocktail franks
2 cans sauerkraut (48 ounces each), rinsed and drained
4 cans (12 ounces each) Reed German potato salad

Mix all ingredients and simmer in a Dutch oven or electric skillet for approximately two hours.

JANET'S SAUSAGE SKILLET
grocery list
- ☐ Oscar Meyer miniature cheese cocktail franks
- ☐ Sauerkraut
- ☐ Reed German potato salad

ELEGANT PORK CHOPS

Oven temperature: 350 degrees

4 large pork chops
1 teaspoon salt
1/2 teaspoon pepper
3 tablespoons olive oil

SAUCE:
2 tablespoons olive oil
1 onion, chopped
1 clove garlic, minced
1 tablespoon butter
1 tablespoon flour
2/3 cup milk
3 tablespoons Gorgonzola cheese
1 tablespoon white wine

ELEGANT PORK CHOPS
grocery list
- ☐ Pork chops
- ☐ Olive oil
- ☐ Onion
- ☐ Garlic
- ☐ Butter
- ☐ Flour
- ☐ Gorgonzola cheese
- ☐ White wine

Season the chops with the salt and pepper. Brown in the olive oil in a skillet. Put into a baking dish and place in oven for about 20 minutes while you make the sauce.

In a saucepan, melt the butter. Add the chopped onion and sauté till soft. Add the garlic and butter and cook until butter is melted. Add the flour, milk and white wine and simmer a minute until it thickens. Serve over chops.

Sandwiches

SLOPPY CHICKEN

The first time I had this delicious sandwich was at a dinner after my brother, Reverend Phillip Hatfield, was installed in the last church he served. It has special memories for us.

28-ounce can boneless chicken or 2 pounds cooked
   chicken, bones removed
1 can cream of chicken soup
1 can cream of mushroom soup
1 stack Ritz or Town House crackers (or substitute store brand)
15-ounce can chicken broth

Mix all ingredients in slow cooker. Cover and cook on low five to six hours and serve on buns.

SLOPPY CHICKEN
grocery list
☐ Boneless chicken
☐ Cream of chicken soup
☐ Cream of mushroom soup
☐ Crackers
☐ Chicken broth

BBQ CHICKEN FOR BUNS

Oven temperature: 375 degrees

6 cups cooked chicken (about 3 pounds fresh, boneless breast)
2 cups diced celery
1 cup chopped onion
1 cup chopped green pepper
4 tablespoons butter
2 cups ketchup
2 cups water
2 tablespoons brown sugar
4 tablespoons vinegar
2 teaspoons dry mustard or 1 tablespoon prepared mustard
Salt and pepper

BBQ CHICKEN for BUNS
grocery list
☐ Chicken, fresh or cooked
☐ Celery
☐ Onion
☐ Green pepper
☐ Butter
☐ Ketchup
☐ Brown sugar
☐ Vinegar
☐ Dry or prepared mustard

If using fresh chicken, put pieces on a baking sheet and drizzle with a little olive oil. Sprinkle with salt and pepper. Cover loosely with foil and bake in the oven at 375 degrees for approximately 35 to 45 minutes. Dice and measure about 6 cups. Mix all ingredients and cook in slow cooker for approximately 6 hours on low.

HAM BBQ

1 pound smoked ham, diced
1 cup cola
1 cup ketchup

Cook in slow cooker eight hours on low.
Serve on hamburger buns.

HAM BBQ
grocery list
☐ Smoked ham
☐ Cola
☐ Ketchup

FOREMAN GRILLED HAM & CHEESE

Sourdough bread or other thick-sliced flavorful bread
Sliced ham
Sliced Cheddar or Swiss cheese
Basil pesto (found in the ethnic food
section of your grocery store)
Sliced tomato

If you have a Foreman grill, plug in to preheat.

Spread the outside of two slices of bread with a little olive oil. Place a slice of ham, a slice of cheese and a slice of tomato on one piece of bread. Spread the other slice of bread with a little of the basil pesto. Place this slice on top of the other slice of bread and put into Foreman grill, nonstick pan or grill. When using a pan or grill, cover the sandwiches for about two or three minutes to make sure the cheese melts.

SPICY HOT DOGS

2 pounds hot dogs
1 cup chili sauce
1 cup barbecue sauce
8-ounce can jellied cranberry sauce

Place the hot dogs in a slow cooker. Mix all other ingredients and pour over the hot dogs. Cook on low for about two hours.

ENGLISH MUFFIN PIZZAS

Oven temperature: 350 degrees

2 pounds ground chuck
1½ teaspoons salt
1/4 teaspoon pepper
1½ teaspoons oregano
1/2 teaspoon garlic salt
14-ounce jar Ragu Pizza Quick sauce
8 ounces Velveeta cheese
4 ounces Mozzarella cheese
English muffins

Brown ground chuck with the salt and pepper (add a little chopped onion to the ground chuck if you like) and drain off grease. Add oregano, pizza sauce and Velveeta cheese; simmer, stirring often until cheese is melted. Spoon mixture on muffin halves. Bake five minutes. Sprinkle with Mozzarella cheese and put back into the oven until cheese melts.

STUFFED FRENCH BREAD

Oven temperature: 375 degrees

1- pound loaf French bread
1½ pounds ground chuck
1/2 teaspoon onion powder
2 dashes celery salt
1/2 teaspoon salt
1/4 teaspoon pepper
1/4 teaspoon dry mustard OR
    1/2 teaspoon prepared mustard
1 beaten egg
2½ cups shredded Cheddar cheese*, divided

STUFFED
FRENCH BREAD
grocery list
☐ French bread
☐ Ground chuck
☐ Onion powder
☐ Celery salt
☐ Dry or prepared mustard
☐ Egg
☐ Cheddar cheese

Cut bread in half lengthwise and hollow out both sides leaving the crust as a shell. Keep crumbs to use for filling.

Brown the ground chuck with salt and pepper (add chopped onions to the ground chuck if you like), onion powder and celery salt, and drain well. In a large bowl mix the meat with the reserved bread crumbs, dry mustard, egg and 1½ cups cheese. Mix well.

Fill hollowed out halves of bread with mixture, put back together and wrap in foil. Bake for about 30 to 45 minutes. Before serving, top with remaining cheese and heat until warmed through and cheese melts.
*Use part Velveeta if you like.

TUNA MELT

Flavorful bread like rye or sourdough
1 large can light tuna
3 ribs of celery, chopped fine
Onion, if you like
1/2 cup mayonnaise or salad dressing depending on your taste
1 teaspoon mustard
Slices of Cheddar cheese
Butter

TUNA MELT
grocery list
☐ Flavorful bread
☐ Tuna
☐ Celery
☐ Onion
☐ Mayonnaise
☐ Cheddar cheese
☐ Mustard
☐ Butter

If you have a Foreman grill, plug in to preheat.

Butter one side of each slice of bread. Mix tuna, celery, onion and mayonnaise. Spread tuna mixture on unbuttered side of one slice of bread and top with one slice of cheese. Add second slice of bread, butter side out. Grill in a Foreman grill if you have one, or in a nonstick pan or on a griddle. Cook both sides until lightly browned.

BEEF FRENCH DIP

3 pounds rump roast
1 package dry au jus gravy mix
1 teaspoon garlic powder
1 teaspoon onion powder
1/2 teaspoon salt
1/4 teaspoon pepper
1/2 cup dry white wine (or water)
2 cups beef broth

BEEF
FRENCH DIP
grocery list

☐ Beef rump roast
☐ Au jus gravy mix
☐ Garlic powder
☐ Onion powder
☐ White wine (optional)
☐ Beef broth

Place all ingredients in slow cooker. Cover and cook on low for at least 6 to 7 hours. Take the meat out and remove any chunks of fat. Shred the beef. Return to the slow cooker and add more beef broth if it seems dry. Serve on buns of your choice.

MEATBALL SUBS

Oven temperature: 350 degrees

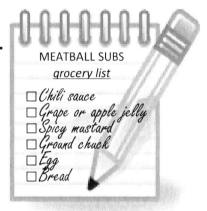

MEATBALL SUBS
grocery list

☐ Chili sauce
☐ Grape or apple jelly
☐ Spicy mustard
☐ Ground chuck
☐ Egg
☐ Bread

SAUCE:
3/4 cup chili sauce
1/2 cup grape or apple jelly
2 teaspoons brown spicy mustard

Mix and put into the slow cooker. Cover and cook on high while preparing meatballs.

MEATBALLS:
2 pounds ground chuck
1 egg
2 slices bread torn into crumbs (Roll pieces in your hands until they fall apart.)
1½ teaspoons salt
1/4 teaspoon pepper

Mix all ingredients. Use a small ice cream scoop to form meatballs. Put on a cookie sheet lined with foil and bake approximately 20 minutes. Drain meatballs and put them into the sauce in the slow cooker. Let simmer for approximately three hours on low.

Put meatballs into sub buns. Top with sauce and sprinkle with Mozzarella cheese.

TANGY BBQ SANDWICHES

3 pounds boneless chuck roast
1 cup barbecue sauce
1/2 cup apricot preserves
1/2 cup chopped green peppers
1 small onion, chopped
1 tablespoon Dijon or salad mustard
1 tablespoon brown sugar

TANGY BBQ SANDWICHES
grocery list
☐ Boneless chuck roast
☐ Barbecue sauce
☐ Apricot preserves
☐ Green peppers
☐ Dijon or salad mustard
☐ Onion
☐ Brown sugar
☐ Hamburger buns

Cut meat into several pieces and place in slow cooker. Mix all ingredients and pour over roast. Cook on low 6 to 8 hours. Remove meat and slice thin or cook until it shreds. Return to slow cooker and mix with sauce. Serve on hamburger buns.

HEARTY ITALIAN SANDWICHES

1½ pounds ground chuck
1½ pounds bulk Italian sausage
2 large onions, chopped
2 green peppers, chopped
2 large sweet red peppers, chopped
1 teaspoon salt
1/4 teaspoon pepper
Shredded Monterey jack cheese
8 to 10 sub buns, depending on size

HEARTY ITALIAN SANDWICHES
grocery list
☐ Ground chuck
☐ Italian sausage
☐ Onions
☐ Green peppers
☐ Sweet red peppers
☐ Monterey jack cheese
☐ Sub buns

Brown ground chuck and sausage together. Drain fat. Place one-third of the onions and peppers in a slow cooker. Top with half of the meat. Repeat layers, sprinkling with salt and pepper.

Cover and cook on low six to eight hours or until vegetables are tender. To serve, spoon beef mixture onto rolls and top with cheese.

DILLY ROAST BEEF SANDWICH

One serving:
3 tablespoons cream cheese, softened
1/8 teaspoon each of dill weed, garlic powder and pepper
2 slices bread
2 slices cooked roast beef
Tomato slices
Alfalfa sprouts

DILLLY ROAST BEEF
SANDWICH
grocery list
☐ Cream cheese
☐ Dill weed
☐ Garlic powder
☐ Bread
☐ Roast beef
☐ Tomatoes
☐ Alfalfa sprouts

Mix cream cheese, dill, garlic powder and pepper. Spread on one slice of bread. Top with beef, tomato and sprouts and the remaining slice of bread.

SAVORY TURKEY BURGERS

1 pound ground turkey
1/4 cup egg substitute
1/4 cup dry bread crumbs
1 teaspoon steak sauce
1 teaspoon spicy brown mustard
1/4 teaspoon thyme
Dash of pepper

SAVORY TURKEY
BURGERS
grocery list
☐ Ground turkey
☐ Egg substitute

SAVORY TURKEY
BURGERS
grocery list
☐ Ground turkey breast
☐ Egg substitute
☐ Bread crumbs
☐ Steak sauce
☐ Brown mustard
☐ Thyme
☐ Buns

Make into burgers and grill or pan-fry. Serve on buns with tomato and lettuce.

QUICK SUPPER DOGS

Oven temperature: 350 degrees

1 tube refrigerated pizza dough
8 to 10 hot dogs
Hormel bacon bits
Chopped onion
Shredded cheddar cheese
Mustard and ketchup

QUICK SUPPER DOGS
grocery list
☐ Refrigerated pizza dough
☐ Hot dogs
☐ Bacon bits
☐ Cheddar cheese
☐ Mustard
☐ Onion
☐ Ketchup

Slice each hot dog lengthwise, but not all the way through. Stuff each one with the toppings of your choice -- cheese pieces, onions, fried bacon, etc. Put the hot dog back together and wrap each one in a piece of pizza dough, just enough to cover. Bake on baking sheet for approximately 10 minutes.

GRILLED CHICKEN FAJITAS

3 whole boneless chicken breasts (6 halves)
1/2 cup olive or vegetable oil
1/2 cup red wine vinegar
1/3 cup lime juice
1/4 cup finely chopped onion
2 cloves garlic, minced
1 teaspoon sugar
1 teaspoon dried oregano
1/2 teaspoon salt
1/4 teaspoon pepper
1/4 teaspoon ground cumin
Warm flour tortillas
Salsa

GRILLED CHICKEN FAJITAS
grocery list
☐ Skinless, boneless chicken breasts
☐ Olive or vegetable oil
☐ Red wine vinegar
☐ Lime juice
☐ Onion
☐ Garlic
☐ Sugar
☐ Oregano
☐ Cumin
☐ Flour tortillas
☐ Salsa

Mix all ingredients except chicken breast halves, tortillas and salsa. Put into a zippered plastic bag along with the chicken. Turn to coat evenly and put into the refrigerator overnight to marinate.

Grill the chicken breasts and slice into strips. Serve on warm tortillas with salsa and other toppings of your choice, such as shredded cheese, shredded lettuce and diced tomato.

CHICKEN FAJITA WRAP

This is a recipe my oldest daughter, Holly, came up with when we owned a food service. It was a favorite of most of our customers.

CHICKEN FAJITA WRAP
grocery list
☐ Chicken fajita strips or fresh chicken
☐ Flavored tortillas
☐ Ranch dressing
☐ Colby jack cheese
☐ Tomato
☐ Lettuce
☐ Chunky salsa or picanti sauce

Purchase chicken fajita strips or make your own by grilling marinated chicken breasts (see recipe for Grilled Chicken Fajitas (above).

Purchase flavored tortillas (tomato basil or southwest wraps work well.) Spread each tortilla wrap with MexiRanch dressing (recipe below)

On each tortilla, place a layer of shredded lettuce. Top with diced tomatoes.
Add a layer of warm or cold chicken fajita strips. Top with shredded Colby-jack cheese.
Roll up and cut diagonally in half.

MEXIRANCH DRESSING:
Mix 1 cup ranch dressing and 2 tablespoons picanti sauce or chunky salsa.

BROILED OPEN-FACE BURGERS

My mother-in-law often made these sandwiches for her family of 9 children on Sunday nights after church.

Oven temperature: 400 degrees

1 pound ground chuck (DO NOT cook.)
1 teaspoon dry onion or 2 teaspoons finely minced onion
2 tablespoons mayonnaise
3 tablespoons ketchup
1/2 teaspoon salt
1/4 teaspoon pepper

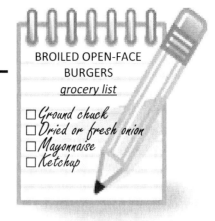

BROILED OPEN-FACE BURGERS
grocery list

☐ Ground chuck
☐ Dried or fresh onion
☐ Mayonnaise
☐ Ketchup

Mix the raw ground chuck with the other ingredients and spread thinly on buns. Bake approximately six minutes. Add shredded cheese to the mixture if you like, or top with cheese while sandwiches are still hot.

HAMBURGER CHEESE LOAF

Oven temperature: 350 degrees

1 pound ground chuck
1 teaspoon salt
1/4 teaspoon pepper
1 tablespoon Worcestershire sauce
1/4 cup ketchup or chili sauce
1/2 cup finely minced onion or 1 tablespoon dry onion
1/2 cup corn flake crumbs (buy prepared, or crush flakes at home)
1/2 cup evaporated milk
Swiss cheese slices
2 loaves French bread

HAMBURGER CHEESE LOAF
grocery list

☐ Ground chuck
☐ Worcestershire sauce
☐ Ketchup or chili sauce
☐ Onion, dry or fresh
☐ Corn flake crumbs
☐ Evaporated milk
☐ Swiss cheese
☐ French bread

Preheat oven to 350 degrees. Mix all ingredients except cheese and French bread. Cut French bread loaves in half lengthwise and spread with meat mixture. Bake 25 minutes, then top with Swiss cheese, return to oven and bake approximately two minutes until cheese is melted.

PIZZA BURGERS

1 pound ground chuck
1/2 cup finely minced onion or 1 tablespoon dry onion
1/4 teaspoon pepper
1 teaspoon salt
1 teaspoon oregano
1 teaspoon basil
1 cup tomato sauce
1 cup shredded mozzarella cheese
Buns

PIZZA BURGERS
grocery list

☐ Ground chuck
☐ Fresh or dry onion
☐ Oregano
☐ Basil
☐ Tomato sauce
☐ Mozzarella cheese
☐ Buns

Lightly brown the ground chuck and onion together. Drain and add all the other ingredients. Spread on buns and broil until cheese is bubbly.

TUNA PUFFS

12-ounce can of light tuna or albacore tuna, drained
2 tablespoons chopped green pepper
2 teaspoons minced onion or 1/2 teaspoon dry onion
2 teaspoons Worcestershire sauce
1 teaspoon mustard
1½ cups mayonnaise
Tomato slices
8 hamburger buns, split
1 cup American cheese, shredded

TUNA PUFFS
grocery list
- ☐ Tuna
- ☐ Green pepper
- ☐ Onion, fresh or dried
- ☐ Worcestershire sauce
- ☐ Mustard
- ☐ Mayonnaise
- ☐ Buns
- ☐ Fresh tomato
- ☐ American cheese

Mix tuna, green pepper, onion, Worcestershire sauce, mustard and 1/2 cup mayonnaise. Spread each half bun with tuna mixture. Top each with a tomato slice.

Mix remaining 1 cup mayonnaise and 1 cup shredded American cheese. Divide among sandwiches, placing about two tablespoons on top of tomato slices. Broil until lightly browned.

FRENCH-TOASTED SANDWICHES

8 slices flavorful, thick-sliced bread
1 jar Cheez Whiz or store brand jarred cheese
Sliced ham or turkey
1 egg, beaten
1/2 cup evaporated milk
1/2 cup water
1 teaspoon mustard
1/2 teaspoon salt
2 tablespoons butter
1/3 cup vegetable oil

FRENCH TOASTED SANDWICHES
grocery list
- ☐ Thick sliced bread
- ☐ Jarred cheese
- ☐ Ham or turkey
- ☐ Egg
- ☐ Evaporated milk
- ☐ Mustard
- ☐ Butter
- ☐ Vegetable oil

Mix egg, milk, water, mustard and salt in shallow bowl and set aside. Spread half of bread slices with cheese. Top with meat and second slice of bread. Heat oil and butter in a skillet over medium heat. Dip sandwiches in egg mixture. Brown on both sides in oil and butter, turning once. Add more oil and butter as needed.

SLOPPY JOE

3 pounds ground chuck
2 cans tomato soup
1 large onion, diced
2 tablespoons mustard
1/2 cup brown sugar
1 tablespoon Worcestershire sauce
2 teaspoons salt
1/2 teaspoon pepper
1/2 cup ketchup

SLOPPY JOE
grocery list
- ☐ Ground chuck
- ☐ Tomato soup
- ☐ Onions
- ☐ Mustard
- ☐ Brown sugar
- ☐ Worcestershire sauce
- ☐ Ketchup

Brown the ground chuck with the seasonings and the chopped onion. Drain the grease and add the mustard, ketchup, Worcestershire sauce, tomato soup and brown sugar. Simmer on low approximately 15 minutes.

Rice and Pasta

DUTCH RICE

2 cups rice
4 cups water
4 cups whole or 2% milk
Sugar
Cinnamon
Butter

DUTCH RICE
grocery list

☐ Rice
☐ Whole or 2% milk
☐ Butter
☐ Sugar
☐ Cinnamon

Put the rice and cold water in a large Dutch oven or other heavy pan and bring to a boil. Turn the heat to low and cook slowly until most of the liquid is gone. Add the milk and continue to cook on low until the rice has absorbed the milk and is soft.

To eat, spread a portion on a plate and top with butter, sugar and cinnamon.

CATHY'S GARDEN SPAGHETTI

10-ounce package frozen broccoli
10-ounce package frozen vegetable medley
1/4 cup onion, chopped
1 clove garlic, minced, or 1 teaspoon garlic powder
3 tablespoons butter
1/4 cup flour
1 chicken flavored bouillon cube
1/2 teaspoon dried thyme
2 cups fat-free milk
6 slices American cheese, cut into pieces
1/2 pound dry whole wheat spaghetti, cooked and drained

CATHY'S GARDEN SPAGHETTI
grocery list
☐ Broccoli
☐ Vegetable medley
☐ Onion
☐ Garlic or garlic powder
☐ Butter
☐ Flour
☐ Chicken flavored bouillon
☐ Dried thyme
☐ Fat-free milk
☐ American cheese
☐ Whole wheat spaghetti

Sauté the onion in the butter in a large saucepan until tender.
Add the minced garlic and cook for 1 minute. Stir in the flour, bouillon and thyme. Gradually add the milk. Over medium heat, cook and stir until the mixture thickens. Add the cheese and stir until melted.

Put the frozen vegetables in a colander and run hot water over them until they are thawed and softened. Add thawed and drained vegetables to the cheese sauce and heat through. Serve over the cooked spaghetti.

RICE OLE'

RICE OLE'
grocery list
- ☐ Ground chuck
- ☐ Onion
- ☐ Beef granules
- ☐ Lawry's seasoning salt
- ☐ Garlic powder
- ☐ Chili powder
- ☐ Rice
- ☐ Tomato sauce
- ☐ Salsa
- ☐ Sour cream

2½ pounds ground chuck
1¼ cups onion, chopped
1 tablespoon beef bouillon granules
1 teaspoon salt
1/4 teaspoon pepper
1 teaspoon Lawry's seasoned salt
1 teaspoon garlic powder
2 tablespoons chili powder
2 cups rice
2 (8-ounce) cans tomato sauce
3 cups water
Salsa

Brown the ground chuck, onion and seasonings in a Dutch oven
or large skillet. Add the rice, tomato sauce and water. Cook uncovered over very low heat, stirring often, approximately 15 minutes. Cover and let stand approximately 30 minutes until rice is soft and liquid is absorbed. Serve with salsa and sour cream.

FOUR CHEESE PASTA

FOUR CHEESE PASTA
grocery list
- ☐ Whole wheat pasta
- ☐ Crushed or pureed tomatoes
- ☐ Heavy cream
- ☐ Parmesan or Romano cheese
- ☐ Swiss or Fontina cheese
- ☐ Ricotta cheese
- ☐ Mozzarella cheese
- ☐ Fresh basil
- ☐ Basil pesto
- ☐ Butter

Oven temperature: 400 degrees

1 pound penne pasta, whole wheat or regular
2 cups crushed or pureed tomatoes
2 cups heavy cream
1/2 cup Parmesan or Romano cheese
1/2 cup Swiss or Fontina cheese
3 tablespoons Ricotta cheese
8 ounces shredded Mozzarella cheese
8 basil leaves
1 tablespoon basil pesto
1 tablespoon butter

Cook the pasta according to the package directions and drain well. Set aside.

In a large bowl, mix the pureed tomatoes, cream, 8 ounces of the shredded Mozzarella, and the Swiss and Ricotta cheese and mix well. Slice the basil leaves into thin shreds and add to the mixture. Add 1 teaspoon salt and 1/2 teaspoon pepper and mix well. Add the cooked pasta, stir, and pour into a baking dish. Top with the rest of the Mozzarella cheese. Bake for approximately 1/2 hour or until heated through and slightly browned on top.

.

ZITI WITH GORGONZOLA SAUCE

ZITI with
GORGONZOLA SAUCE
grocery list
☐ *Gorgonzola cheese*
☐ *Cream*
☐ *Chicken stock*
☐ *White wine*
☐ *Ziti pasta*
☐ *Butter*
☐ *Fresh parsley*

6 ounces gorgonzola cheese, crumbled
1½ cups heavy cream or half and half cream
1/2 cup chicken stock
1/3 cup dry white wine
2 tablespoons butter
1 teaspoon salt
1/4 teaspoon pepper
3/4 pound ziti pasta
2 tablespoons chopped fresh parsley
1/4 cup shredded Parmesan

In a bowl, mash the gorgonzola with a fork. Add the cream a little at a time, whisking, until the mixture is fairly smooth. (Some lumps will remain.)

In a saucepan, bring the chicken broth and the wine to a boil and cook until reduced to 1/2 cup, about five minutes. Add the butter. Reduce the heat to moderately low and add the cheese mixture. Cook and stir until the sauce thickens slightly, about three minutes. Add the salt and pepper.

Cook the ziti pasta according to package directions. Drain and toss with the sauce, Parmesan and parsley.

BAKED ZITI

BAKED ZITI
grocery list
☐ *Ziti pasta*
☐ *Olive oil*
☐ *Onion*
☐ *Crushed tomatoes*
☐ *Bay leaf*
☐ *Mozzarella cheese*
☐ *Garlic*
☐ *Ricotta cheese*
☐ *Parmesan cheese*
☐ *Basil pesto*

Oven temperature: 350 degrees

1 pound ziti pasta
2 tablespoons olive oil
1 tablespoon olive oil
1 onion, chopped
2 cloves garlic, minced
2 cups canned crushed tomatoes in thick puree
1/2 teaspoon salt
1 bay leaf
1/2 teaspoon pepper
1 cup ricotta cheese
1½ cups shredded mozzarella cheese
1/3 cup grated Parmesan cheese
1/2 cup basil pesto

Cook the pasta according to directions on the package. Drain and rinse with cold water and set aside.

In a saucepan, heat the 2 tablespoons oil and add the chopped onion and cook approximately five minutes. Add the garlic and cook, stirring, for 30 seconds. Add the tomatoes, salt and bay leaf. Bring to a simmer over medium heat and cook until very thick, about 10 minutes. Stir in the pepper and remove the bay leaf. Set aside.

In a bowl, combine the ricotta, 1 cup of the mozzarella, approximately 1/2 of the Parmesan, and the pesto. Put half of the cooked pasta into a prepared 8"x8" baking pan and top with about 1/3 of the tomato sauce. Spread the ricotta mixture on the sauce in an even layer. Cover with the remaining pasta and then the remaining sauce. Top with the remaining 1/2 cup mozzarella and drizzle with the remaining tablespoon of olive oil. Bake until bubbling, about 30 to 45 minutes.

PENNE PASTA WITH SHRIMP & VEGETABLES

3/4 cup olive oil
2 tablespoons olive oil
1½ tablespoons lemon juice
1½ teaspoons paprika
1¾ teaspoons ground cumin
1/4 teaspoon ground ginger
1 teaspoon dried oregano
1/2 teaspoon salt
1/4 teaspoon black pepper
3/4 cup canned pureed tomatoes
1/2 cup chopped flat leaf parsley
1 pound penne pasta
1 pound medium shrimp, shelled
1/2 pound fresh mushrooms
1 small zucchini, diced

PENNE PASTA with SHRIMP & VEGETABES
grocery list
- [ ] Olive oil
- [ ] Lemon juice
- [ ] Paprika
- [ ] Ginger
- [ ] Oregano
- [ ] Cumin
- [ ] Pureed tomatoes
- [ ] Fresh parsley
- [ ] Penne pasta
- [ ] Shrimp
- [ ] Mushrooms
- [ ] Zucchini

In a large bowl, whisk together the 3/4 cup olive oil and the lemon juice along with the paprika, cumin, ginger, oregano, salt and pepper. Stir in the crushed tomatoes and the flat leaf parsley.

Cook the penne pasta according to package directions until almost done, approximately 12 minutes, then add the shrimp and cook about two minutes more. Drain.

In a sauté pan, heat the 2 tablespoons olive oil and sauté the vegetables for approximately five minutes. Add to the tomato sauce and toss all together with the penne pasta. Heat on low heat approximately five minutes or until the sauce is heated through.

HAMMY SPAGHETTI

4 large ears corn, or 3 cups frozen corn
15-ounce can creamed corn
1/2 cup half and half OR whole milk
3 tablespoons flat leaf parsley
1 teaspoon salt
1/4 teaspoon pepper
1 pound spaghetti
1/2 pound smoked ham, cut into thin strips
2 tablespoons butter, cut into pieces

HAMMY SPAGHETTI
grocery list
- [ ] Fresh or frozen corn
- [ ] Creamed corn
- [ ] Milk or half and half
- [ ] Flat leaf parsley
- [ ] Spaghetti
- [ ] Ham
- [ ] Butter

Mix the corn, parsley, cream, salt and pepper.

Cook the pasta according to package directions and drain, reserving 1/2 cup of the water. Toss the pasta with the reserved water, the corn mixture, ham and the butter. Heat through on medium heat, stirring as needed. If sauce is too thick, add a little more cream or water.

RIGATONI WITH ANDOUILLE

1 pound andouille sausage
  or other spicy sausage such as hot Italian
1 tablespoon olive oil
1 onion, chopped
2 ribs celery, chopped
1 large green pepper, chopped
2 cloves garlic, minced
16-ounce can crushed tomatoes
1 tablespoon tomato paste
8-ounce can tomato sauce
1¼ teaspoons salt
1/2 teaspoon pepper
1 pound rigatoni

RIGATONI WITH
ANDOUILLE
grocery list

☐ *Andouille or other*
   spicy sausage
☐ *Olive oil*
☐ *Onion*
☐ *Celery*
☐ *Green pepper*
☐ *Garlic*
☐ *Crushed tomatoes*
☐ *Tomato paste*
☐ *Tomato sauce*
☐ *Rigatoni pasta*

Remove casings from sausage and cut meat into pieces. In a large
frying pan, heat the oil over medium heat. Add the sausage and cook, stirring for 3 minutes. Stir in the onion, celery, green pepper and garlic. Cover the pan and cook over medium low heat, stirring occasionally until the vegetables are soft, about 10 minutes. Add the tomatoes, tomato paste, tomato sauce, salt and pepper. Cover and simmer for approximately 15 minutes. Cook the pasta according to package directions and drain. Toss with the sauce.

SIMPLE CHICKEN & PASTA

1/3 cup walnuts
8 tablespoons olive oil
4 skinless boneless chicken breasts, about 1 pound
2 teaspoons salt
1/4 teaspoon salt
1/4 teaspoon pepper
Pinch of pepper
2 tablespoons red wine vinegar
1/2 pound bow tie pasta
2 tablespoons chopped flat leaf parsley

SIMPLE CHICKEN &
PASTA
grocery list
☐ *Walnuts*
☐ *Olive oil*
☐ *Skinless, boneless*
   chicken breasts
☐ *Wine vinegar*
☐ *Bow tie pasta*
☐ *Flat leaf parsley*

Flatten chicken breasts by placing them between two layers of plastic wrap and pounding the meat with the flat side of a heavy pan or rolling pin.

In a nonstick skillet toast the walnuts over medium heat stirring until lightly browned, about five minutes. Remove the nuts from the pan and chop. In the same pan, heat 2 tablespoons of the oil over medium heat. Season the chicken breasts with the 2 teaspoons salt and 1/4 teaspoon pepper. Cook the breasts until browned and just done, approximately five minutes. Let rest approximately five minutes, then cut into bite size chunks.

In a glass bowl, combine the remaining 6 tablespoons oil, vinegar, 1/4 teaspoon salt, and the pinch of pepper. Add the chicken.

Cook pasta according to directions on the package and drain. Toss with the walnuts, chicken and vinaigrette mixture and top with chopped flat leaf parsley.

THAI SPAGHETTI

3 tablespoons plus 1 teaspoon soy sauce
2 tablespoons plus 2 teaspoons lime juice (from about 2 limes)
1 tablespoon vegetable oil, plus 1 tablespoon more if needed
4 cloves garlic, minced
3/4 teaspoon ground ginger
3 boneless, skinless chicken breasts (about 1 pound in all)
1/2 cup chunky peanut butter
1 cup canned chicken broth
1/2 teaspoon sugar
1/2 teaspoon salt
1/8 teaspoon dried red pepper flakes or to your taste
1 pound spaghetti
3 green onions, chopped
1/3 cup peanuts

THAI SPAGHETTI
grocery list

☐ Soy sauce
☐ Lime juice
☐ Vegetable oil
☐ Garlic
☐ Ginger
☐ Boneless, skinless chicken breasts
☐ Chunky peanut butter
☐ Chicken broth
☐ Sugar
☐ Red pepper flakes
☐ Spaghetti
☐ Green onions
☐ Peanuts

In a shallow glass dish, combine the 3 tablespoons soy sauce, 2 tablespoons lime juice, 1 tablespoon of the oil, the garlic and the ginger. Add the chicken, turn to coat and let marinate at least 10 minutes or longer if you have the time.

In a saucepan, combine the remaining 1 teaspoon soy sauce and the 2 teaspoons lime juice, the peanut butter, chicken broth, sugar, salt and red pepper flakes. Pour the marinade from the chicken into the saucepan and bring just to a simmer over medium heat, whisking until smooth.

Cut the chicken crosswise into slices and sauté in the remaining 1 tablespoon oil over medium heat approximately five to eight minutes until just done. (You can also use grilled chicken breasts or chicken from a deli for this dish.)

Cook the pasta according to the directions on the package and drain. Toss the pasta, chicken and chopped green onions all together and top with the chopped peanuts.

SWEET POTATO TIES

2 tablespoons olive oil
1 onion
1 large sweet potato (approximately 1/2 pound)
1/4 cup water
1 teaspoon dried sage
1/8 teaspoon cayenne
1/2 teaspoon salt
16-ounce can crushed tomatoes
8-ounce can tomato sauce
1 tablespoon tomato paste
1/2 pound Canadian bacon
1 pound bow tie pasta

SWEET POTATO TIES
grocery list

☐ Olive oil
☐ Onion
☐ Fresh sweet potato
☐ Water
☐ Sage
☐ Cayenne
☐ Crushed tomatoes
☐ Tomato sauce
☐ Tomato paste
☐ Canadian bacon
☐ Bow tie pasta

Peel sweet potato, cut in half lengthwise, then cut crosswise into 1/4-inch slices. Peel onions, cut in half and cut into thin slices.

Sauté the onion and sweet potato in the oil over medium heat. Add the water. Cover and cook until the onions are soft, about five minutes. Stir in the sage, cayenne, salt, tomato sauce, tomato paste and tomatoes. Reduce the heat. Cover and simmer until the sweet potato is tender and sauce is thickened, about 15 minutes. Add the Canadian bacon and remove from the heat. Cook the pasta according to directions on the package. Drain and mix with the sauce.

SPAGHETTI BOLOGNESE

1/4 pound bacon, cut into pieces
1 onion, chopped
1/2 pound ground beef
2 cups canned chicken stock
1/2 cup red wine OR substitute more chicken stock
2 tablespoons tomato paste
1 teaspoon dried oregano
1 teaspoon dried basil
1 teaspoon salt
1/4 teaspoon black pepper
1/2 cup half and half
1 pound spaghetti

SPAGHETTI
BOLOGNESE
grocery list

☐ Bacon
☐ Onion
☐ Ground Beef
☐ Chicken stock
☐ Basil
☐ Red wine (optional)
☐ Tomato paste
☐ Oregano
☐ Half and half
☐ Spaghetti

Heat the butter in a sauté pan over low heat.

Fry the bacon approximately three minutes. Add the onion and cook until it starts to soften. Stir in the ground beef and cook until the meat is no longer pink. Add the broth, wine, tomato paste, oregano, basil, salt and pepper. Simmer, stirring occasionally, until the sauce thickens, about 25 minutes. Stir in the cream and remove from the heat. Cook the pasta according to directions on the box, drain and toss with the sauce.

TEX-MEX PASTA

2 tablespoons olive oil
1 pound ground beef
2 teaspoons chili powder
1 teaspoon ground cumin
10-ounce can tomatoes with green chilies
 such as Ro-Tel brand
1 teaspoon salt
1/4 teaspoon ground black pepper
1 teaspoon garlic powder
16-ounce jar chunky salsa
1 pound cavatappi or other pasta of your choice
2 teaspoons lime juice
1/4 cup chopped flat leaf parsley
8 ounces Cheddar cheese

TEX-MEX PASTA
grocery list

☐ Olive oil
☐ Ground beef
☐ Chili powder
☐ Cumin
☐ Canned tomatoes with
    green chilies
☐ Garlic powder
☐ Salsa
☐ Pasta
☐ Lime juice
☐ Parsley
☐ Cheddar cheese

Heat the oil in a sauté pan. Add the ground beef and cook until browned. Stir in the chili powder, cumin, salt and pepper. Add the salsa and tomatoes and simmer over low heat to allow the flavors to combine. Cook pasta according to directions on the box, drain and toss with the lime juice, parsley and 1 cup of the cheese. Stir until the cheese is melted. Sprinkle with the remaining cheese.

CHEESE TORTELLINI WITH SAGE SAUCE

8 tablespoons butter
3 cloves garlic, minced
1 teaspoon ground sage
1 teaspoon salt
1/4 teaspoon pepper
1 cup half and half
1/2 cup chicken broth
8 ounces Monterey jack cheese, shredded
1 pound cheese-filled tortellini
Flat leaf parsley if desired

Melt the butter in a sauté pan and add the garlic, cooking slowly until it is soft. Stir in the sage, salt and pepper. Heat one minute. Add the cream and chicken stock. Cook pasta according to directions on the package. Drain and toss with the sage sauce and Monterey jack cheese.

Vegetables & Beans

KAREN'S BAKED BEANS

1/2 pound bacon
1/4 cup onion, chopped
1 large can Campbell's pork and beans
1/4 cup brown sugar
1/4 cup ketchup
4 tablespoons unsulphured molasses

KAREN'S BAKED
BEANS
grocery list

☐ Bacon
☐ Onion
☐ Pork and beans
☐ Brown sugar
☐ Ketchup
☐ Molasses

Dice bacon and fry in a skillet until pieces are crisp. Remove meat from skillet. Sauté the onion in the bacon grease. Put the bacon and onion in a large saucepan and add the remaining ingredients. Cook uncovered on low heat for approximately one hour stirring often until thickened.

MOM'S POTATO SALAD

6 to 8 large potatoes
1 teaspoon salt
1/4 teaspoon pepper
1/3 cup sweet relish
4 large stalks celery, diced
1/2 red onion, diced fine
6 hard boiled eggs
1 cup mayonnaise
1/2 cup Henri's dressing
3 tablespoons granulated sugar
1 tablespoon mustard

MOM'S POTATO
SALAD
grocery list

☐ Potatoes
☐ Relish
☐ Celery
☐ Onion
☐ Eggs
☐ Mayonnaise
☐ Henri's dressing
☐ Sugar
☐ Mustard

Boil the potatoes and cool. Cut into small bite-size pieces and put into a large bowl. Peel the hard boiled eggs and chop into small pieces and add to the potatoes. Chop the celery and onion and add to the potatoes and eggs. Mix the mayonnaise, mustard, Henri's dressing, granulated sugar, salt, pepper, and sweet relish. Add to the potato mixture and stir. (Instead of Henri's dressing, use all mayonnaise, or part mayonnaise and part salad dressing if you prefer.)

SUMMER SQUASH & ZUCCHINI CASSEROLE

SUMMER SQUASH &
ZUCCHINI CASSEROLE
grocery list

☐ Yellow squash
☐ Zucchini squash
☐ Cream of chicken soup
☐ Sour cream
☐ Grated carrot
☐ Herb stuffing mix
☐ Butter

Oven temperature: 350 degrees

6 cups chopped yellow summer squash and zucchini mixed
1/4 cup chopped onion
1 can cream of chicken soup
1 cup sour cream
1 cup grated carrot
6-ounce package herb stuffing mix
1/2 cup butter

Cook squash and onion in small amount of boiling water for five minutes and drain. Mix sour cream and cream soup. Stir in the carrot. Fold mixture into the squash.

Mix stuffing and butter and spread half of it in a 7"x12" baking dish. Spread the vegetable mixture on top of the stuffing. Top with the remaining stuffing mixture. Bake 30 minutes until heated through

.

OLD-FASHIONED DUTCH MOUSE

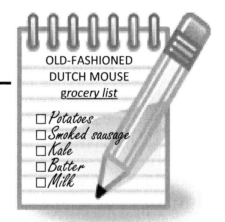

OLD-FASHIONED
DUTCH MOUSE
grocery list

☐ Potatoes
☐ Smoked sausage
☐ Kale
☐ Butter
☐ Milk

6 to 8 medium boiling potatoes
1 pound ring of smoked kielbasa
   OR roasted sausage or mettwurst sausage
1 can kale, drained
4 tablespoons butter
1/2 cup whole or 2% milk
1 tablespoon salt
1/4 teaspoon pepper

Peel and halve potatoes and cover with cold water. Add the salt and bring to a boil. Add the sausage and continue to boil until the potatoes are fork tender. Drain in a colander. Put the sausage on a plate, cut into serving pieces and cover with foil.

Heat milk, but do not boil. Mash the potatoes with the butter and warmed milk. Add the drained kale and stir. Serve with the sausage.

SWEET POTATO SIDE DISH

Oven temperature: 350 degrees

1/2 cup butter, melted
3 cups mashed sweet potatoes
1 cup granulated sugar
2 eggs
1 teaspoon vanilla
1/3 cup whole or 2% milk
1/2 cup packed brown sugar
1/4 cup flour
1/2 cup chopped toasted pecans
2½ tablespoons butter, melted

Mix the 1/2 cup melted butter, sweet potatoes, granulated sugar, eggs, milk and vanilla.Put into a casserole dish.

Mix the flour, brown sugar, 2½ tablespoons butter and nuts in a small bowl and sprinkle on top of the sweet potato mixture. Bake uncovered approximately 30 to 40 minutes.

EASY ROASTED VEGETABLE CHEESE PIZZA

Oven temperature: see pizza box

Two commercial frozen cheese pizzas, 12" to 14"
1 box Zataran's Herb Rice Mix
4 ounces cream cheese
1 pound mozzarella cheese
Roma tomatoes
Bell peppers, green, red and yellow
Red onion

Prepare the rice mix according to package directions. Add the cream cheese and half of the mozzarella cheese to the hot rice.

Thinly slice Roma tomatoes, bell peppers and red onions.

Place the frozen pizza on a baking sheet. Spread each pizza with half the rice mixture. Top each with half the remaining cheese. Top pizza with the sliced tomatoes, green peppers and red onions. Drizzle with a little olive oil. Bake according to frozen pizza directions or until the vegetables are roasted to your taste.

CHRIS' SWISS POTATO PIE

Oven temperature: 400 degrees

6 medium potatoes
6 tablespoons butter, melted
1 teaspoon salt
1/4 teaspoon pepper
1 teaspoon parsley
1½ cup diced Swiss cheese
1 cup cooked, cubed ham
1 medium onion, grated
3 eggs
1/2 cup milk

Boil potatoes in water until fork tender. Drain and mash with the butter, salt, pepper and parsley. Spoon two-thirds of the potatoes into sides and bottom of greased two-quart casserole.

Combine cheese, ham and onion. Spoon into potatoes that are in the casserole dish.

Beat together eggs and milk and pour over the ham mixture. Spread the remaining potatoes on top, sprinkle with paprika if you like. Bake for 35 to 40 minutes at 400 degrees.

DOUBLE STUFFED PEAR POTATOES

Oven temperature: 400 degrees

2 sweet potatoes
2 white potatoes
3 fresh pears
1/2 cup milk
6 tablespoons butter
1 teaspoon salt

Bake potatoes until fork tender, about 45 minutes. Cool slightly.

Peel 3 pears and cut into cubes. Cover with water and bring to a boil. Boil just until tender and drain.

Scoop out the inside of each of the potatoes and set the shells on a baking sheet. Mash the potato pulp with the pears and milk, butter and salt .Spoon the mixture back into the shells and top with the following mixture:

1/2 cup brown sugar
1 teaspoon cinnamon
1 tablespoon butter

Mix till crumbly and sprinkle on the potatoes. Put back into the oven and bake for approximately 30 minutes until tops are bubbly.

152

Salads

FIVE CUP SALAD

1 cup sour cream
1 cup coconut
1 cup pineapple, drained
1 cup maraschino cherries, drained and cut in half
1 cup mandarin oranges, drained

Combine all ingredients and chill overnight or at least six hours.

FIVE CUP SALAD
grocery list

☐ Sour Cream
☐ Coconut
☐ Pineapple
☐ Maraschino Cherries
☐ Mandarin Oranges

PANZANELLA SALAD

3 tablespoons extra virgin olive oil
1 small French bread loaf, cut into cubes (about 6 cups)
1 teaspoon kosher salt
2 large ripe tomatoes, cut into cubes
1 hot house cucumber, seeded and sliced
1 red bell pepper, seeded and cut into cubes
1 yellow bell pepper, seeded and cut into cubes
1/2 red onion, cut in half and thinly sliced
20 large fresh basil leaves, coarsely chopped
3 tablespoons capers, drained

PANZANELLA SALAD
grocery list

☐ Olive oil
☐ French bread
☐ Tomato
☐ Cucumber
☐ Red bell pepper
☐ Yellow bell pepper
☐ Red onion
☐ Fresh basil
☐ Capers

SALAD:
Heat the olive oil in a sauté pan and add the bread and salt. Cook over low to medium heat, tossing frequently for about 10 minutes or until bread cubes are evenly browned. Add more oil as needed.

In a large bowl, mix the tomatoes, cucumber, red peppers, yellow pepper, red onion, basil and capers. Add the bread cubes and toss with the vinaigrette. Season with salt and pepper.

VINAIGRETTE DRESSING:
1 teaspoon minced garlic
1/2 teaspoon Dijon mustard
3 tablespoons white wine vinegar

1/2 cup extra virgin olive oil
1/2 teaspoon kosher salt
Fresh ground black pepper

Mix everything except the olive oil then drizzle the olive oil over the other ingredients while whisking all together.

TACO SALAD

1 small head lettuce, chopped
1 pound ground beef
1 teaspoon garlic powder
1 teaspoon salt
1/4 teaspoon pepper
1 onion, chopped
2 packages taco seasoning
16-ounce bottle Thousand Island salad dressing
1/2 cup salsa
15-ounce can red kidney beans, drained and rinsed
16 ounces shredded Cheddar cheese
1 pound bag of Nacho tortilla chips such as Doritos
2 or 3 tomatoes, diced
2 green onions, diced

TACO SALAD
grocery list

☐ Lettuce
☐ Ground beef
☐ Garlic powder
☐ Onion
☐ Taco seasoning
☐ Thousand Island
☐ Salsa
☐ Kidney beans
☐ Cheddar cheese
☐ Doritos
☐ Tomatoes
☐ Green onions

Fry the ground chuck with the chopped onion, garlic powder, salt and pepper. Add one package of the taco seasoning. Drain meat mixture and set aside.

Mix the Thousand Island dressing and salsa with 2 tablespoons of taco seasoning from the remaining package.

Put the chopped lettuce in a large bowl, toss with the kidney beans, ground beef mixture, diced green onions, diced tomatoes, Cheddar cheese and as many of the Doritos as you like. Serve immediately.

HOLLY'S ORANGE SALAD

3-ounce package orange gelatin dessert
2 cups small curd cottage cheese
10-ounce can mandarin oranges, drained
1 cup crushed pineapple, drained
8 ounces whipped topping

DAD'S CHERRY
GELATIN SALAD
grocery list

☐ Cherry gelatin dessert
☐ Cherry pie filling
☐ Whipped topping

Mix the dry gelatin dessert into the cottage cheese in a medium-size bowl. Add the remaining ingredients and stir well.
Chill for one hour before serving.

DAD'S CHERRY GELATIN SALAD

6-ounce package cherry gelatin dessert
2 cups boiling water
1can cherry pie filling
Whipped topping

Dissolve the gelatin dessert in the 2 cups of boiling water. Add the cherry pie filling. Put into a 9"x13" dish and chill in refrigerator. Cut in squares to serve.

HOLLY'S ORANGE
SALAD
grocery list
☐ Orange gelatin
☐ Cottage cheese
☐ Mandarin oranges
☐ Pineapple
☐ Whipped topping

Orange Spinach Salad, recipe p. 18

Breads

JANET'S BANANA BREAD

*My daughter Janet is quite sure she is not a good cook.
If you make her recipe for banana bread given here
you will know this isn't true!*

Oven Temperature: 350 degrees
(Makes two loaves)

1 cup vegetable oil
2 cups granulated sugar
4 eggs
6 to 8 very ripe (or rotten) bananas, mashed
6 tablespoons sour milk or buttermilk
4 cups flour
2 teaspoons baking soda
1 teaspoon baking powder
1 teaspoon salt
1 teaspoon vanilla
1 cup chopped nuts, if desired

JANET'S BANANA BREAD
grocery list
☐ Vegetable oil
☐ Sugar
☐ Bananas
☐ Buttermilk
☐ Eggs
☐ Flour
☐ Baking soda
☐ Baking powder
☐ Vanilla
☐ Nuts (optional)

Mix all ingredients in order given just until combined. Pour into two oiled one-pound loaf pans and bake approximately 40 to 50 minutes .
(It works well to freeze very ripe bananas in the skins in a plastic bag until you need them.)

ROSE'S BRAN MUFFINS

Oven temperature: 400 degrees

1 quart buttermilk
4 eggs, beaten slightly
3 cups sugar
5 cups flour
5 teaspoons baking soda
15 ounce box raisin bran cereal
1 cup vegetable oil
2 teaspoon salt

ROSE'S BRAN MUFFINS
grocery list
☐ Buttermilk
☐ Sugar
☐ Flour
☐ Baking Soda
☐ Raisin Bran cereal
☐ Eggs
☐ Vegetable oil

Pour milk over the cereal and let set for 30 minutes. Add
the other ingredients.Bake in muffin cups 15 to 20 minutes.

JOAN'S ROLLS

Oven temperature: 325 degrees

1/2 cup very warm water
2 tablespoons (or 2 packages) yeast
1 teaspoon sugar
2 cups whole milk
2 eggs
2/3 cup sugar
8 tablespoons butter (or substitute vegetable shortening,
    but don't substitute margarine)
2 teaspoons salt
7 cups flour

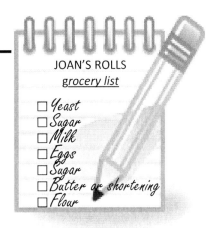

JOAN'S ROLLS
grocery list

☐ Yeast
☐ Sugar
☐ Milk
☐ Eggs
☐ Sugar
☐ Butter or shortening
☐ Flour

Heat the milk and shortening until bubbles start to form on the edge of the pan, but don't bring it to a boil. Pour into a large mixing bowl and add the 2/3 cup sugar and salt. Let cool to room temperature.

While the milk is cooling, add the yeast to the water and sprinkle with the 1 teaspoon sugar. Stir with a small whisk and let stand for a few minutes until it starts to foam.

Add the eggs to the milk mixture along with 2 cups of the flour and beat with an electric mixer until well mixed. Add the yeast mixture and 2 cups more of the flour and mix with the mixer until smooth.By hand, add the rest of the flour and stir until well mixed.

Grease a large bowl with butter or shortening, turn the dough into the bowl and cover with a clean towel. Let rise until doubled, approximately one hour depending on the room temperature.Turn out onto a floured surface and cut into dinner rolls (I use a juice glass) and place on a baking pan or into pie pans. Cover and let rise approximately 45 minutes. Bake approximately 17 to 18 minutes until lightly browned.

BREAD MACHINE WHOLE WHEAT ROLLS

BREAD MACHINE
WHOLE WHEAT ROLLS
grocery list

☐ Oil
☐ Sugar
☐ Dry milk
☐ Bread flour
☐ Whole wheat flour
☐ Yeast

Oven temperature: 350 degrees

Put the ingredients in the bread machine bowl in the order given:
1 1/2 cup water at 80 degrees
2 tablespoons oil
1/4 cup brown sugar
1 teaspoon salt
2 tablespoons dry milk
2 1/2 cup white bread flour
2 cups whole wheat flour
1 tablespoon active dry yeast

Set bread machine program to "dough" and turn on to mix. When machine rising cycle is complete, turn out on a lightly floured surface. Divide into pieces and shape. Place in a greased baking pan. Cover and let rise in a warm place for 1 hour until double in size. Bake approximately 25 minutes. Makes approximately 20 rolls.

157

MARK'S PARMESAN BREAD

Oven temperature: Broil

1 large loaf French bread
2 sticks butter, melted (don't substitute margarine)
1 cup grated Parmesan cheese

Slice the bread into 1-inch thick pieces. Dip each piece in the melted butter and place on a baking sheet. Top with the grated Parmesan cheese. Put under the broiler for approximately two minutes or until browned and crisp. Watch closely while in the broiler to keep bread from burning.

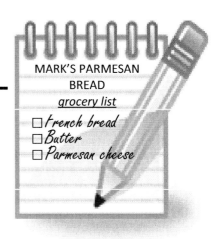

MARK'S PARMESAN BREAD
grocery list
☐ French bread
☐ Butter
☐ Parmesan cheese

BEER CHEESE TRIANGLES

Oven temperature: 450 degrees

2 cups packaged biscuit mix such as Bisquick
1/2 cup shredded sharp Cheddar cheese
1/2 cup beer

In a mixing bowl, stir together the biscuit mix and shredded cheese. Make a well in the center and add the beer all at once. Stir just till mixture clings together. Knead lightly on a floured surface five strokes. Roll or pat dough into a 6" circle. Cut into triangles using a pizza cutter, or cut into biscuits using a biscuit cutter or small juice glass. Bake 8 to 10 minutes.

BEER CHEESE TRIANGLES
grocery list
☐ Biscuit mix
☐ Shredded cheese
☐ Beer

FIESTA BISCUITS

Oven temperature: 425 degrees

2 cups biscuit mix, such as Bisquick
1/2 cup shredded Cheddar cheese
2 tablespoons chopped pickled jalapenos
2/3 cup milk
4½ teaspoons chili seasoning mix
2 tablespoons butter, melted

FIESTA BISCUITS
grocery list
☐ Biscuit mix
☐ Cheddar cheese
☐ Pickled jalapenos
☐ Milk
☐ Chili seasoning mix
☐ Butter

Mix the biscuit mix, chopped jalapeno, chili seasoning mix and cheese. Add the milk and mix until moistened. Pat into an 8" baking pan and drizzle with melted butter. Bake 15 to 17 minutes, or until a toothpick inserted in the middle comes out clean.

EASY RAISIN BREAD

Oven temperature: 350 degrees

EASY RAISIN BREAD
grocery list
- ☐ Yeast
- ☐ Sugar
- ☐ Flour
- ☐ Mace
- ☐ Raisins
- ☐ Evaporated milk
- ☐ Nuts
- ☐ Butter
- ☐ Vegetable oil
- ☐ Eggs

2½ tablespoons yeast
   OR 3 packages yeast
2 cups lukewarm water
2 tablespoons sugar
5 pounds flour
2½ cups sugar
1 tablespoon mace
1 tablespoon salt
1 pound raisins
13-ouncecan evaporated milk
1 cup nuts
3 sticks butter
1/2 cup vegetable oil
5 eggs

Dissolve the yeast in the water and add sugar.

Combine remaining ingredients and add yeast mixture. Mix well. Place dough in a large greased mixing bowl and turn to coat. Allow to rise for at least two hours. Punch down and let rise two more hours. Oil and coat with sugar six loaf pans, each 9"x5", or use seven loaf pans, each 8½"x4½". Divide the dough evenly and put into the pans and let rise two more hours or until the bread is up to the top of the pans. Bake at 350 degrees for one hour. Turn off oven. Let loaves stand in oven for 15 minutes.

VIENNA BREAD

Oven temperature: 450 degrees

VIENNA BREAD
grocery list
- ☐ Sugar
- ☐ Yeast
- ☐ Flour
- ☐ Vegetable shortening

2½ cups warm water (not hot)
1 tablespoon sugar
1 tablespoon salt
1 tablespoon dry yeast or 1 package
8 cups flour, sifted
2 tablespoons soft vegetable shortening

Measure water, sugar and salt into a large mixing bowl. Add yeast and stir to dissolve. Add 2 cups flour and beat until blended. Stir in 2 tablespoons soft shortening and remaining flour, mixing with your hands. Turn out on board and knead until smooth and elastic. Put in a greased bowl and turn dough to coat both sides. Cover with a towel and let rise until double in bulk.

Divide dough into two parts. Form into balls and set them on the board again and cover. Let rest 15 minutes. Shape into two oblong loaves and place on a greased baking sheet sprinkled with corn meal. Cover and let rise free from drafts until double. Brush with cornstarch glaze. Make 4 diagonal gashes on top of loaves and sprinkle with poppy seeds. Bake for 10 minutes at 450 degrees, then lower heat to 400 degrees and bake until done, approximately 30 to 40 minutes.

CORNSTARCH GLAZE:
1/2 cup cold water
1 teaspoon cornstarch
1/2 teaspoon salt

GRANNY'S BUNS

Oven temperature: 375 degrees

1 package yeast
or 1 tablespoon dry bulk yeast
3/4 cup sugar
1 cup warm water
2 teaspoons salt
1/2 cup vegetable oil
1 egg
2 cups milk
5½ cups flour

Dissolve yeast in 1/4 cup sugar in warm water for 5 minutes. Add salt, remaining sugar and oil to mixture. Beat egg and milk together and add to yeast mixture. Gradually stir in flour to form a soft dough. Knead dough on a floured surface for five to eight minutes, until smooth and elastic. Place in a greased bowl, cover and allow to rise until double in bulk, approximately three hours. Punch down and let rise again, about one more hour. Shape dough into pieces the size of a golf ball. Press balls flat onto a greased baking sheet. Let rise an additional two hours. Bake 15 to 18 minutes.

CHEESY BISCUITS

Oven temperature: 350 degrees

1/4 pound (1 stick) butter
2 egg yolks, well beaten
5 ounces grated Swiss cheese
1½ teaspoons prepared mustard
dash of cayenne pepper
1 cup flour

Cream butter with an electric mixer. Add egg yolks and mix well. Gradually blend in cheese, mustard and pepper. Beat in flour until blended. Mixture will be a stiff dough.

Roll out on a floured board and cut into circles with a biscuit cutter or small juice glass. Place on an ungreased baking sheet and bake for 20 minutes.

GRANDMA'S POPPYSEED BREAD

Oven temperature 350 degrees

1 yellow cake mix
2 tablespoons poppy seeds
3.4-ounce package instant coconut cream pudding
4 eggs
1/2 cup vegetable oil
1 cup hot water

Mix all ingredients together until moist, put into 2 (8"x5") baking pans and bake approximately 35 minutes or until toothpick inserted in top comes out clean. Remove from oven, turn out onto racks and let cool.

Desserts

GRANDMA'S EASY BUTTERSCOTCH PIE

Purchase a frozen prepared pie crust that is ready to bake. Bake according to directions.

1/4 cup granulated sugar
1/2 cup brown sugar
1/3 cup flour
2 cups whole milk (don't use 2% or fat-free in this recipe)
3 egg yolks
1 teaspoon vanilla
1½ tablespoons butter (Don't substitute margarine in this recipe.)
1/4 teaspoon salt
Whipped topping

GRANDMA'S EASY
BUTTERSCOTCH PIE
grocery list
☐ Prepared pie crust
☐ Sugar
☐ Flour
☐ Milk
☐ Eggs
☐ Vanilla
☐ Whipped topping

Mix the granulated sugar and brown sugar in a saucepan. Add the milk, salt and egg yolks and beat well. Cook on medium heat until the mixture comes to a boil, stirring constantly. Boil for two minutes. Remove from the heat and add the butter and vanilla. Pour into the prepared pie crust. When cool, top with whipped topping.

DAD'S ALMOND TART

Oven temperature: 450 degrees

2 frozen, unbaked pie crusts
3 egg yolks
1 tablespoon almond flavoring
1/2 cup flour
1/2 cup whole milk (don't use 2% or fat-free for this recipe)
1½ cups granulated sugar
1/4 teaspoon salt

DAD'S ALMOND TART
grocery list
☐ Frozen pie crusts
☐ Eggs
☐ Almond flavoring
☐ Flour
☐ Milk
☐ Sugar

Mix the egg yolks, sugar and almond flavoring well. Add the milk, flour and salt and pour into the prepared frozen pie crusts. Bake at 450 degrees for 10 minutes, then turn the oven down to 350 degrees and continue to bake for another 20 minutes or until tarts are set.

BUTTER PECAN DESSERT

Oven temperature: 350 degrees

1½ cups graham cracker crumbs
3 tablespoons butter, melted
2 tablespoons granulated sugar
2 packages instant vanilla pudding, 3.4 ounces each
1½ cups whole milk (NOT 2% or fat-free)
1 quart butter pecan ice cream, softened
8 ounces whipped topping
2 Hershey candy bars or 4 Heath candy bars, chopped

BUTTER PECAN DESSERT
grocery list
☐ Graham cracker crumbs
☐ Instant vanilla pudding mix
☐ Butter
☐ Sugar
☐ Milk
☐ Butter pecan ice cream
☐ Whipped topping
☐ Hershey or Heath candy bars

Mix the graham cracker crumbs, melted butter and granulated sugar and press into a 9"x13" baking dish. Bake for 10 minutes and cool completely.

Beat the pudding with the milk. Add the ice cream and pour into the crust. Spread whipped topping over all and top with chopped candy bars. Put into the freezer to set.

FRUIT MAGIC

Oven temperature 350 degrees

1 can cherry pie filling
1 package Jiffy yellow cake mix
1/4 cup butter or margarine, melted
1/2 cup walnuts, chopped

FRUIT MAGIC
grocery list
☐ Cherry pie filling
☐ Jiffy yellow cake mix
☐ Butter
☐ Walnuts

Spread the pie filling in an 8"x8" baking dish. Sprinkle the dry cake mix over top of the pie filling. Drizzle the butter over the cake mix and sprinkle the walnuts on top. Bake approximately 40 minutes or until it begins to brown.

EASY COCONUT MACAROONS

Oven temperature: 350 degrees

2 (8-ounce) packages shredded coconut
14-ounce can sweetened condensed milk
2 teaspoons vanilla

EASY MACAROONS
grocery list
☐ Shredded coconut
☐ Sweetened condensed milk
☐ Vanilla

Mix ingredients. Drop from teaspoon onto well-greased cookie sheet. Bake in 350 degree oven for 10 to 12 minutes. Cool slightly before removing from rack.

ALMOND POUND CAKE

Oven temperature: 350 degrees

4 eggs
2 cups granulated sugar
1½ cups vegetable oil
1 can evaporated milk
3 cups plus 2 tablespoons flour
1½ teaspoons baking soda
1 teaspoon salt
1 cup almond paste, softened

ALMOND
POUND CAKE
grocery list

☐ Sugar
☐ Vegetable oil
☐ Evaporated milk
☐ Flour
☐ Baking soda
☐ Almond paste

Mix the eggs, granulated sugar and oil. Add milk and stir to blend. Add flour, baking soda and salt. Grate the soft almond paste into the mixture with a box grater so it will be in small pieces. Mix with an electric mixer until well incorporated. Pour into a tube pan that has been well sprayed with food release spray. Bake for 1¼ hours.

REFRIGERATED CHEESECAKE

REFRIGERATED
CHEESECAKE
grocery list

☐ Graham cracker
   crumbs
☐ Butter
☐ Sugar
☐ Lemon gelatin dessert
☐ Evaporated milk
☐ Cream cheese
☐ Pineapple
☐ Sugar
☐ Vanilla

CRUST:
1½ cups graham cracker crumbs
3 tablespoons melted butter or margarine
2 tablespoons granulated sugar

FILLING:
3 ounce package lemon gelatin dessert
1 can evaporated milk
8-ounce package cream cheese, softened
1 small can crushed pineapple, drained well
1 cup granulated sugar
2 teaspoons vanilla

Put evaporated milk, bowl and mixer beaters into freezer to chill.

Mix the gelatin with 1 cup hot water. Chill until syrupy but not set.

Whip the milk using chilled bowl and beaters. Mix together the cream cheese, sugar and vanilla. Add the pineapple and cooled gelatin. Fold in the whipped milk. Put into the crust and chill overnight.

SNICKERDOODLES

Oven temperature: 400 degrees

1½ cups sugar
1 cup butter, softened
2 eggs
1/2 teaspoon salt
2¾ cups flour
2 teaspoons cream of tartar
1 teaspoon baking soda

SNICKERDOODLES
grocery list
☐ Sugar
☐ Cinnamon
☐ Butter
☐ Cream of tartar
☐ Baking Soda
☐ Eggs
☐ Flour

Cream sugar and butter. Add the eggs and mix well. Add the dry ingredients and mix thoroughly.

MIX:
2 tablespoons sugar
2 teaspoons cinnamon

Form dough into balls and roll sugar/cinnamon mixture. Bake on ungreased cookie sheet at 400 degrees 12 to 15 minutes. They should be slightly brown.

CATHY'S RUSSIAN TEA CAKES

Oven temperature: 400 degrees

CATHY'S RUSSIAN TEA CAKES
grocery list
☐ Butter
☐ Sugar
☐ Vanilla
☐ Flour
☐ Walnuts

1 cup butter, softened (don't use margarine for this recipe)
1/2 cup powdered sugar
1 teaspoon vanilla
2¼ cups flour
1/4 teaspoon salt
3/4 cup chopped walnuts

Mix the butter, powdered sugar and vanilla. Add the flour and salt. Mix well. Add nuts and chill the dough.

Roll dough into small balls, about the size of a walnut. Put on a baking sheet and bake approximately 12 minutes. While still warm, roll in more powdered sugar. Cool, then roll in powdered sugar again.

CHOCOLATE LAYER DESSERT

CHOCOLATE LAYER
DESSERT
grocery list
- ☐ *Chocolate graham crackers*
- ☐ *Instant chocolate or vanilla pudding mix*
- ☐ *Evaporated milk*
- ☐ *Half and half or milk*
- ☐ *Whipped topping*
- ☐ *Fudge ice cream topping*

1 box of chocolate graham crackers
2 (3.4 ounce) packages instant chocolate OR vanilla pudding
1 (12 ounce) can evaporated milk
Half and half, or whole milk
8 ounces whipped topping, thawed
4 ounces whipped topping, thawed
12 ounce jar fudge ice cream topping

Mix the pudding with the cream and milk. Fold in the 8 ounces whipped topping.

Put a layer of chocolate graham crackers on the bottom of a 9"x13" pan. Top with half of the pudding mixture. Put another layer of graham crackers on top of the pudding mixture. Top with the rest of the pudding mixture. Cover the last layer of pudding with another layer of graham crackers. Top with the fudge ice cream topping and 4 ounces whipped topping. Refrigerate at least 4 hours before serving.

EASY MICROWAVE FUDGE

EASY ROCKY ROAD
FUDGE
grocery list
- ☐ *Chocolate chips*
- ☐ *Butter*
- ☐ *Sweetened condensed milk*
- ☐ *Miniature marshmallows*

12 ounce package chocolate chips
2 tablespoons butter
1 can sweetened condensed milk
Nuts, if desired

Microwave the chocolate chips and butter in a bowl for approximately two minutes depending on the power of your microwave. Add the sweetened condensed milk and stir until thickened. Add nuts, if desired. Pour into an 8"x8" pan to set. Cut into pieces about one-inch square. (You may substitute other flavors of chips.)

RICH LAYER DESSERT

Oven temperature: 350 degrees

1 cup flour
1 stick butter
1/2 cup nuts, chopped
8-ounce package cream cheese, softened
2 cans chocolate pudding
1 cup powdered sugar
1 teaspoon vanilla
8 ounces whipped topping

Mix the flour, butter and nuts together and spread in a 9"x13" baking pan. Bake for 15 minutes. Let cool completely.

Mix the cream cheese, powdered sugar and vanilla, and fold in the whipped topping. Spread over the crust. Spoon the pudding on top and garnish with more whipped topping. Chill.

LAYER
DESSERT
grocery list

☐ Flour
☐ Butter
☐ Canned chocolate pudding
☐ Cream cheese
☐ Nuts
☐ Powdered sugar
☐ Vanilla
☐ Whipped topping

MADELINE CAKE

Oven temperature: 350 degrees

3 eggs
1 cup sugar
1 cup flour
1 cup butter
1 tablespoon almond flavoring

MADELINE
CAKE
grocery list
☐ Almond flavoring
☐ Powdered sugar
☐ Eggs
☐ Sugar
☐ Flour
☐ Butter

Combine the eggs, sugar and flour in a mixing bowl. Melt butter and pour over egg mixture. With mixer on low, blend ingredients well and add almond flavoring. Continue to beat for five minutes. Beating the air in is the only leavening. Spread in a lightly greased 9"square pan and bakefor 25 minutes. While the cake is still warm, spread on the following glaze:

GLAZE:
1/2 cup powdered sugar
1 tablespoon hot water
Pinch of salt
1/2 teaspoon almond flavoring

INDEX